Urban Capitalists

STUDIES IN INDUSTRY AND SOCIETY
GLENN PORTER, GENERAL EDITOR

Published with the assistance of
The Eleutherian Mills-Hagley Foundation

1.   Burton W. Folsom, Jr.
*Urban Capitalists: Entrepreneurs and City Growth
in Pennsylvania's Lackawanna and Lehigh Regions, 1800-1920*

Urban Capitalists

Entrepreneurs and City Growth in Pennsylvania's
Lackawanna and Lehigh Regions, 1800-1920

Burton W. Folsom, Jr.

The Johns Hopkins University Press
Baltimore and London

The Johns Hopkins University Press, Baltimore, Maryland 21218
The Johns Hopkins Press Ltd., London

Library of Congress Cataloging in Publication Data

Folsom, Burton W
    Urban capitalists.

    (Studies in industry and society; 1)
    Bibliography: p. 181
    Includes index.
    1. Cities and towns—Pennsylvania—Growth—Case studies.
    2. Urbanization—Pennsylvania—Case studies.
    3. Capitalists and financiers—Pennsylvania—History.
    4. Lackawanna Valley, Pa.—Economic conditions.
    5. Lehigh Valley—Economic conditions.
I. Title.
II. Series.
HT371.F64   338.9748'22   80-8864
ISBN 0-8018-2520-2

To My Parents

Contents

List of Illustrations

Maps

Figure

Photographs

List of Tables

Foreword

This book inaugurates both a new series of publications and a new cooperative undertaking by The Johns Hopkins University Press and the Regional Economic History Research Center. The Center encourages and coordinates research into the economic history of the Middle Atlantic region, with particular focus on the social context and consequences of economic change. It is a part of the Eleutherian Mills-Hagley Foundation, a complex of institutions that collectively represents a major national cultural resource devoted to the presentation and interpretation of America's industrial and technological history. Other components of the Foundation are: the Hagley Museum, an indoor-outdoor museum in the historic and industrially important Brandywine Valley; the Eleutherian Mills Historical Library, a research library housing extensive manuscript, pictorial, and imprint collections that focus on the economic past of the Middle Atlantic states; and the Hagley Graduate Program, an M.A./Ph.D. program operated jointly with the University of Delaware to train students for academic posts or careers in museums and historical agencies.

This publications series with The Johns Hopkins University Press is a part of the Center's efforts to disseminate the fruits of research into the history of our region and to strengthen the broader understanding of American economic and social history as a whole. We anticipate that the Studies in Industry and Society series will consist of contributions that relate aspects of American economic and industrial history to the history of other important social institutions, such as politics, labor, the family, and science and technology. Although we expect that many of these studies will deal—as the initial one does—with our region, we also hope to include some outstanding books that are thematically relevant but are not necessarily restricted to this portion of the United States.

Burton Folsom's *Urban Capitalists* is a particularly appropriate book with which to begin the series. In recent years the Regional Economic History Research Center has sponsored, through the generous support of the National Endowment for the Humanities and the Andrew W. Mellon Foundation, a program of research fellowships. Professor Folsom was among our first fellows, and he played an active and effective role in our conferences, colloquia, and informal discussions, as well as contributing an essay to the third volume of our *Working Papers* series. We are very glad to have the opportunity to be associated with the publication of this book by a former Center fellow.

Urban Capitalists makes a real contribution to the history of economic development, to urban history, and to the history of this region. It combines narrative and generalization well, and it has a clear and strong relevance to broad questions of the process of city formation, the creation and functioning of elites, and the role of entrepreneurship in economic development. It does not, of course, supplant or fundamentally call into question the utility of the existing substantial body of geographical theory concerning urban systems and hierarchies among towns and cities. It is, however, an exceedingly valuable comparative case study that adds an important dimension to the prevailing theoretical constructs of geographers and urban historians. It demonstrates that factors such as locational advantage were not always decisive in determining which city in a region would be the major one. The quality of local leadership could sometimes make a real difference within the constraints established by large-scale changes in the surrounding economic and political systems. The study serves to remind us that massive, impersonal historical forces do not always determine events; sometimes people do.

The book also advances our understanding of the process of elite formation and the interrelationships among urban hierarchies. Folsom's data on the backgrounds and the "recruitment" of urban leaders in Pennsylvania are particularly valuable. Folsom's treatment of this topic will be of interest to all those concerned with social mobility and the regional aspects of social change. By looking at several related communities at once and tracing movements among them, he is able to document the process by which vital new cities attracted talented and mobile people in the nineteenth century. For all these reasons, this study is a good one with which to launch the new series; it not only adds to our knowledge of the economic and social history of the Middle Atlantic region, but it also makes contributions to much wider topics and issues.

I am grateful to all who have played key roles in the creation of this new series. First on the list is the book's author, Burt Folsom, whose help, patience, and good humor were invaluable. I must also express my appreciation to others whose support and good will were critical: Walter J. Heacock, general director of the Eleutherian Mills-Hagley Foundation; Henry Y. K. Tom, social sciences editor for The Johns Hopkins University Press; and the members, past and present, of the Center's Academic Advisory Board.

GLENN PORTER

Director, Regional Economic History Research Center
Eleutherian Mills-Hagley Foundation

Preface and Acknowledgments

Entrepreneurs have built America into the number one industrial power in the world. Our economic growth has been so spectacular and so steady over the last 150 years that we often take it for granted. We just assume that our success was bound to happen the way it did. We seem to think we were destined for affluence. Yet on closer inspection we must acknowledge the laws that gave us so many freedoms and the entrepreneurs who used this openness to create something new. This book takes a close look at the rapid transformation of two Pennsylvania regions from primitive farming societies to coal and iron centers. It is a book about entrepreneurs who took risks, the cities they built, and the regions they conquered.

Many people helped me in the making of this book and I want to thank them. First is Frederick Luebke, my teacher and long-time advisor, who has given me excellent guidance for over a decade; more important, he has given me his friendship. Edward J. Davies was my roommate for four years in graduate school. We spent countless hundreds of hours talking about history in general and Scranton and Wilkes-Barre in particular. We worked together, laughed together, endured each other, and somehow we both made it through. Lee Benson was my roommate for two summers at the Regional Economic History Research Center. He has been a good critic of my book and a fount of ideas and information. My thinking on entrepreneurs and city growth is much sharper for having talked so much with him. Aileen Kraditor has been helping me with my work for some time now; I listen to her because she makes me make sense. Samuel Hays, Julius Rubin, and Van Beck Hall all helped me write this book. Professor Hays taught me much about social history; Professor Rubin sparked my interest in economic development; and Professor Hall wrote a useful four-page single-spaced critique of an earlier draft of this work. Thomas Cochran, Louis Galambos, and Harold Livesay all have read this book; I hope I am worthy of their confidence. Glenn Porter and Bill Mulligan helped me fight the battle to get this book published. I wielded the pen, they slew the dragons, and we've launched a series of books on regional history.

I've been lucky in my research to have had three excellent sources of information on Scranton and Bethlehem. The late Robert C. Mattes, director of the Lackawanna Historical Society, talked with me for hours about Scranton and its entrepreneurs. Mr. Mattes was a great-grandson of one of Scranton's founding families. His many stories gave me a personal sense of what it was like to live in Scranton around the turn of the century. Mr. William Lewis is the current director of the Lackawanna Historical Society; he knows Scranton well and I have learned from him too. Finally, Ruth Linderman Frick of Bethlehem is a great-granddaughter of Asa Packer's. She and I spent a wonderful afternoon talking about the history of Bethlehem. She helped me understand the Packer group and their way of life in the late 1800s.

Martha McCallon and Betty Ingrum typed much of this book. That they did so with skill was a relief; that they did so without complaining was divine. Many others have helped me stumble toward completion. Walter and Sophie Sagrera, Karen LaFrance, Bill and Ruth Hammond, Joe Rishel, Robert Doherty, Tony Freyer, Harold Cox, James Hammack, and Harold Kuyper are a few of them.

Three institutions have shown faith in this book by giving me grants. The most helpful has been my three summers of aid at the Regional Economic History Research Center at the Eleutherian Mills-Hagley Foundation. The Committee on Institutionally Sponsored Research at Murray State University has also helped with a summer grant. Finally, the Intercollegiate Studies Institute gave me a Richard Weaver Fellowship, for which I am grateful.

Special thanks go to my family. I thank my parents, to whom this book is dedicated, for instilling in me an entrepreneurial spirit. Anita Prince Folsom was first my student, is now my wife, and has always been my marvelous critic. When she first skipped my class I knew she had the good taste and the sense of adventure to endure my courtship.

Urban Capitalists

Introduction

Evaluating the impact of the individual on history, economist Robert Thomas contended that "individual entrepreneurs . . . *don't matter!*" After this startling remark, Thomas said further that "innovations . . . do not come about as the product of individual genius but rather as the result of more general forces acting in the economy." A short time later, historian Harold Livesay insisted that "individual people do make history and that understanding how they do it is what historians do best."[1] Even allowing for possible misunderstandings caused by overstatement, departmental chauvinism, and alleged misquotation (the rallying cry of those who have been discredited), it seems likely that one of these gentlemen is wrong. In this book I will try to show which one I think it is and why.

The extent to which a great man or group of men can shape change in society has been a perennial historical problem ever since the Victorian days of Thomas Carlyle. Few people seriously believe that entrepreneurs impose themselves "as jack-in-the-boxes who emerge miraculously from the unknown to interrupt the real continuity of history." A more realistic description of an entrepreneur would be one who is "at once a product and an agent of the historical process, at once the representative and the creator of social forces which change the shape of the world and the thoughts of man."[2] In short, an entrepreneur is an innovator: someone who changes the factors of production to create something new. During the last couple of decades the weight of evidence seems to be that such individuals are very few in number and that they reflect "general forces acting in the economy" more than they mold them.[3]

Assessing the role of entrepreneurs in creating change is no small task. Merely developing a rigorous test case, not to mention researching it, requires a clear justification of the time period, the place, and the events selected for study. Since the industrial revolution has profoundly shaped the lives of all Americans, the beginning of iron and coal development will broadly provide the events and time period for this study. For places I have chosen Pennsylvania's Lackawanna and Lehigh valleys, two oddly named regions that witnessed America's first successful use of anthracite to smelt iron ore and later America's first successful mass production of iron rails.

In a sense this book is an urban history because it focuses on those urban capitalists who built the cities and created the factories and railroads to tie these Pennsylvania regions to the outside world. Cities became the lifeline of early industrial America. Cities received entrepreneurs, capital, and laborers and pumped out coal and manufactured goods through trade arteries to outside markets. Transportation links were vital to cities with pretentions to empire, and the urban competition for railroads, industries, and population was keen. The creation of cities and their regional rivalries for economic dominance are crucial ingredients in the making of industrial America in general and in the Lackawanna and Lehigh valleys in particular.[4] The story of urban capitalism in these Pennsylvania regions, then, is a chapter (though not the only one) in the story of entrepreneurs and the growth of cities throughout America.

The Lackawanna and Lehigh valleys occupied mountainous terrain, rich in coal, limited in iron, and contoured by partially navigable rivers leading to the coast. Man's conquest of these regions was surely inevitable. In the 1700s, Indians roamed these lonely valleys and usually dismissed the scattered coal as useless black stones. So did most of the early settlers who beat back the Indians and farmed the land. By the early 1800s, the "black stones" were competing with wood as a local fuel. The invention of the hot blast (to smelt iron with anthracite) and technological advances in canal building provided the two regions with a valuable export, transportation to outside markets, and a rush of entrepreneurs seeking the main chance.[5]

Yet throughout this sequence of events there was wide latitude for the interplay of human talents. At one level, individuals, small firms, and large companies all entered the anthracite fields to exploit the available resources. In their competition with each other and with other fuels (charcoal, timber, and bituminous coal), it was by no means predetermined which capitalists would establish profitable industries. Adding to the anxiety, it was not clear in the mid-1800s which locations, if any, would emerge as major cities to centralize the factors of production. The importance of cities as catalysts to regional development made urban development a key to the future prosperity of eastern Pennsylvania. The remarkable and unlikely emergence of Scranton and Bethlehem as regional capitals signaled the capability of the Lackawanna and Lehigh valleys to generate coal and iron development—a tour de force long-awaited by American businessmen who wanted American independence from English manufacturing. The rise of Scranton, within a regional urban network, is the starting point for analyzing this landmark achievement in American urban and economic history.

Historians have sadly neglected the region as a focus for explaining the rise of industrial society in America. Urban historians, in particular, have rarely strayed from the individual city as their unit of analysis.[6] Such an approach is understandable because cities were catalysts for economic development. Such an approach is undesirable, however, because cities often operated in the context of the region. The region, not the isolated city, may be the fundamental unit of economic and social organization. In this arena there occurs the development of the primary export and competition among the cities and towns to create industry and transportation and to attract population. Unlike other urban histories, then, this study describes the process of urbanization within regional systems of cities.

With historians providing little guidance for studying regional development, one must turn to geographers and economists for explicit theory on the creation of urban systems. Geographers especially have been active in trying to explain urban location and regional growth. Influenced by *environmental determinism* they have usually argued that impersonal forces—terrain, river sites, natural resources, and market areas—largely explain where cities and towns are located in America. An example of this approach is central place theory, the notion that cities and towns of similar sizes perform similar functions and are equally spaced from each other to provide for equal market areas for consumers.[7] This equidistant pattern of the spacing of towns will, according to central place theorists, take the shape of hexagons, and the region will be linked together by cities with specific economic ties.[8] Some geographers have contended that this model of urban growth fits the development of certain areas of the United States, especially a flat, relatively homogeneous plain like that in Iowa and South Dakota.[9]

In this model, man is primarily, if not purely, an economic animal; he responds "rationally" to his environment and calculates markets and economic advantages successfully before deciding where to build cities and towns. According to geographer Allan Pred, "until relatively recently economic geographers, like geographers in general . . . failed or refused to regard any spatial distribution, or array of economic features on the landscape, as the aggregate reflection of individual decisions." Pred further observes that

> some economic geographers were instead content to indirectly deal with the influence of behavior by accepting the environment-stimulus and behavioral-response generalizations of the "environmental determinists" and their successors, the "probabilists" and "possibilists." (Whatever the school of thought turned to, generalizations seldom descended to the level of individual decision-making). Other economic geograpers were presumably consciously or unconsciously willing to accept Carl Sauer's contention that: Human geog-

raphy . . . unlike psychology and history, is a science that has nothing to do with individuals but only with human institutions or cultures.[10]

Since many, if not all, regions in America do not conform to the model of central place theory, geographers have tried to explain why these deviations exist.[11] In doing so they have rarely used entrepreneurship to interpret city formation and urban growth. Instead they use the concepts of initial and locational advantage to explain city growth in its regional setting.[12] Cities with initial advantage are those that first appear in the region, and some grow rapidly because of their "early lead." Cities with locational advantage are those strategic sites at the junction of rivers or those placed near valuable natural resources. Cities with initial or locational advantages, in this point of view, have an edge in the regional competition for people and industries.[13]

If these geographers are right in their description of urbanization and regional development, then the range of entrepreneurship in the growth of American cities is very small. The human factor is a given in regional development; capitalists will inevitably be drawn to certain locations, and they will then export something using the available resources of the region in a rational economic manner. Allan Pred makes explicit this "fundamental behavioral implication of virtually all past and subsequent location theory": that urbanization can best be "theoretically analyzed by assuming that the units involved act in the guise of 'absolutely rational' unerring 'economic man.'"[14]

Other social scientists have contributed mightily to the notion that impersonal forces govern individual behavior. Bernard Schwartz, a sociologist, has seen in his field "a natural tendency . . . to reduce the 'isolated individual' to as rudimentary a model as possible, thus allowing full scope to social structure as a determining factor." Among psychologists, B.F. Skinner seems to celebrate the inability of the individual to shape the world around him. "Every discovery of an event which has a part in shaping a man's behavior," contends Skinner, "seems to leave so much the less to be credited to the man himself; and as such explanations become more and more comprehensive, the contributions which may be claimed by the individual himself appear to approach zero." Skinner concludes that "science ultimately explains behavior in terms of 'causes' or conditions which lie beyond the individual himself."[15]

Many economists follow these social scientists in making entrepreneurship a dependent variable. Robert Thomas, who was quoted earlier, did indeed remark that "individual entrepreneurs, whether alone or as archetypes, *don't matter!*" Thomas further said that

if indeed they do not matter, the reason, I suggest, is that the supply of entrepreneurs throughout American history, combined with institutions that permitted—indeed fostered—intense competition, was sufficiently elastic to reduce the importance of any particular individual . . . . This is not to argue that innovations don't matter, only that they do not come about as the product of individual genius but rather as the result of more general forces acting in an economy.

Refering again to entrepreneurs and economic development, Thomas poses the following parallel.

Let us examine an analogy from track and field; a close race in the 100-yard dash has resulted in a winner in 9.6 seconds, second place goes to a man whose time was 9.7, and the remaining six runners are clustered below that time. Had the winner instead not been entered in the race and everyone merely moved up a place in the standings, I would argue that it would only make a marginal difference to the spectators; to be sure they would be poorer because they would have had to wait one-tenth of a second longer to determine the winner, but how significant a cost is that? That is precisely the entrepreneurial historians task, to place the contributions of the entrepreneur within a marginal framework. Generally such historians have viewed their entrepreneur as the fastest man on earth racing against one-legged men. The historical record of the United States in my opinion suggests . . . that at best the marginal contribution of any one man was small. In short, the individual entrepreneur is no more important and probably no less than the other factors of production.[16]

Some economic historians have observed the trend to downplay the capacity of people to shape the world around them. Louis Galambos calls this the emerging "organizational school of history." He thinks that "organizational history will, no doubt, stress the role of environmental forces acting on the individual." He predicted that future historians would put less emphasis . . . on the individual's effort to shape his own historical context. In part, this will be a product of behavioral models which tend to fix one's attention on the more general, environmental factors instead of the unique individual."[17] Harold Livesay has also noticed "the tendency to focus on institutions instead of people" and observes that "this kind of history seem[s] trendy and therefore attractive." He concludes, however, that "individual people do make history and that understanding how they do it is what historians do best."[18]

Earlier economic historians, oddly enough, granted American entrepreneurs a prominent place in economic development. Arthur Cole, founder of the Research Center in Entrepreneurial History at Harvard University, said that "to study the entrepreneur is to study the central figure in modern economic development, and, to my way of thinking, the central figure in economics."[19] Joseph A. Schumpeter also stressed the role of entrepreneurs in economic development. Like Cole, Schumpeter saw the entrepreneur as an innovator creating markets and taking risks. He spoke of the "creative response" of industrialists who "do something . . . that is outside the range of existing practice," something that "cannot be predicted by applying the ordinary rules of inference from the pre-existing facts." This "creative response changes social and economic situations for good," and "shapes the whole course of subsequent events and their 'long-run' outcome." Schumpeter concluded that "whether we emphasize opportunity or conditions, the responses of individuals or of groups, it is patently true that in capitalist society objective opportunities or conditions act through entrepreneurial activity, analysis of which is at the very least a highly important avenue to the investigation of economic changes in the capitalist epoch."[20]

Nonetheless, the burden of proof is on historians to show when and under what circumstances entrepreneurs can shape urban-economic development. As Robert Thomas observed, "the proper unit of study for entrepreneurial history is the competitive environment."[21] To the economic historian, this "competitive environment" is the industry; to the urban historian it is the region.

Within the region, cities and towns vie in a "competitive environment" for population and industry. To many geographers and economists environmental forces dictate the results of this urban competition. We can find out whether this is true or not by looking at the collective entrepreneurship of economic leaders in key cities and towns in a region.[22] Do urban elites ever display a "creative response" in the competition for population and industry? Can they overcome environmental forces and a lack of natural resources to create city growth and shape regional development in an unexpected way? If we compare urban leadership we can test the location theory of geographers, evaluate the entrepreneurial theories of the economists, and explore regional development all at the same time.[23]

Method and Definition

Since historians are supposed to study the evolution of society over time, they are in a unique position to help us understand the rise of industrial America. Historians can test the environmental determinism of many geographers and economists by doing case studies of regional urbanization over time.

This book will explore the evolution of industrial society through the study of economic elites and urban development in two Pennsylvania regions, the Lackawanna and Lehigh valleys, at three points: 1850, at the outset of coal and iron exporting; 1880, after the first stage of economic development and before the emergence of national corporations; and 1920, after the creation of a national market through large corporations. Neither the regions nor the time periods will receive equal attention. The bulk of my effort will go toward describing the rise of an urban network in the Lackawanna Valley from 1850 to 1880. The Lehigh Valley and the 1920 time period will be used to help me compare different regions at different stages of development.

In a study of regional development, the term *region* must be carefully defined. Yet this is surprisingly hard to do. Social scientists might all agree that a region is larger than a city and smaller than a nation; but there the agreement ends. Some have used *region* to signify a multistate area nearly resembling a section, while others have used a mere county for regional analysis. Market areas and exports seem to be important in classifying a region, but different cities within a region sometimes have different market areas for different products; furthermore, these market areas, and sometimes the exports, change over time. So, the complexity of economic activity in America prevents perfection in any regional analysis. But the development of industrial society in contexts broader than that of the individual city means we must try some sort of regional analysis.

Recognizing these problems, I use the criteria of *export*, *terrain*, and *economic network* in defining the perimeters of the Lackawanna and Lehigh regions. During the 1840s and 1850s, the Lackawanna and Lehigh valleys became regions as they underwent coal and iron development. The processing and exporting of these commodities involved core areas, where the minerals or initial key towns were located, and a hinterland (or periphery), which was tied into the core by supplying it food, manpower, and capital for development. In the Lackawanna Valley this evolving region *roughly* comprised Lackawanna County (the coal-producing core) and Wayne, Susquehanna, and parts of Bradford and Wyoming Counties east of the Susquehanna River. The Lehigh Valley *roughly* consisted of Carbon, Lehigh, and Northampton Counties—all of which spanned the Lehigh River. In the Lehigh Valley, the ore deposits were scattered throughout the region and urbanization took place along the river, so here the core area is the towns along the river, the hinterland is the rest of the three counties. The coal-producing Wyoming Valley is introduced for comparisons, and its core is Luzerne County; its hinterland is *roughly* Columbia County and the parts of Bradford and Wyoming Counties west of the Susquehanna River (see map A).

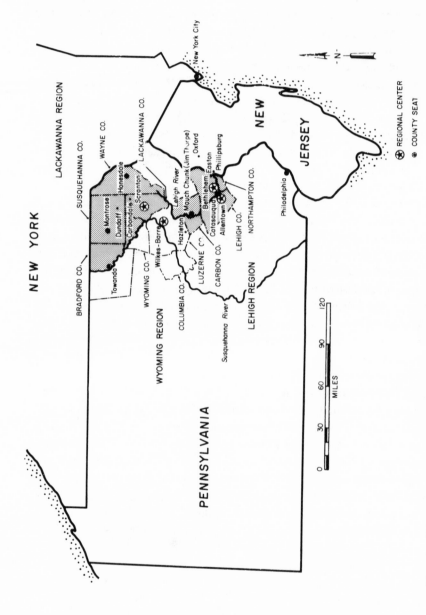

Map A. The Lackawanna, Wyoming, and Lehigh Regions

1

The First Towns in
Northeast Pennsylvania, 1800–1850

Pennsylvania has been the industrial heartland of America. From the steel mills at Pittsburgh to the seaport at Philadelphia, Pennsylvania has been blessed with abundant resources that have supported factories throughout the state. In fact, America's industrial revolution in coal and iron began in Pennsylvania—at Scranton, in the Lackawanna Valley. There American ingenuity combined the available coal and iron to challenge England's world dominance in manufacturing. The story of the Lackawanna region tells us much about America, and perhaps even more about how regions and cities develop in a capitalist economy.

The Lackawanna Valley was not always a coal center. From the 1760s, when the first settlers arrived, to 1825 it was purely an agricultural frontier. Coal, in fact, did not dominate as the region's export until the 1850s. In myth-making about our frontier heritage we emphasize the rural, individualist, and isolationist features of our westward movement. Yet in the early settlement of the Lackawanna Valley (and elsewhere), what stands out is the quick creation of towns, cooperation among prominent urban families, and competition among towns for trade, transportation, and people. Building log cabins, tilling the soil, and beating back Indians may have been everyday drama for the first settlers, but visions of land speculation and boom towns filled their dreams.[1]

Newcomers to this Pennsylvania frontier migrated in clusters from Connecticut and New York; they seem to have been motivated by land shortage and lack of opportunity back east. Carving out Luzerne, Susquehanna, Bradford, and Wayne Counties, they built county seats at Wilkes-Barre, Montrose, Towanda, and Bethany. Then they grew wheat and corn, and raised cattle and sheep, on the land nearby. They shipped some of the farm surplus down the Susquehanna or Delaware rivers to markets as far away as Philadelphia. Even so, the small population of the Lackawanna Valley had little wealth and very small towns. The four towns that did exist, however, became focal points of economic and social activity. Urban dwellers performed the administrative tasks of county government and provided agricultural and commercial services for miles around. With bustling market places, specialized services, and men on the make, towns were places of opportunity and the centers of civilization in northeast Pennsylvania.[2]

Before the development of the coal trade in the 1820s, the main boroughs in northeast Pennsylvania were county seats: Wilkes-Barre in Luzerne County, Towanda in Bradford County, and Montrose, in Susquehanna County. Dundaff, also in Susquehanna County, was created as a commercial center in the 1820s. County histories written in the nineteenth century go into great detail about life in all of these towns and how it changed over time. We can use these histories and other information to reconstruct the economic and social life in northeast Pennsylvania.[3]

As it happened, Wilkes-Barre, Towanda, Montrose, and Dundaff had many similarities in their development. For example, the first three of these towns initially grew because they were county seats. They needed lawyers, judges, and clerks to resolve civil and property disputes in the county. Building the court house and printing the legal proceedings gave jobs to more newcomers. The need for county officials—road commissioner, sheriff, justice of the peace, and postmaster—gave jobs (usually part-time) to more townsfolk. These administrators and their families guaranteed these county seats a base to grow from.[4]

The county seats also became natural centers for commerce and services. Small businessmen just logically located there. For example, some townsfolk catered to the local farmers by building and operating grist mills, saw mills, tanneries, and even carding factories. Others satisfied needs for transportation and services: They became wagon makers, saddle and harness makers, and operators of livery stables, hotels, and taverns. Physicians took care of the sick and the undertaker took care of their mistakes. Ministers and teachers came to satisfy religious and secular needs. In many ways, merchants were the key to the local economy; before the building of turnpikes and canals they were the town's main contact with the outside world. Merchants had the arduous chore of bringing to town hundreds of pounds of goods on horseback from New York City or Philadelphia. By the 1830s, Wilkes-Barre, Montrose, Towanda, and Dundaff each held at least 300 people—a large enough population to support a new group of specialists. These often included a boot and shoe maker, a gunsmith, a tailor, a milliner, a bookseller, and a cabinet maker. There were two signs that a town had come of age: a turnpike (or canal) and a bank. The turnpike brought more ties and trade with the outside world; the bank meant that capital could be mobilized to shape the town's future.[5]

Economists call this continued urban growth and expansion of services a "multiplier effect." The need for some jobs creates a new need for other jobs, all of which results in continued population expansion. During prosperous times this cycle of growth accelerated, but during periods of depression it reversed itself: Investment was halted, businesses failed, and towns lost population. Most townsfolk had much at stake in creating prosperity—high real estate values, high wages and low unemployment, investment opportunities, and more specialized laborers that provided urban consumers an array of services. With so much at stake, towns vied competitively for industries; they depended heavily on entrepreneurs—those people who generated capital and created local industries.[6] Tracing the establishment of local industries and the migration of entrepreneurs, then, helps us understand how towns grow.

The entrepreneurs in northeast Pennsylvania's first towns often reveal a striking similarity in the way they created capital. First, land speculators and farmers vigorously sought to form a new county, with their turf selected as the new county seat. If and when this political decision occurred, the building of streets and the dividing of lots rewarded the patient landowner with a profit. Since more growth meant more demand for their land, the urban dwellers started local businesses to trade with the farmers nearby. This involved an emerging elite, often a few interrelated families, in a quest to bring transportation to their town. Such transportation, in the form of turnpikes and canals, would increase trade and prosperity for town and countryside alike. Observing this symbiotic process, Henry Clay noted that "the benefit resulting from a turnpike road made by private associations is divided between the capitalist, who receives his toll, the land through which it passes and which is augmented in its value, and the commodities whose value is enhanced by the diminished expense of transportation."[7]

New turnpikes, canals, and later railroads broadened a town's trading area; in doing so they also brought towns into competition with each other for the same urban markets, rural hinterland, and even nearby entrepreneurs. Such urban competition resulted in both winners and losers. An example of how this worked was the colonial rivalry between Baltimore and Charlestown.

> Charlestown and Baltimore are nearly of the same age, and for a long time after the former was laid out they were rivals, and continued to be such until about the time of the Revolutionary War, when the latter, owing to the trade with the western part of the State and the superior facilities for foreign commerce, outstripped the former, and it gradually sank into obscurity and neglect. Many of the inhabitants who had erected substantial houses in

Charlestown tore them down and shipped the material to Baltimore, where it was used in the construction of other buildings; thus the successful rival gained what the unsuccessful one lost, and as the one diminished, the other increased in size.[8]

The study of local elites provides a useful technique for exploring urban competition and growth. In the preindustrial towns of northeast Pennsylvania, the elite may be defined as the town's businessmen, those who accumulated capital for local investment. Few people met this simple standard and, as a rule, the smaller the town the smaller the elite. A description of these four towns and their elites helps set the stage for studying the massive coal development in northeast Pennsylvania after 1850.[9]

Located strategically on the Susquehanna River, Wilkes-Barre was the first town in northeast Pennsylvania; it would later become the regional center of the state's Wyoming Valley. When Wilkes-Barre was established in the 1770s, it had to beat back challenges from Forty Fort to become the county seat of spacious Luzerne County. The early settlers, primarily Connecticut Yankees, serviced the thinly settled population and administered land claims until statehood and Indian removal spurred greater settlement. By the early 1800s, the social, economic, and political leaders in Wilkes-Barre had formed a tight kinship network described in chapter five. Economic success in early Wilkes-Barre came only to those who were part of this social and familial group.[10]

The elite of early Wilkes-Barre used the town's good location on the Susquehanna River to promote trade and local growth. Some of these entrepreneurs started country stores in nearby hamlets and became middlemen in a trade extending from Philadelphia to the Wyoming Valley. Politicians in Wilkes-Barre helped their city by influencing the state legislature to widen and deepen the Susquehanna River to increase the flow of commerce to and from Wilkes-Barre. By 1850, when transportation and marketing advances made rapid coal production possible, Wilkes-Barre had a cohesive elite and a 2,700 population. Wealthy members of the town's kinship group, not outside investors, became prime movers for coal development in Wilkes-Barre and the Wyoming Valley.[11]

As settlers trickled in to northeastern Pennsylvania, new counties were carved from Luzerne County.[12] Entrepreneurs created new towns to handle the administrative duties of county seats and the commercial tasks of servicing nearby agriculture. By the early 1800s, the new counties of Bradford, Susquehanna, and Wayne formed the northeastern border of Pennsylvania. Their county seats, Towanda, Montrose, and Bethany (later Honesdale), actively sought business and population. Wilkes-Barre's longevity, of course, had allowed that town time to generate wealth and population through an active elite. As Pennsylvania's northeast filled out, though, the new county seats each carved out small hinterlands within their county and began the slow process of elite formation and urban growth.

Montrose and Towanda, the hubs of Susquehanna and Bradford Counties, underwent similar patterns of growth and development. Founded as county seats in 1812, both towns were the centers of their counties. As the farmland of northeast Pennsylvania filled with settlers, Montrose and Towanda expanded their commercial services. Both towns, for example, established their first local banks in the mid-1830s; in that decade the number of lawyers in each town visibly increased. By the 1850s, after two generations of growth, Montrose and Towanda each held about 1,000 population.[13]

Two names stand out in the early history of Montrose—Post and Jessup. These two families came from Long Island, New York, in the early 1800s, and spearheaded the commercial development of Montrose. As large landowners, the Post family promised some of their land free if the state would agree to make it the seat of Susquehanna County. Having done this, Isaac Post became Montrose's first merchant. He also led the fundraising to build a turnpike from Montrose to outside markets. He and his brother David helped organize the first county government. Thereafter the Post brothers worked together as merchants, hotel owners, turnpike investors, and even members of the board of directors on the Bank of Susquehanna, Montrose's first financial institution. In local politics, Isaac served as state legislator and associate county judge; David was elected justice of the peace. Their cousin, Yale-educated William Jessup, was one of the county's first lawyers. Starting his career in county government, Jessup soon developed a large law practice, which included the training of dozens of lawyers throughout northeast Pennsylvania. From 1838 to 1851, Jessup served as district judge in Pennsylvania for three counties. Not neglecting the business life of Montrose, Jessup served with three of his Post cousins on the board of directors of the Bank of Susquehanna.[14]

Jessup and the second generation of Posts in Montrose continued investing the wealth that their families had created. Isaac Post's eldest son, William L., became president of the Bank of Susquehanna in the early 1840s; another son, Isaac L., cofounded the banking house of Post, Cooper, and Company a decade later. Jessup, meanwhile, became a railroad promoter and also trained three of his sons and two of Isaac Post's sons to become lawyers. By 1850, Judge William Jessup was the second largest wealthholder in Montrose. The Post and Jessup families seem to have proven the quip that "Montrose businessmen have Yankee shrewdness and look out for the main chance."[15] Jessup shrewdness, after 1850, would be applied to coal development in the Lackawanna Valley.

In Montrose, then, as in Wilkes-Barre, the family was an important institution for raising and investing capital. The Posts and Jessups took the following steps.

First, they came to Montrose and immediately began speculating in land. Second, they gained skills in law and business and used their knowledge and capital to invest in various local enterprises. Third, they educated their children, and gave them capital to start banks and law firms. Other members of the town's small commercial elite did some of the same things. Edward Fuller was a landholder and the county's first sheriff. His son George became the town's first U.S. congressman. He also built up the family fortune with his brother. Together, they started a hotel as well as a dry goods and grocery business. Secku Meylert, the son of a German banker, parlayed fifty acres of land into an estate of over one thousand acres by operating a store and managing several large tracts of land for outside investors. Shortly after Meylert died in 1849, his sons Amos and Michael started a bank.[16]

The story of early Towanda is like the story of Montrose. A small elite made money first in land speculation; then they gravitated toward law, banking, and large landholding. Finally, after 1850, much of this money ended up invested in the Lackawanna coal fields.

Founded as the seat of Bradford County in 1812, Towanda was located on the Susquehanna River, later enlarged into the North Branch Canal. One of the town's founding fathers was Epithalet Mason, who was elected as county auditor, deputy sheriff, record of deeds, and county road commissioner. By the early 1830s, Mason and his son Gordon were investing in thousands of acres of land in Bradford County. From the returns on land, Gordon Mason seems to have raised the capital to launch a career in banking. In 1850, he started a banking house in Towanda with two other partners. By 1863 he had dropped that venture to become the initial president of the First National Bank of Towanda. Alert to new opportunities, his capital and banking skills helped finance city growth in the Lackawanna coal fields in the 1850s.[17]

Two other prominent Towanda capitalists were Joseph Kingsbury, a banker and landholder, and his son-in-law, George Sanderson, a lawyer and state senator. Kingsbury, an early merchant of Bradford County, invested some of the income from his large farm estate in the county's first bank, the Towanda Bank. In the late 1830s he became that institution's president. Migrating to northeastern Pennsylvania from Massachusetts, George Sanderson, with an eye for the main chance, married the banker's daughter in 1835. He went into law and business and ranked as Towanda's fourth largest wealthholder by 1850. He must have been popular as well as prominent: In the next year he was elected as Bradford County's state senator—an office that would broaden his political contacts and would soon lead him and the Kingsburys to investments in the emerging Lackawanna coal region.[18]

As county seats, Towanda and Montrose had clear advantages in competing for growth and business. They were limited in their expansion though by the sparse farm settlement in Pennsylvania in the early 1800s. Only one other major town, Dundaff, had formed in either of these counties before the 1840s. Yet despite not being a county seat, Dundaff temporarily drew more people than did either Montrose or Towanda.[19]

Dundaff, like Montrose, was created from the migration of several New England families. The leader of this group of Connecticut Yankees was Gould Phinney, who made his fortune investing in tin plate during the War of 1812. Turning to land speculation, Phinney bought several large tracts of land on the Milford and Owego turnpike south of Montrose. With capital and transportation, Phinney built a town on his land and named it Dundaff. He convinced several cousins and friends to join him; in 1824, Phinney and his associates tied their futures to the new town of Dundaff. The versatile Phinney does not seem to have been modest or cautious. He established a store, a tavern, a grist and saw mill, a stage line, and a blacksmith and wagon shop. As one observer noted, Phinney "was practically the proprietor of Dundaff" and "gave employment to many."[20]

For a while Phinney's enterprises brought people to Dundaff. The need for new urban services gave Phinney's sons, cousins, and friends a chance to invest. One son, Thomas Phinney, became a lawyer; another son, Elisha, established a store, an axe factory, and a tannery. Their cousins, Horace, Alexander, and Jaman Phelps served as a merchant, a physician, and a tanner. Fellow newcomers Charles Welles became a local merchant, John Wells established a carding factory and became a clothier, and Thomas Wells served as the cashier of Gould Phinney's bank. By 1828, the town of Dundaff had almost 300 people; it rivaled the county seat of Montrose for trade and surpassed it in population.[21]

Phinney was not one to think small. Beating Montrose merely whetted his appetite for regional conquest. He seemed to think that Dundaff could rise to supremacy in northeast Pennsylvania by becoming the seat of a new county carved out of the emerging coal field to the south. Phinney's future, then, became closely linked with that of his new town—and he persistently endeavored to secure the success of both. In 1825, just one year after moving to Dundaff, Phinney opened the Northern Bank, then the only financial institution in Susquehanna County. Six years later Phinney colluded with his Phelps cousins to open a glass factory in Dundaff. They employed scores of persons to make window glass from the sand around nearby Crystal Lake.[22]

Yet, despite the bustle of economic activity Dundaff ultimately lost out. After the early 1830s, the town's population declined, local investment plummeted, and leaders went elsewhere. Its problem was the development of the nearby Lackawanna coal fields to the south of Dundaff in the late 1820s. New Yorkers built the new towns of Honesdale and Carbondale as transportation points for coal shipped by the new Delaware and Hudson Canal Company (hereafter the D&H). When this happened, Carbondale became the center for investment in the newly-created Lackawanna coal region. Susquehanna and Bradford counties were barely outside the coal fields below, so the Phinney clan desperately tried to coax the D&H to build its canal to Dundaff and make that town its Pennsylvania headquarters. When this failed, "Dundaff . . . descended to occupy the position of a small country trading point," and Carbondale was touted as "the undoubted future emporium of northeastern Pennsylvania." As one observer of this competition noted

> Dundaff . . . exerted an influence which caused it to be widely known. But it is difficult to overcome natural obstacles when competing towns, in addition to the advantages of location, receive the impetus connected with extensive transportation facilities. In such an uneven struggle it is with towns, as with men, a question of the survival of the fittest. The one contending against the modern railway must go to the wall. Notwithstanding the efforts of Dundaff to avert such a fate, . . . after 1840 the claims of the new town of Carbondale to become the business center of this part of the state were fully conceded.[23]

So Dundaff was tied to farming and a turnpike, Carbondale to coal and a canal. The gradual shift from mixed farming to coal development transformed economic and social life in northeastern Pennsylvania. This process created the new Lackawanna coal region and made Bradford and Susquehanna counties this region's hinterland. As the fall of Dundaff and the rise of Carbondale indicate, coal mining also dramatically altered the patterns of city growth in northeastern Pennsylvania. After 1830, urban competition for entrepreneurs and industry was shaped by the emergence of coal as a primary export.[24]

The development of coal tantalized capitalists in New York City to extend their empire into neighboring Pennsylvania. In the 1820s, the D&H dug the canal about 100 miles from their city to the tip of the Lackawanna Valley.[25] This accomplishment was one step in the dramatic rise of New York City as America's first multiregional center. It started in the 1810s when New Yorkers built the Erie Canal 363 miles across the state to tap new western markets. In that same decade New York shippers boldly cornered the carrying trade for Southern cotton; then they centralized British-American trade in Liverpool and New York City.[26] As New York City's empire expanded, its entrepreneurs flourished and its population spiralled to provide new local services. Its urban domination continued well into the twentieth century as New York investors took the risks that made their city the financial center of the United States. One

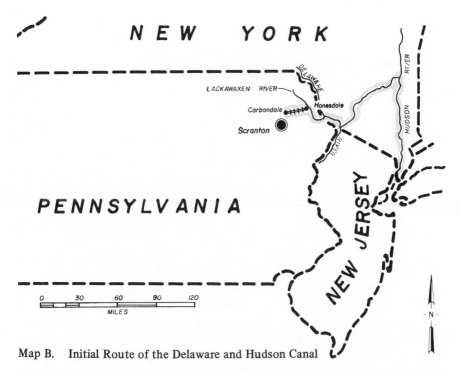

Map B.   Initial Route of the Delaware and Hudson Canal

of these risks was the digging of the Delaware and Hudson Canal in the 1820s to bring the Lackawanna coal east from Pennsylvania to New York City.[27]

Actually entrepreneurs from both New York City and Philadelphia began to speculate in coal during the War of 1812. Timber scarcity had caused a rapid rise in wood prices. After the war anthracite continued to be used because it was readily available and potentially cheap, if only it could be transported efficiently from the Lackawanna Valley to markets on the east coast. Politicians in Pennsylvania and New York removed this bottleneck by approving state funds to build canals to the rich coal lands. The New York legislators granted the D&H a charter to build a canal almost 100 miles from the Hudson River to Rondout, New York, to the Lackawaxen River, up to Carbondale, at the eastern edge of the Lackawanna coal fields. The Pennsylvania legislature, which later sponsored internal improvements throughout the state, gave the funds to widen the Lackawaxen River in Pennsylvania.[28]

Building the canal generated jobs and excitement throughout eastern Pennsylvania; in 1829 the D&H shipped the first coal from Carbondale to New York City. Soon the prices of coal dropped and this spurred demand: Tonnage on the D&H increased from 7,000 in 1829 to 110,000 in 1833. New York investors received the coal profits, but the Lackawanna Valley had a marketable export in coal and a growing town in Carbondale. Because of the booming coal traffic, the industrial towns of Honesdale and Carbondale quickly surpassed the nearby agricultural towns of Towanda, Montrose, and Dundaff.[29]

As the shipping point at the head of the Delaware and Hudson Canal, Honesdale grew rapidly and passed 2,000 population by 1850. The town was named for Phillip Hone, the mayor of New York City, who promoted the canal in the 1820s. Honesdale's founder and wealthiest citizen was Jason Torrey, a speculator in Wayne County land almost from the county's creation in 1798. Unlike most land investors, Torrey had to win the county seat battle twice: first, to have it located in Bethany, where he was a large landholder; and second to have it changed to the new town of Honesdale. The land in Honesdale, at the head of the canal, offered better opportunities for investment and growth than did Bethany—an observation not missed by Jason Torrey, even though he seemed committed to Bethany. So in routing the new canal, Torrey worked closely with the D&H. When the plans for the canal were revealed, Torrey owned the upper half of Honesdale and the D&H owned the lower half.[30]

With the land question settled, Jason Torrey and his family joined the D&H in generating business in Honesdale. Torrey's son John, who succeeded his father as the wealthiest man in the city, built a flour mill and became vice-president and director of the Honesdale Bank. Another son, Stephen, joined his brother as a bank director and was also city treasurer. Their brother-in-law, Henry Seely, was president of the Honesdale bank; their nephew, Charles Weston, comanaged the Honesdale Mill. A close associate of the Torreys was lawyer and local newspaper editor Ebenezer Kingsbury, who became prominent as speaker of the Pennsylvania Senate. He used his influence to help the Torreys relocate the seat of Wayne County at Honesdale. The Torrey capital and talent that helped build Honesdale would help build a regional center in the Lackawanna Valley after 1850.[31]

Honesdale dominated economic life in Wayne County, but the D&H invested far more in Carbondale. In the 1830s and 1840s, some thought Carbondale would become the "grand emporium of northeast Pennsylvania." First, as the earliest town in coal fields, it had what geographers call "initial advantage," or head start. Second, Carbondale also had "locational advantage." The town was on the northeastern tip of the Lackawanna coal field and was close to New York City. All future towns in the northern anthracite field—the Lackawanna and Wyoming valleys—would have a greater distance to market their coal. Third, Carbondale had plenty of exportable anthracite, which was becoming popular in American and world markets. And the D&H made Carbondale the center for coal shipment by pouring capital into a canal and railroad from New York City to the anthracite fields. Fourth, as the largest town for a hundred miles around, Carbondale began to attract people from nearby farms and villages.[32]

Carbondale seemed destined to become a major industrial city. The D&H hired scores of people to build a gravity railroad from its coal land at Carbondale to its shipping point at Honesdale. After this, hundreds of people flocked to Carbondale to work for the D&H. They mined and transported coal, dug shafts and pumped water from the mines, and broke the coal into marketable sizes. The D&H then centered in Carbondale its "linkage industries," those related to the production of coal. These included machine and car shops, to make engines and later locomotives; repair and paint shops, which were especially needed after fires; and a lumber department, which used its saw mill to make railroad cars, tracks, and mine shafts. The need for workers brought to Carbondale not only hundreds of migrants from the countryside nearby but also an influx of foreigners. By 1850, twenty-year-old Carbondale was almost twice the size of Wilkes-Barre, which was emerging as the regional capital of the Wyoming Valley. In the Lackawanna region, Carbondale was five times as large as Montrose and Towanda, and sixteen times bigger than Dundaff.[33]

Despite Carbondale's many advantages it lost out in the urban competition during the 1850s.[34] The new city of Scranton, sixteen miles from Carbondale, emerged in the 1850s as the regional center of the Lackawanna Valley. Carbondale, "the grand emporium of northeast Pennsylvania," seems to have stagnated for three reasons.

First, as a company town Carbondale never developed a strong local elite that could build new industries. By contrast, Wilkes-Barre, the center of the adjacent Wyoming Valley, had existed as a regional service center before coal development. It had an indigenous elite and the local capital to finance coal operations. In Carbondale, the D&H owned the railroad and most of the coal land; few independent entrepreneurs could afford to invest in coal. Carbondale was therefore inflexible and, unlike Wilkes-Barre, became almost entirely dependent on the D&H and New York capital. As at least one observer noted in 1880, "the prosperity of Carbondale has always depended on the amount of work done by the Delaware and Hudson Canal Company."[35] Since the owners of the D&H channeled the profits of anthracite coal elsewhere, Carbondale did not become wealthy despite its initial growth. Some outside investment can help make a city prosper. But total outside ownership almost never does. Entirely dependent on New York capital, local Carbondalers were unable to chart a future for their town.

Second, the environment in Carbondale was not healthful or conducive to business and trade. Most industrial cities in the nineteenth century were hardly paragons of cleanliness and safety but Carbondale was among the dingiest. Fires periodically gutted whose sections of the city destroying property, buildings, and lives. Mines caved in from time to time; the most serious collapse buried sixty miners (fourteen died) in forty acres of subterranean caverns. If the fires and mines didn't get you, a flood might. One flood, caused by a poorly planned reservoir, surged through main street filling the mines, taking lives, and annihilating buildings and houses.

In light of these disorderly influences it is startling to discover that before 1851 Carbondale had no fire or police department. In that year, after an unusually severe fire "laid waste to the greater portion of the city above the public square," Carbondale's shortsighted leaders finally decided to get some "means of protection against fire or outlaws." The dedication of Carbondale's new civil servants seems to have been slim because another fire soon ravaged the city, this time "entailing a considerable loss" to William Richmond's coal car factory and George L. Dickson's mercantile firm among other damage. This new city government apparently made no provision for sanitation; as one resident complained in 1875, "another inconvenience is that citizens have no convenient place to dump their coal ashes, or empty . . . rubbish." Such a perilous environment prevented a stable business climate and must have repelled potential investors from the city limits of Carbondale.[36]

The third explanation of Carbondale's failure is that the small economic elite that did exist there did not have strong loyalties to this city. The weakness of these ties is certainly understandable. The hazards of fire, flood, and crime forced businessmen to load up on insurance and cross their fingers if they expected to survive. Also, the prospects of upward mobility through the D&H made ambitious men focus on the company and not on Carbondale. The superintendent of engineering for the D&H, James Archbald, was the town's first mayor. The owner of the town's flour mill, Edward Weston, was chief surveyor of lands for the company. The operator of Carbondale's foundry, Thomas Dickson, worked years for the D&H; his father was superintendent of its machine shop. These men tied their fortunes to the D&H, not to Carbondale, as their migration would later indicate.[37]

By 1850, no town in the Lackawanna Valley had shown the strength to harness the capital and talent in northeast Pennsylvania; urbanization, in the region, therefore, was fragmented and decentralized among the old commercial towns of Towanda, Montrose, and Dundaff and the new industrial towns of Honesdale and Carbondale. The elites in these towns usually invested as families in local real estate and in small urban enterprises. They shunned the riskier, more expensive investments that would use the abundant deposits of anthracite. New Yorkers did make these investments, however, so the lion's share of the coal profits went to entrepreneurs outside the Lackawanna Valley. A similar occurrence at the opposite end of the country took place when outside owners in the silver mining regions in Nevada brought their wealth to the city of San Francisco. Without a regional center, the Lackawanna Valley was also in danger of having its economic future determined by outsiders in board rooms in New York City.

TABLE 2.1. Genealogy of the Scranton Group

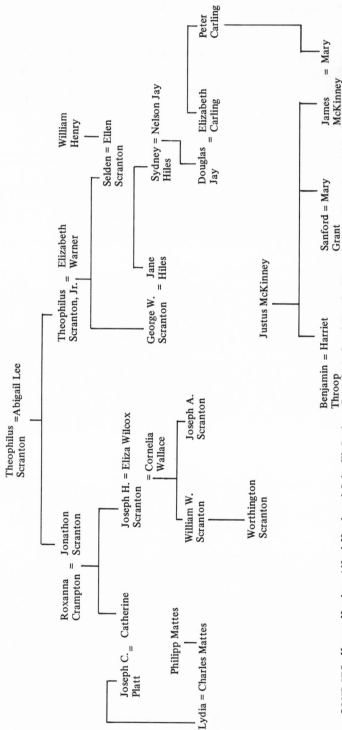

SOURCES: Horace Hayden, Alfred Hand, and John W. Jordan, *Genealogical and Family History of the Wyoming and Lackawanna Valleys, Pennsylvania* (New York and Chicago, 1906), 2:140–42. Hitchcock, *History of Scranton and Its People*, 2 vols. (New York City, 1914) 1: 88, 180; 2:11; Frederick L. Chapman, *Portrait and Biographical Record of Lackawanna County, Pennsylvania* (New York and Chicago, 1897), pp. 600, 697; George B. Kulp, *Families of the Wyoming Valley, Biographical, Genealogical, and Historical Sketches of the Bench and Bar of Luzerne County, Pennsylvania* (Wilkes-Barre, 1885), 3: 1299.

2

From Nails to Rails:
The Scrantons' Improbable Experiment
Creates a City

During the 1840s the Lackawanna Valley would be the battleground where American independence from English iron would be fought and won. This masterpiece of entrepreneurship was largely the work of George, Selden, and Joseph Scranton who, after much experimenting, became the first Americans to mass-produce rails.[1] In doing so they harnessed talent, capital, and technical expertise from within their families and friends, investors in small towns in the Lackawanna Valley, and outsiders from New York. Two ironies are striking: First, the Lackawanna Valley with its thinly scattered, low quality ore deposits was hardly a natural setting for manufacturing; second, in the competition for urban growth the winning city of Scranton did not exist until the 1840s. Only splendid entrepreneurship could have created such an unlikely result.

The migration of the visionary Scrantons to northeast Pennsylvania began in the late 1830s, when William Henry, a trained geologist, scoured the area looking for the right ingredients for ironmaking—water power, anthracite coal, iron ore, lime, and sulphur. Henry found these elements in small quantities throughout the Lackawanna Valley so he falsely assumed they all existed there in abundance. Playing a hunch, Henry took an option to buy 500 acres of land at present-day Scranton and build a blast furnace on it. At first he sought the necessary $20,000 for the scheme from New York and England; but the high risk of his daring experiment frightened away even the hardiest of speculators. Finding greater faith from his family, Henry received support from his son-in-law, Selden T. Scranton, and Scranton's brother George, both of whom were operating the nearby Oxford Iron Works in Oxford, New Jersey. Originally from Connecticut the wide-ranging Scrantons tapped their credit lines and picked

25

George W. Scranton

up additional capital from Sanford Grant, a merchant from Belvidere, New Jersey, and Philipp Mattes, a banker from Easton, Pennsylvania. With almost $20,000 raised the project began in 1840. The Scrantons made the equipment for the blast furnace at their Oxford Iron Works. Then they sent it to Henry, who assembled it on their plot of land in the remote Lackawanna Valley. After a year and a half of futile tinkering, the group finally built the right blast furnace and found the right combination of ores, lime, and sulphur to make pig-iron.[2]

The next problem the Scrantons faced was how to market the iron successfully and still keep control of the enterprise in the family. The high transportation costs and the limited demand for their product threatened either to sink the project or to throw it, if it did work, into outside control. When William Henry lost credibility George Scranton took charge. His plan: to convert the pig-iron into nails. Such a bold venture into manufacturing would not be cheap. The need for a rolling mill and a nail factory upped the ante to $86,000. Desperate for credit, George Scranton coaxed some of this money from New York mercantilist John Howland. Yet this jeopardized the family's ownership. So he placed his greatest reliance on his two first cousins Joseph H. and Erastus C. Scranton, who

Joseph H. Scranton

had left Connecticut to become merchants in Augusta, Georgia. These Southern cousins had encouraged the ironmakers right from the start by sending the profits of their own business to the Lackawanna Valley. So by 1843 George Scranton got his $86,000 and kept family control as well.[3]

Forging ties to one another through intermarriage, the Scranton group long managed to keep a majority of the company stock within their family. For example, when Sanford Grant weakened, he sold his share to Joseph H. Scranton. Later, when more capital was needed, Joseph Scranton's brother-in-law, Joseph C. Platt, came to the Lackawanna Valley from Connecticut to manage the company store.[4] When Philipp Mattes' son Charles married Joseph Platt's sister, all original members of the industrial project were related, as shown in table 2.1. With enough money at last, the Scrantons began making nails in 1843.

The nail factory failed miserably. First, no rivers or rails helped market its product. Dependent on land transportation, the Scrantons transferred the nails on wagons to Carbondale and Pittston and there shipped them to other markets. Second, no one wanted the Scrantons' nails because they were poor in quality. The low grade ores in the Lackawanna Valley provided only brittle and easily breakable nails. Faced with bankruptcy, the Scrantons contemplated the conversion of the nail mill into a rolling mill for railroad tracks. Yet experienced Englishmen dominated the world production of rails in the 1840s and no American firm dared to challenge them. After floundering in the production of nails, however, the Scrantons decided that a lucrative rail contract might be the gamble that could restore their lost investment.[5]

As fate would have it, in 1846 the nearby New York and Erie Railroad had a contract with the state of New York to build a rail line from Port Jervis to Binghamton, New York. When England had a rail boom and English manufacturers refused to supply the Erie with the needed rails, the Scrantons had their chance. They traveled to New York and boldly persuaded the board of directors of the New York and Erie to give their newly formed company the two year contract for producing 12,000 tons of T-rails. Impressed with the Scrantons, and desperate for rails, the directors of the New York and Erie advanced $90,000 to the eager Scrantons to construct a rolling mill and to furnish the necessary track.[6]

The construction of the mill and the making of thousands of tons of rails seemed impossible. Not just because no Americans had done it before. Or even because the Scrantons had so little equipment to do it. The logistics alone defied success. The Scrantons would first have to learn how to make the rails they promised to provide. Then they would have to import some ore and much limestone into the Lackawanna Valley to make the rails. Then, because they lacked a water route to the Erie line, they would have to draft dozens of teams of horses to carry finished rails from the rolling mill scores of miles through the wilderness to New York right where the track was laid. It is no wonder the New Yorkers wanted to back out at the last moment. Yet somehow, in less than a year and a half, the Scrantons did it. On December 27, 1848, with just four days before the expiration of the Erie's charter, the Scrantons fulfilled their contract and completed the rail line. In doing so, they won the confidence of New York investors and a profit for their family enterprise.[7]

The Scrantons, the New Yorkers, and the nation benefited from mass-produced American rails. On the eve of the Scranton experiment, Nicholas Biddle, the former president of the Bank of the United States, observed that "with all the materials for supplying iron in our own hands, the country has been obliged to pay enormous sums to Europeans for this necessary article. . . . This dependence is horrible." This "costly humiliation," Biddle urged, "ought to cease forever." The Scrantons broke the English domination of rail production and established their iron works as an enterprise of the future.[8]

In 1853, with the full confidence of New York investors, the Scrantons incorporated an $800,000 iron and coal company; they also made plans to build their own rail transportation to connect Scranton to New York City and also to markets westward. With their locally owned enterprises as a base, the Scrantons were starting to build a major industrial city.[9]

The gradual growth of the Scrantons' iron works during the 1840s, from making nails to rails, taxed their ingenuity to raise money, to import lime and ore from outside sources, to learn new techniques of ironmaking, and to maintain control over the future of the company. Trying to achieve success and local-group ownership, the Scrantons eagerly sought capital from three different sources: family and friends, New York capitalists, and investors from small towns in the Lackawanna Valley.

The first and best sources were friends and kinsmen. A valuable ally of the Scrantons was ironmaster Joseph J. Albright, the uncle of Selden Scranton. Albright had worked with the Scranton brothers in New Jersey at the Oxford iron furnace in the mid-1830s; afterward he managed two iron works in the Lehigh Valley and one in Virginia. Through correspondence and personal visits with the Scrantons, Albright advised and encouraged them in the making of iron. He loaned them money and personnel; he even sold his nephews wagons, mules, and equipment when they ran short.[10] Two other Scranton allies, later to become relatives, were brothers John and James Blair. As founders of the Belvidere Bank in New Jersey, the Blairs had backed the Scrantons in their early ironmaking days in Oxford; the bankers even served as a market by purchasing the Scrantons' nails. In the 1840s and afterward, further financing by the Blairs preserved local group control of the fledgling enterprise.[11]

Capital supplied from within the Scranton group was helpful but hardly adequate. Since few investors could afford the thousands of dollars needed to operate nail makers and rolling mills, the Scrantons desperately needed backing from a second source: New York capitalists. Through the development of the D&H, New Yorkers had already seen the profitability of exporting Lackawanna Valley coal; in the nation's largest city there were many investors who could afford to risk the necessary capital. Howland and Company and Phelps, Dodge, and Company, with close ties to the Erie Railroad, took this chance. Through their loans to the Scrantons, the New Yorkers became partners in the Scrantons' enterprise.[12]

Like the Scrantons, John Howland, Anson and John J. Phelps, and William Dodge were all Connecticut men, which seems to have provided a bond of trust among the various interests.[13] As an investor in the Scranton iron works and as a partner in the Erie Railroad, William Dodge was especially valuable in getting the Scrantons their major rail contract with the Erie. Among the New Yorkers, John J. Phelps even had some direct knowledge of the potential of the Lackawanna Valley. Phelps had lived in Dundaff in the 1830s and was the son-in-law of Gould Phinney, the city father of this Pennsylvania town. So New York capital again became part of the economic life of the Lackawanna Valley when the Scrantons expanded their iron works and built rails to tie them to outside markets.[14]

In the early 1840s, before the Scrantons could get New York capital, they relied on a third and final source: investors in and around the Lackawanna

Valley. When the Scrantons selected land in the Lackawanna Valley for their experiment in ironmaking, most northeast Pennsylvanians doubted the wisdom of the scheme. This skepticism appeared to be confirmed by the Scrantons' early failures to perfect an anthracite furnace to smelt the iron ore. To attract any investment, then, required diligent salesmanship, and this task brought the Scrantons in contact with the elites in the nearby towns of Towanda, Montrose, and Carbondale. Listening to the Scranton promise of an industrial empire in the Lackawanna Valley interested them, alerted them to the Scranton plan, and coaxed from them a modicum of capital. The Scrantons eagerly accepted all they could get, which included small loans from the Towanda Bank and the Bank of Susquehanna. In Carbondale, the Scrantons received another small loan from Charles Pierson, a foundry owner and the wealthiest man in town. Another Carbondaler, James Archbald, the superintendent of the D&H, corresponded wistfully with George Scranton about building canal transportation from the Scranton iron works to Carbondale. Small loans and good wishes aside, though, the Scranton venture was too steep for these small town investors.[15]

The Scrantons tried to recruit talented personnel in the Lackawanna Valley to their cause. In the 1840s, they could not hope to uproot the wealthier urban gentry in northeast Pennsylvania, whose land speculations and capital investments committed them to their small towns. As the Scrantons' enterprise developed they were able to recruit some venturesome personnel nearby. For example, Charles Fuller, the son of a tavernkeeper and the first sheriff of Montrose, became the Scantons' bookkeeper in 1848 and later grew prosperous with them. Edward Kingsbury, the son of a state senator, lawyer, and newspaper editor in Honesdale, became a clerk and later assistant treasurer for the Scrantons. William Manness, who came to the Lackawanna Valley from New Jersey about the same time as the Scrantons, joined them in erecting their first blast furnace; he later became their superintendent of building. Finally, the Scrantons got help from physician Benjamin Throop, who came to the Lackawanna Valley from upstate New York, via Honesdale, shortly after the Scrantons' arrival. Throop records the loyal support he gave the new industrialists in a book written much later, and some of his claims are clearly born out in the Scranton correspondence.[16]

Not everyone wished the Scrantons well. And this is what made their success so unlikely. First, there was the generally negative reaction from entrepreneurs in Wilkes-Barre, who thought the rise of a new city would threaten their hegemony in northeast Pennsylvania. The Scrantons logically tried to secure loans in Wilkes-Barre, the oldest and largest city in northeast Pennsylvania. But the businessmen there rarely helped, and they often hurt. For example, in the 1850s the Scrantons tried to get a railroad charter for a new line, the Liggett's Gap, from the state legislature; Wilkes-Barre's able and influential politicians thwarted the Scrantons because the new rail line threatened Wilkes-Barre's trade dominance of the Susquehanna River through the North Branch Canal. Referring to Wilkes-Barre as "the old harlot of iniquity," a concerned lawyer advised the Scrantons that those associated with the North Branch Canal in Wilkes-Barre and the D&H in Carbondale "all make common cause against [the] Liggett's Gap [Railroad]."[17]

Not only did politicians in Wilkes-Barre hamper iron production and delay rail completion, they prevented the Scrantons' emerging industrial city from becoming a county seat. The new city of Scranton happened to be situated in the eastern end of Luzerne County. So wily politicians in the county seat of Wilkes-Barre used statewide influence to delay for decades the creation of a new county. Even the prestige and influence of George Scranton in the Pennsylvania senate and U.S. Congress during the 1850s could not force the division of Luzerne County. So while the Scrantons were trying to promote their new town as a mecca of industrial opportunity, the town's administrative business was being diverted to the county seat of Wilkes-Barre. Summarizing Wilkes-Barre's general "policy of obstruction" Benjamin Throop observed that

> during all these early struggles, Wilkes-Barre had the advantage. The Lacka-
> wanna Valley was poor, and had its fortune still to make; Wilkes-Barre had
> inherited considerable wealth from its former generations. The public-spirited
> men here were, most of them, new-comers and unknown. Those of the
> opposition had prestige and influence.[18]

Possibly even more damaging than the opposition from Wilkes-Barre's politicians was the hostility from many local farmers near Scranton. These old settlers liked the prospects of improved transportation to get their crops to market, but many did not want to see the "machine" transform their "garden" into an industrial community.[19] One contemporary described their fears sarcastically as follows:

> There were then, as there are yet, and as there always will be, a debilitated,
> but croaking class of persons who by some hidden process manage to keep
> up a little animation in their useless bodies, who gathered in bar-room cor-
> ners, and who, with peculiar wisdom belonging to this class while discussing
> weighty matters, gravely predicted that "the Scrantons must fail!"[20]

Even before the Scrantons arrived, several of these farmers had formed an ad hoc committee and denounced "*blackleg drivellers*, in the shape of incorporated companies."[21]

The local squabbles with the old settlers regularly kept the Scrantons from fully attending to their iron works. Recognizing this problem early the Scrantons donated land and labor to help build the old settlers a church. Through a company store the industrialists enthusiastically traded goods and produce with nearby farmers. Desperate for credit, though, the Scrantons were barely surviving in the early 1840s and had to seek extensions on local loans. At one point William Henry wrote that "we have not twenty-five cents in hand. . . . The credit of the concern [is] impaired." He added that "this suspense and uncertainty is worse where our credit is concerned than almost any other mode of proceeding." George Scranton felt the same way. At one point he described himself as being "worried most to death for fear we can't meet all [credit obligations]. I cannot stand trouble & excitement as I once could. I don't sleep good. My appetite is poor & digestion bad. . . . If we can succeed in placing Lacka. out of debt it would help me much." During some of the Scrantons' darker moments "every petty claim of indebtedness was urged and pressed before the justices of the township with an earnestness really annoying."[22]

Disputes with the old settlers over land and credit, then, persisted as the Scrantons verged for years on bankruptcy without successfully producing nails or rails. At one extreme a vindictive local merchant threatened to "break . . . down" the Scrantons' company store by "selling goods very cheap"—if necessary by "giving away his goods." At the other end, legend has it that after the Scrantons' brittle nails were rejected by New York merchants, Selden Scranton immediately sold quantities of the "practically worthless" product to unsuspecting old settlers. Such feuding seems to have been commonplace; even when the Scrantons finally received the rail contract from the Erie, many farmers withheld the use of their mules and horses to prevent delivery of the rails.[23] Under these conditions one can hardly argue that the location at Scranton was inevitably destined for urban glory. It was not.

The Scranton industrialists, as a group, contrast sharply with the old settlers. The industrialists were younger than the prominent old settlers; they had come from a different part of the country, primarily New Jersey; they were more urbane and educated; and, as Presbyterians, Whigs, and temperance men they differed in cultural heritage.[24] Their industrial vision contrasted with the rural agricultural orientation of some old settlers. In short, the industrialists were more cosmopolitan than the old settlers.[25] While the latter, with their narrow view of life, brooded about annual harvests and local affairs, the industrialists built railroads to the outside world and produced iron and coal for a national market. While the traditional farmers found comfort in the holding of land, the modern industrialists invested and expanded. By 1850, despite resistance from old settlers, the Scrantons were creating a successful city with their Lackawanna iron works. Newcomers looking for jobs made changes too—even in the renaming of the town. By 1850, as one contemporary noted, "the old village names of Capoose and Slocum Hollow were disowned and forgotten by newcomers . . . for the briefer name of Scranton."[26]

The Scrantons could not hope to launch a city-building venture without transportation to outside markets. After completing their rail contract with the Erie Railroad in 1848, the Scrantons planned to lay rails to tie their new city to markets throughout New York. The D&H in Carbondale had been profitably supplying New York City and the Hudson Valley with coal since the 1820s, so the demand for anthracite had been proven.[27]

With the confidence of New York investors, the Scrantons proposed two railroads: the Liggett's Gap, which has already been mentioned, and the Delaware and Cobb's Gap. The Liggett's Gap line, running from Scranton fifty-six miles north to connect with the Erie at Great Bend, would permit Scranton to supply coal to the farms in the Genessee Valley in upstate New York; the Delaware and Cobb's Gap route, running sixty-four miles east to the Delaware River at Stroudsburg, would give the Scrantons a potential outlet for coal to New York City. By backing two lines the Scrantons gave themselves two markets for Lackawanna Valley coal. This brought them into formal competition with the North Branch canal in Wilkes-Barre and the D&H in Carbondale. The building of two rail lines, then, was a logical sequel to the Scrantons' superb iron works. The railroad itself became a market for Scranton iron, it provided an outlet for Scranton coal, and it promoted trade for Scranton city.[28]

The two railroads were primarily a joint venture of Scranton and New York capital. The lucrative contract for building the Erie Railroad gave the young industrialists capital to invest nearly on a par with the wealthy New Yorkers. John J. Phelps of New York was president of the Liggett's Gap line, but George Scranton was its general agent, and the Scranton group controlled five of the directorships. Phelps and Dodge capital were also conspicuous in the Delaware and Cobb's Gap line, but George Scranton was its president, and three of his relatives held seats on the board of directors. The two railroads were surveyed and built from 1850 to 1853; and then both were consolidated into one line, the Delaware, Lackawanna, and Western Railroad (hereafter D.L.&W.) with George Scranton as its first president. In 1853, flushed with success, the Scrantons also incorporated their iron works as the Lackawanna Iron and Coal Company (hereafter L.I.&C.) and elected Selden T. Scranton as president.[29]

In building the D.L.&W., the Scrantons received valuable assistance from leaders in nearby Montrose, Dundaff, and Towanda who knew their areas well and saw how a railroad would aid local economic development. So they helped the Scrantons with the surveying and the legal technicalities of buying right-of-way passage through farmland. Lawyer William Jessup and landholder Michael Meylert, both of Montrose, seem to have been especially useful to the Scrantons in persuading obstinate farmers to grant right-of-way privileges to the railroad. Elisha Phinney of Dundaff was George Scranton's assistant in surveying and constructing the Liggett's Gap railroad, the northern line of the D.L.&W. Finally state senator George Sanderson of Towanda helped the Scrantons overcome legislative obstacles, which probably concerned chartering the combined rail lines into the D.L.&W.[30]

With sizable ownership in the iron works and the railroad, the Scrantons were heavily committed to the growth of their new locality. In their correspondence, they clearly viewed industrial and urban growth as symbiotic. Their investment in real estate and housing multiplied in value after the success of their iron works and the arrival of a railroad. The Scranton group originally bought a 503 acre tract for $8,000 in 1840. As mere coal land that acreage was worth at least $100,000 by the mid-1850s. As improved land much of it was worth even more. The Scrantons had laid out streets, sold lots, and built mansions for themselves and company houses for their workers. The Scrantons' industrial success, then, created vast wealth for the group in real estate appreciation alone.[31]

The local ownership of industry and real estate was a primary reason that Scranton supplanted Carbondale during the 1850s as the largest town in the Lackawanna Valley. In this decade Scranton began to develop coal-related industries, such as engine manufacturing and gunpowder production, to supplement the growing L.I.&C. and the D.L.&W. So even though Carbondale was the first town in the Lackawanna Valley—and sixteen miles closer to New York City than Scranton was—its leaders could not make their town grow. Scranton emerged from the 1850s with a clear advantage in city building. The Scranton group held controlling ownership of the L.I.&C. until the 1870s, when the majority of stock fell into New York City hands. Initially dominating the D.L.&W., the Scranton group long held stock in it. So when coal mining and manufacturing became profitable, and when migrants came to Scranton for jobs, the local entrepreneurs, as well as New York City investors, shared in the benefits.[32]

Two forces helped the city of Scranton emerge as the capital of the Lackawanna Valley. First, the Scranton group openly promoted the economic opportunity of their rapidly growing city. They conscientiously urged capitalists in nearby towns to come and invest. Second, the visible success of the iron works and railroad was an alluring advertisement to entrepreneurs in the Lackawanna Valley and beyond: They migrated without being asked. As a result Scranton centralized much of the talent and capital in the region and used these resources to accelerate its rate of growth even further.

Actually the Scrantons had been urging entrepreneurs to come to their iron works almost since the time of their own migration in the early 1840s. During those bleak early years, when the Scrantons tried to avoid bankruptcy more than they tried to create a city, only their best friends took them seriously enough to join them. By the early 1850s, though, with an iron works and a railroad as visible symbols of achievement, the Scrantons lured several men of means from nearby towns into their industrial lair. These investors found plenty of opportunity because during the 1850s Scranton grew by almost one thousand persons per year. The city needed specialized professionals with capital. Specifically, Scranton needed bankers to concentrate wealth and loan capital to future investors; merchants and agricultural processors to supply dry goods and food to the burgeoning population; real estate developers to build houses and local transportation; lawyers to settle civil disputes, property claims, and to provide corporate assistance. The Scrantons themselves established the city's water works, but within their small group they could not hope to develop their iron and railroad industries and still satisfy the urban needs of a growing population.[33]

After much prompting, lawyer and former state senator George Sanderson moved from Towanda to Scranton in 1855. Sanderson had worked amicably with George Scranton in the Pennsylvania senate in the early 1850s and may have known him a decade earlier; at that time the Scrantons received a loan from the Towanda Bank, whose president was Sanderson's father-in-law, Joseph Kingsbury. Once in Scranton, Sanderson founded the city's first banking house, Sanderson and Company, with his brother-in-law and fellow Towanda migrant Burton Kingsbury. Sanderson must have made a lot of money banking because he later branched into real estate and local transportation development. In fact, he eventually built a whole suburb in his new home town.[34]

The second banking house in Scranton, Mason and Meylert, represented a combination of capital from Towanda and Montrose. One founder was Gordon F. Mason, who had been a land speculator, state senator, and banker in Towanda. Mason secured capital for the Scranton bank from two other Towanda businessmen, Christopher Ward and John Laporte, both of whom were among the town's wealthiest citizens. Mason's partners in Scranton were brothers Michael and Amos Meylert, who were from a family of bankers and large landholders outside of Montrose. Michael Meylert had already been useful to the Scrantons in securing right-of-way passage for the Liggett's Gap Railroad. This concentration of capital from Scranton's two northern county seats would be useful to the new industrial town. The Meylerts' ties to Scranton would be solidified when Amos Meylert's daughter married Joseph Scranton's son.[35]

Also from Montrose in the mid-1850s came merchant George Fuller, the brother of the Scrantons' bookkeeper, Charles Fuller. In Montrose, Fuller had been a merchant and U.S. congressman; in Scranton Fuller opened a dry goods store with his two sons George and Isaac. The sons inherited the business and son George A. Fuller cemented ties to his new city by marrying George Scranton's daughter, by becoming a bank director, and later by becoming president of the

Board of Trade. The Fullers must have felt right at home in Scranton when descendants of Montrose's founding families, including three sons of William Jessup and two grandsons of Isaac Post, settled in Scranton to practice law and invest in banks, insurance, and trolleys. The elder William Jessup remained in Montrose as a district judge and the most prominent man in the community. Yet he, too, felt the lure of opportunity in Scranton; he "engaged in rail and coal operations in Luzerne County," as president of the shortlived Lackawanna Railroad and chief attorney for the Scranton's profitable D.L.&W. line.[36]

The quality of urban services in Scranton improved with the migration of Elisha Phinney from Dundaff to Scranton. As the eldest son of the founder of Dundaff, Phinney developed agricultural services in his father's town by founding an axe factory and a tannery. In the early 1850s, Phinney worked as the assistant superintendent to George Scranton in building the northern line of the D.L.&W. Whether by urging or by choice, Phinney moved to Scranton in 1856 and established a wholesale flour and feed business to supply food to the industrial city's expanding population. Phinney later became president of a meat packing company and, like his father in Dundaff, a bank president. The presence of Phinney in Scranton, like that of the Masons and Sandersons from Towanda, and the Jessups, Posts, Meylerts, and Fullers from Montrose, marked a significant transfer of capital southward from the old commercial towns to the young industrial center of the Lackawanna Valley.[37]

The biggest catch that the Scrantons reeled in was James Blair of Belvidere, New Jersey. A friend, relative, and business partner of the Scrantons for decades, Blair, with his millionaire brother John, had backed the Scrantons in their lean years in New Jersey before their harvest in the Lackawanna Valley. In 1865, whether by conscious choice or friendly persuasion, James Blair moved to Scranton with hundreds of thousands of dollars in search of investments. With little delay he started his own bank and trolley company to add to the partnerships he already had with his Scranton friends.[38]

By attracting outside capital, the Scrantons were receiving men who would make the investments to help prevent bottlenecks and dislocations in the expanding urban economy. The arrival in Scranton of real estate developers, wholesale food producers, trolley builders, insurance agents, and bankers among others, were important for insuring an acceptable quality of life to sustain high morale and rapid growth.

Despite the clear opportunities for those with capital, not all such men responded to the Scrantons' siren call. Few, if any, Wilkes-Barre investors moved to Scranton. The older city was becoming the regional capital of the adjacent Wyoming Valley, and their city's entrepreneurs tied themselves to profitable investments there. Even an occasional friend of the Scrantons would balk at the uprooting and uncertainty endemic to migration. For example, merchant Phillip Walter of Nazareth resisted an apparently elaborate courtship from his Scranton relatives in 1852: He was reluctant "to pull [up] stakes and move" from "my long cherished *home*" because "I might fail." After a visit to Scranton, in which Walter sold hundreds of dollars worth of merchandise to an expanding population, he confessed that "I was quite enchanted with your place, and the great, though undeserved, esteem in which I was held by many of the inhabitants." Walter also admitted that he "certainly could not find a place anywhere where I would rather go than to Scranton." He further acknowledged that "my sons . . . would likely find openings for business in such a thriving place as Scranton appears to be and will yet become." Other men of means saw these advantages and settled in Scranton. But Walter avoided getting "carried away by the admiration of your thriving place" by his reluctance to uproot and his haunting fear that "still I might fail." Winnowing out the conservative and the weak at heart, Scranton seems to have attracted a select set of venturesome leaders to guide its industrial growth.[39]

Unlike Carbondale, Scranton attracted outside entrepreneurs. The prospects of lucrative iron manufacturing drew the original industrialists, but Scranton needed much more than scanty and poor-quality iron deposits to become a city. An imported elite gave Scranton a solid base from which to grow. These migrants became the bankers, lawyers, real estate agents, and independent coal operators who bolstered the town's elite and created more capital for local development. They did not jump in at the beginning, however, because the initial risks were high. Only after the Scrantons proved themselves through their iron works and railroad were they able to attract capital and talent to their city.[40]

3
The Making of a Regional Capital:
Scranton, 1850–1880

From 1850 to 1880, the city of Scranton filled with people. The long shot that the Scrantons risked their fortunes on was paying off big at last. An iron industry and a railroad gave the city its start; coal and manufacturing kept it going. By 1880, Scranton had over 45,000 people and was easily the largest city in northeast Pennsylvania. Coal mining had so increased that Scranton earned the nickname "The Anthracite Capital of the World." Such expansion was no accident of geography. Nor was it inevitable. Scranton became the premier anthracite city because its founding fathers made the critical economic and political decisions that led to rapid urban growth. Some of these pioneer industrialists made great fortunes from their industrial experiment; more important, they also made an open economic system with opportunities for many newcomers.

Using manufacturing to build a city was never easy for the Scrantons. When William Henry surveyed the 503 acres that the industrial pioneers bought in 1840, he hoped that this land contained iron ore, lime, and coal in abundance. As usual he was wrong. From the start the lime turned out to be almost nonexistent; it had to be imported from Danville, up the North Branch Canal to Pittston, and then by wagon seven miles to Scranton. The iron-ore deposits were less plentiful than expected, poor in quality, and expensive to mine. Furthermore, after committing themselves to a specific piece of land, the Scrantons found a richer ore bed three miles away. They practically went bankrupt, sinking more capital into this additional land, and transporting its ore. During the 1840s and 1850s, the desperate Scrantons had almost exhausted these and other ore deposits in the Lackawanna Valley. Then they had to import the bulk of their iron as well as the necessary lime. Refering to the Scrantons' need to import ore from central Pennsylvania and New Jersey, a writer in the *Iron Manufacturer's Guide* observed in 1859: "The absence of anthracite iron deposits . . . was a bitter disappointment to the first manufacturers of iron with stone anthracite coal." The Scranton group was in the improbable position of having to import iron ore and lime to establish a city based on the export of iron products.[1]

Faced with the dearth of lime and iron ore, the Scrantons turned to exporting anthracite coal, an abundant local resource that was popular as a home heating fuel and as a coking material for manufacturing. The Scrantons marketed their coal through the D.L.&W., which had mining privileges, and the newly formed Scranton Coal company, which represented another combination of capital from entrepreneurs in Scranton and New York City. Using the D.L.&W., the Scrantons carved out a market for their coal in upstate New York; the D&H and the Pennsylvania Coal Company already dominated the coal trade to New York City while the North Branch Canal sent coal to Philadelphia. The Scrantons' decision to mine coal as well as make rails was logical and wise; in making this shift they were further directing the economic development of their city.[2]

As the Scrantons discovered, political decisions, as well as entrepreneurial skill and tenacity, can make or break a city. They learned this the hard way when they tried to charter the D.L.&W. in the state legislature. Several interests in Pennsylvania, especially those in Wilkes-Barre, opposed the chartering because they feared the competition to their own transportation systems.[3]

From 1850 to 1880, Scranton faced two overpowering political needs: to be chartered as a city, with spacious boundaries, and to become the seat of a new county. Scranton's politicians had to get both of these to make their city work. Businessmen and politicians planned the growth of their city and created industrial, recreational, and residential districts. Spacious urban boundaries gave them freedom to build, expand, and grow. And the citizens got better urban and social services: Fire departments, sanitation and health services, water companies, and road builders all operate more effectively, and with lower costs, in a large urban setting. To protect people from rampant fires and contagious diseases, wide political jurisdiction is essential. In decentralized urban areas, where several towns and villages are adjacent to each other, overlapping political bureaucracies and social services result. They mean inefficiency, waste, and high fixed costs. Eager to avoid such a fate, a newspaper editor in Scranton concluded in 1866 that "a city charter is our greatest need . . . it will promote the peace, convenience, and wealth of the people within the proposed limit of the city."[4]

Two older hamlets, Providence and Hyde Park, feared the hegemony of their close industrial neighbor. Both hamlets had local pride: The citizens of Providence, dreaming of urban expansion, even helped to build a plank road to Carbondale. With prodding from Wilkes-Barre, the people in these boroughs tried to block Scranton's urban expansion, and exploit its industrial opportunities without paying higher taxes. In 1841, even before the Scranton settlement was one year old, Providence and Hyde Park asserted their local autonomy and delayed for seven years Scranton's attempt to secure a federal post office.

With vision and audacity, Scranton's leaders proposed to the state legislature in 1866 that the two older boroughs, and more land as well, be incorporated into Scranton. The astonished leaders in Providence and Hyde Park vigorously protested their absorption, citing as reasons higher taxes for themselves and the miles of rural landscape still separating them from Scranton. Legislators in Wilkes-Barre entered the fray and, "for the convenience of Wilkes-Barre lawyers," amended Scranton's proposed city charter to make the courts in the county seat of Wilkes-Barre the arbiters of Scranton's municipal and civil disputes. The state legislature approved the charter that gave Scranton the big city and gave its administrative services to Wilkes-Barre. This verdict, which fixed Scranton's boundaries at almost twenty square miles, gave Scranton political jurisdiction over the economic development of a large enough area to ensure unhampered urban growth.[5]

The county seat problem proved even more vexing because Wilkes-Barre had so much more influence in the state legislature than did the nearby hamlets of Providence and Hyde Park. As the county seat, Wilkes-Barre continued to siphon legal and administrative work from the younger but twice-as-large city of Scranton. When Scranton agitated for separation from Luzerne County in the 1850s, politicians in Wilkes-Barre secured a law making county separation possible only on a vote of the entire county, not just the seceding section. Naturally people in Wilkes-Barre voted against the separation. Not until the late 1870s was Scranton, led by industrialists and old settlers alike, able to get the law amended and separate their city from Luzerne County. The formation of Lackawanna County in 1878 made Scranton the administrative as well as economic center of the Lackawanna Valley.[6]

In spacious urban boundaries the newly-created county seat of Scranton was at last completely free to grow. Its leaders still had work to do to create a favorable climate for investment and expansion. The Scranton group set a tone of openness by actively recruiting diverse and talented newcomers to their city. Then the local businessmen showed their commitment to openness and growth by establishing a board of trade. This local board of trade organized fragmented groups of businessmen throughout the city to help Scranton grow. It was formed in 1867 as a wholesale merchants association to persuade the D.L.&W. to reduce transportation rates; the founders soon broadened the Board's membership to include "the business community" as a whole. By 1872, scores of the city's prominent businessmen had joined the board of trade. They met together regularly and planned an open environment for Scranton's future industrial expansion. First, they passed out literature advertising the manufacturing and transportation advantages in Scranton. Then they sponsored a law to reduce city taxes for new businesses locating in Scranton. Coal towns are dirty towns, so to entice investors the board campaigned to beautify Scranton. It raised money for a park, a hospital, a library, improved street paving and several bridges.[7]

Scranton was not the first city to start a board of trade; other American cities tried them too. More often than not they failed, or were ineffective, because fragmented economic interests are hard to mobilize for a common cause. Probably some of these divisive antagonisms existed in Scranton, but they did not become the dominant force in the city. The Scranton family introduced the idea of an open economic system and it seemed to catch on. The city's mushrooming growth and the rapid creation of wealth probably converted many doubters to the gospel of openness. The prevailing ideology among Scranton's businessmen seems to have been that the long-run benefits of growth (rise in value of real estate, lower transportation costs, and increased variety of goods available) outweighed the short-run problem of increased competition. An illustration of this view is the tax law that the board of trade promoted to bring industry to Scranton. According to the board of trade, "it is the custom of the city to free new industries from taxation for a period of ten years, . . . such encouragement is given new industries, and it demonstrates the good fellowship and hearty welcome that is extended." Because of the long-run benefits of rapid urbanization, and possibly because of Scranton's tradition of openness, its businessmen were willing to absorb a larger share of the tax burden to bring potential competitors to their city.[8]

Openness was one thing, building the factories was another. Scranton excelled in both. By developing both iron and coal, the Scrantons gave the city two industries from which to expand. Scranton's iron and steel industries were led by the L.I.&C. and employed over 1,500 workers in 1880. The limited ore deposits in the Lackawanna Valley, and the ease of entry into coal mining, eventually made coal the more popular investment; by 1880 another 5,000 persons worked in Scranton's coal mining industries. The active iron and coal industries were a boon to manufacturers. Several entrepreneurs came to Scranton and mobilized the capital and skilled personnel for manufacturing. In 1880, over 2,000 persons were employed in manufacturing of all types and sizes in Scranton. In the 1850s, one newcomer, an immigrant, founded the Dickson Manufacturing Company, which soon employed hundreds of persons to make engines, boilers, and machinery. At first he only made equipment for the large local firms, but within a decade he was exporting machinery and operating a branch plant in Wilkes-Barre.[9]

Dozens of other manufacturers in Scranton exported on a smaller scale or made equipment for local use. They made mining gear and machinery, circular saws, farm tools, tin and slate roofing, iron railings, and carriages. Some shops also specialized in repairing machinery. As Scranton became the manufacturing center of northeast Pennsylvania, many foundry operators and mechanics found it economical to locate near the source of labor and material. The major operator of a plant making brass castings and files settled in Pittston in 1853, but he moved his operation to Scranton in 1865 because it had "proved to be a better field for the business."[10]

In such an open and free economy, Scranton became a haven for inventions and the technological improvement of industrial goods. Several mechanics tinkered with the making of stoves that only burned anthracite coal. Investors started several of these stove companies beginning in the 1850s. One of these enterprises, the Scranton Stove Company, became profitable after John A. Price patented for it a new and efficient grate. Other local inventors included William G. Doud, a mechanic and relative of the Scrantons', who invented a roofing machine and also a picker for miner's lamps. The owner of the Scranton City Foundry invented and then manufactured a turbine water wheel. The creativeness of Scranton's industrialists increased in the 1880s and included the invention of a durable steel wheel for locomotives and an electric motor for trolleys. When these investors patented and manufactured their products in Scranton, as they often did, they enhanced Scranton's reputation as the manufacturing center of northeast Pennsylvania.[11]

Such innovation and advancement spread to Scranton's secondary industries. Two businessmen started competing power companies, which assisted coal mining and the construction of railroads. One of these men invented a cartridge for dispensing the explosive powder safely. By 1880, Scranton was also the junction of four railroads. This expanded the city's markets, reduced transportation costs, and gave employment to nearly 1,000 persons on railroad car and repair shops. Finally outside capitalists brought clothing factories into Scranton in the late 1870s. These industries became large local employers of women.[12]

The success of these varied industries meant a large growth in Scranton's urban services by 1880. At first, company stores and company housing were common in and around Scranton. Yet eventually small merchants and grocers captured most of this trade. Small construction firms also emerged to pave streets and erect buildings and houses. The clothing factories were, of course, a service as well as an export. The Scranton of 1880 supported nine banks (excluding two that had recently failed), two incorporated insurance companies, and a cemetery association. Unlike most anthracite cities, Scranton had two major food-processing industries: a flour-milling company and a pork packing and provision company. Finally, the expanding technology of the 1850 to 1880 period permitted the creation of gas and water companies, for more efficient utilities, and street railways to get people to and from work.[13]

Scranton's growth from 1,000 people in 1850 to 45,000 in 1880 pulled together a hodgepodge of economic and social groups. The entrepreneurs gave direction and order to city growth but thousands of immigrants, factory workers, and uprooted farmers added to the cultural life of the new city. These people created a variety of institutions to give order and meaning to their lives in Scranton. For example, some of the entrepreneurs and the wealthier citizens formed private social clubs. Many had a definite commitment to voluntarism and community service—they started a YMCA, a Poor Board, a hospital board, and a city militia; for entertainment they began an academy of music and a baseball club. The city's immigrants usually separated into ethnic groups. The Welsh settled in Hyde Park, and the Germans in the south side. They created an array of institutions, such as churches, singing societies, and burial associations. They provided stability while the entrepreneurs provided change.[14]

There are pitfalls in evaluating urban leadership because no one has yet figured out a foolproof way to measure someone's economic influence. One useful criterion is membership on the boards of directors of incorporated companies and the larger limited partnerships.[15] Scranton's incorporated businesses were invariably the showcase enterprises in the city; those elected to their boards of directors in the nineteenth century were usually the largest shareholders. Some of the limited partnerships rivaled the corporations in size and therefore also need to be included. Scranton's incorporated companies and limited partnerships, those with at least $50,00 in paid up capital, amounted to forty-three enterprises. Analyzing the boards of directors (or partners) of these big enterprises excludes small businessmen and includes only those entrepreneurs who shaped Scranton's future by guiding its largest industries, banks, and urban services.[16]

An "economic leader" will be defined as someone holding at least *three* partnerships or directorships—*two* if he was an officer in a company. This standard eliminates small investors and those with narrow economic pursuits. By 1880, after a full generation of industrial growth in Scranton, only forty men qualified as economic leaders. These forty entrepreneurs forged Scranton's economic development by making the major investments that created markets outside of Scranton and urbanization inside. These men were Scranton's captains of industry—to understand their social background is to understand how a regional capital is created.[17]

These forty economic leaders of 1880 can be artificially divided into several groups. First, fourteen of the forty were already active in Scranton by the mid-1850s, before the city was even incorporated as a borough. This tells us that many of those who came early in Scranton's history grew with the city. They applied their skills and sunk their capital into building Scranton; they got rich as the city filled with people. Of these fourteen economic leaders three were part of the original Scranton group; five were long-time friends and relatives of the Scrantons, who had supported them ever since the bleak days of the 1840s; four others came from nearby commercial towns; two were old settlers, men originally tied to the farming economy of the Lackawanna Valley. These fourteen men laid the basis for Scranton's future prosperity.

Three of the fourteen were Scranton's industrial prime-movers—Joseph C. Platt, Charles P. Mattes, and William W. Scranton. They along with the other Scrantons, Henry, and Grant, were young when they directed the city's early industrial operations in the 1840s. In the following decades their individual success ran the gamut from bankruptcy and impoverishment to wealth in the millions. At the wealthy end, Joseph C. Platt and Charles P. Mattes were heavily involved in the economic life in Scranton in 1880. Platt, in fact, held more directorships in Scranton in that year than anyone else. He was president of Weston Mill Company and a director of the L.I.&.C., First National Bank, Dickson Manufacturing Company, Moosic Powder Company, Scranton Stove Works, and People's Street Railway. He was an honorary member of the Scranton Board of Trade and an officer in several social organizations. Charles P. Mattes was vice-president of the L.I.&C. and a director in the Lackawanna Valley Bank. By getting in on the ground level, these two early industrialists grew with their city.[18]

Not all of Scranton's industrial pioneers were as fortunate as these two men. William Henry, the original leader of the group, had left the city in the 1840s after some bad investments. Henry had energy and vision but little ability to time the right investment; he died embittered and impoverished in 1878. Sanford Grant, the first owner of the company store, wilted when faced with business competition and industrial risk. Selling his stock, he left for safer business climes in Belvidere, New Jersey, where he lived, without ulcers or wealth, until his death in the 1880s. Displaying greater fortitude than Grant, Selden Scranton became the first president of the L.I.&C.; five years later, though, he and his brother Charles left to operate a blast furnace in Oxford, New Jersey. Their ironmaking talents ultimately failed them; Selden declared bankruptcy in 1844 and died shortly thereafter. George Scranton, the early leader and driving force behind coal and railroad development, had shrewder business instincts than his brother Selden. George, however, still lost the bulk of his fortune during the Panic of 1857, and had to sell much of his stock in the D.L.&W. at reduced value. Plagued with health problems from overwork during the rugged days of the 1840s, George died in 1861 at age forty-nine. Managing to avoid the pitfalls of his cousins, Joseph H. Scranton lived to be a millionaire and president of the L.I.&C. before his premature death in 1872 at age fifty-nine. He also became the father of the only Scranton son ever to qualify as an economic leader. So after starting at roughly the same position in the 1840s, the original industrialists varied widely in their achievements by 1880.[19]

The wealth of the offspring of the industrial pioneers was almost as fragmented as that of their fathers. For example, George Scranton's sons, William H. and James S., lived in Scranton but exerted no economic influence and do not even seem to have been gainfully employed. William Henry's sons, William and Reuben, fared slightly better in their jobs as lesser officials with the D.L.&W. Selden Scranton was childless. In fact, of the four Scrantons, only Joseph Scranton produced even one heir who qualified as an economic leader. In 1880, this son, William W. Scranton, was the general manager of the L.I.&C., from which he would soon resign to establish the Scranton Steel Company. He was also president of the Scranton Gas and Water Company and the Hyde Park Gas Company, and a director of the Dickson Manufacturing Company and the People's Street Railway.[20]

The Scrantons had several friends and relatives who came to the Lackawanna Valley and made big money. Five of these people invested in or supported the Scranton iorn works in the bleak days of the 1840s and lived to become economic leaders of Scranton in 1880. In the modern parlance "they paid their dues." The most prominent of these men, James Blair, has already been mentioned as a business associate of the Scrantons even before they came to the Lackawanna Valley. When Blair arrived in Scranton he was a banker and an established businessman, eager to exploit the opportunities available in the "Anthracite Capital." In 1880, Blair was a director of Scranton's two largest industries, the D.L.&W. and the L.I.&C. He was also a director of Scranton's two largest locally owned businesses, the First National Bank and the Dickson Manufacturing Company. As a sidelight, he founded the Scranton Savings Bank and the People's Street Railway. Outside of Scranton, Blair held directorships on four midwestern railroads, which were largely dominated by his brother John I. Blair, one of America's wealthiest men.[21]

An uncle and early associate of the Scrantons was Joseph J. Albright, a man still prominent in Scranton's economic life in 1880. Invited by the Scrantons to become the first coal agent for the D.L.&W., Albright did his job well and grew prosperous with the railroad. In the mid-1860s he switched companies and held the same position for the D&H. In addition to his railroad work, Albright was the president of the First National Bank, the city's premiere financial institution. In 1880, Albright's name also appeared on the boards of directors of the Scranton Gas and Water Company, Dickson Manufacturing Company, and Weston Mill Company.[22]

A long-time friend (and distant relative) of the Scrantons was Benjamin Throop, the company surgeon of the L.I.&C. Practicing medicine only part time, Throop became president of the Scranton City Bank and the Scranton Illuminating, Heating, and Power Company. His primary source of wealth, however, seems to have come from local land speculation, which he describes in detail in a book he wrote on the Lackawanna Valley. As Scranton grew, Throop's investments in real estate appreciated rapidly, and with much less risk than was attached to the creation of industrial enterprises.[23]

Two other long-time allies of the Scrantons were economic leaders in 1880: William Manness, the original superintendent of building for the L.I.&C., and Edward Kingsbury, who went from a clerk for the Scranton iron works in 1850 to treasurer of the Scranton Steel Company in 1881. In addition, Manness was a director in the Dickson Manufacturing Company and the Weston Mill Company, while Kingsbury held a directorship on the Scranton Gas and Water Company. Both of these men joined the Scrantons in the lean years and got rich with them in the fat years.[24]

Once Scranton had established an export and built a railroad, the city became a magnet to entrepreneurs in nearby towns. Four wealthy men from Towanda, Montrose, and Dundaff came to Scranton in the mid-1850s and soon became economic leaders there. Two of these four migrants were the father and son team of George and J. Gardiner Sanderson from Towanda. They started Scranton's first banking house in 1855. Their bank prospered as the city grew, and in 1880 they organized the larger Lackawanna Valley Bank. Like other shrewd investors, the Sandersons invested in local real estate; after building a suburb in Scranton they laid the Providence and Scranton Street Railway to get the new suburbanites to and from downtown.[25]

The other two early arrivals to Scranton came from adjacent Susquehanna County: Elisha Phinney, the son of the founder of Dundaff, and George A. Fuller, the son of a congressman from Montrose. Like the Sandersons, both of these men developed Scranton's urban services instead of its industries. Phinney came and started Scranton's first flour and feed company in 1856; by 1880, he was president of both the Merchants and Mechanics Bank and the Stowers Pork Packing and Provision Company, as well as treasurer of the Lackawanna and Susquehanna Coal Company. Phinney came upon hard times after this date but still kept his title as general of the city militia. George A. Fuller, after marrying a Scranton, launched a successful career as a merchant; he also became a director of the Scranton Savings Bank and president of the Scranton Board of Trade.[26] Both of these men were fortunate to have been born into prominent families and smart enough to go south to Scranton.

By 1880, because of the entrepreneurship of these newcomers, the surviving old settlers found that they had to move elsewhere if they wished to continue farming as their life's work. Those who remained seem to have associated with and intermarried among themselves, not with the pioneer industrialists. Several of the surviving old settlers got rich by leasing their farm lands to coal companies. As Scranton industrialized, though, they dwindled in numbers and in influence.[27]

Only those few old settlers who adapted to the changing economy of the Lackawanna Valley carved a niche in industrial Scranton. Two such men, Ira Tripp and William Winton, qualified as economic leaders in 1880. A member of one of the founding families of northeast Pennsylvania, Ira Tripp converted his family's farm to coal land after the 1850s. Tripp was a country merchant before the arrival of the Scrantons; he became a coal operator afterward when they built a city near his coal-laden estate. In 1880, Tripp held two bank directorships and operated his own small Tripp Coal Company.[28]

Although the old settlers were not trained for coal development, some became keenly interested when it became profitable. The enterprising William W. Winton is even a better example of this than Ira Tripp. Migrating to the Lackawanna Valley from upstate New York in the early 1830s, Winton became a landowner, a merchant, and an innkeeper. When the Scrantons arrived, Winton doesn't seem to have helped them much; in fact, in the 1840s his store competed with the Scranton's company store for local trade. When the Scrantons created a market for Lackawanna Valley coal, Winton used some of his capital to launch Scranton's Second National Bank; he used some more capital to buy hundreds of acres of coal land near Scranton. Going into coal mining, Winton cofounded the Winton and Dolph Coal Company. So both Winton and Tripp, held onto their land and changed when the region changed from farming to coal development.[29]

Other than Tripp and Winton, who just barely qualified as economic leaders, few old settlers made any investment in industrial Scranton. In fact, large numbers of them sold their farms before they could make much profit from soaring land prices. Those who tenaciously clung to their land, such as Henry Griffin, Joseph Church, Edward Spencer and Theodore Von Storch, mined the coal themselves or leased the mining rights for large sums of money. So they got

TABLE 3.1. Real and Personal Wealth of Pre-1850 Industrialists, Post-1850 Industrial Migrants, Commercials and Professionals, and Old Settlers Holding $200,000 or More in Scranton in 1870

	Number of Wealthholders	Real Estate Wealth and Percent of Total Wealth	Personal Wealth	Total Wealth
Pre-1850 industrialists[a]	2	$ 130,000 (10%)	$1,190,000 (90%)	$1,320,000
Post-1850 industrial migrants[b]	5	720,000 (34%)	1,341,000 (66%)	2,061,000
Commercials and professionals[c]	2	375,000 (77%)	110,000 (23%)	485,000
Old settlers[d]	4	1,050,000 (89%)	135,000 (11%)	1,185,000

SOURCE: Manuscript Census Returns, Nineth Census of the United States, 1870, Luzerne County, Pennsylvania, National Archives Microfilm Series, M-593, Roll 1368.

[a]Joseph H. Scranton and Joseph C. Platt
[b]James Blair and wife, Horatio Pierce, George Sanderson, Jr., George Sanderson, Sr.
[c]William Winton and Benjamin Troop
[d]Edward Spencer, Henry Griffin, Joseph Church, William Merrifield

rich even though they played little role in directing Scranton's industrial future. They were merely fortunate to own land in the Lackawanna Valley during its early coal development, fortunate that the Scranton group located a city near their property, and fortunate not to have sold their land.[30]

The data in table 3.1 suggest two observations about the ten largest wealth-holders in Scranton in 1870. First, that the Scranton group and the newcomer industrialists to Scranton differed sharply from the old settlers in their invest-ment strategy: The industrialists shunned the conservative policy of land in-vestment and plowed capital into higher risk manufacturing and coal develop-ment. Second, after only two decades of industrialization an enormous amount of wealth had been created in Scranton. According to the manuscript census of 1850, only fourteen persons in the several townships that Scranton would incorporate recorded more than $10,000 in real estate wealth. In 1870, thirty-three men recorded real and personal wealth of at least $100,000 and ten men held $200,000 or more. When the Scrantons marketed an export, built a rail-road, and promoted a city, they had also created opportunities for others. Ironically, some of these "others" became millionaires and some of the Scran-tons ended up with almost nothing.

During Scranton's first generation of urbanization, from 1850 to 1880, its leaders strove to create a favorable atmosphere for economic development. On one hand this required aggressive political maneuvering to get wide city limits and to make Scranton a county seat. On the other hand, the Scranton family and the board of trade promoted freedom of economic opportunity—they urged immigrant and native alike to come and invest. From a base of coal, iron, and railroad industries, Scranton became a center for manufacturing. Investors flourished in Scranton's open environment and they helped to improve industrial productivity. Success came to many of Scranton's early builders, but the city also remained wide open to newcomers with some combination of skill, luck, and capital.

4

The Captains of Industry:
Scranton, 1880

During Scranton's industrialization, it experienced the triumph of laissez-faire capitalism: an influx of people and the stratification of society. A whirlwind of unrestrained business left in its wake paupers as well as millionaires, the fleeting residents and those who found roots, and ethnic grocers nearby the captains of industry. Only a few made fortunes, but a reading of the federal manuscript census clearly suggests that the creation of industry in the Lackawanna Valley generated unknown wealth for thousands of newcomers. By 1880, twenty-six newcomers to Scranton had joined the fourteen industrial pioneers described in the last chapter. Each of these forty qualify as economic leaders because each held at least three directorships (or two if he had an officership). These fittest of the surviving newcomers included nine immigrants, ten native-Americans from Honesdale, Carbondale and the hinterland nearby, four representatives of outside family companies, and three adventurous entrepreneurs who came to Scranton from outside the Lackawanna Valley.

A striking feature of Scranton's 1880 leadership is the presence of nine European immigrants. Protestants from England, Wales, and Germany often formed separate enclaves in Scranton, as did Catholics from Germany, Ireland, and Poland. The successful immigrants in 1880 were mostly English, Irish, German, Scottish, or Canadian Protestants who innovated in the iron and coal industries and who assimilated easily into Scranton's WASPish elite.[1] They had come to America with some combination of technical skills, intelligence, and money. Possibly most important, they had good luck. Since these immigrants usually did not have needed skills, inherited wealth, or lucrative kinship ties, they relied on their own families and exploited any opportunities that Scranton provided. They needed time to make their mark, and when they did they were usually older than their WASP counterparts.[2]

Thomas Dickson

William Connell

John Jermyn

James Archbald

The Dicksons were probably the most prominent immigrants in Scranton in 1880. Thomas Dickson was born in 1824 in Leeds, England, of Scottish parents, James and Elizabeth Linen Dickson. They migrated to Toronto, Canada, in 1832, and soon came to Dundaff, Pennsylvania. In 1836, the Dicksons moved to nearby Carbondale, where Thomas Dickson got his first job as a mule driver for the D&H. He overcame a lack of schooling with tenacity and shrewdness. In the 1840s he bought into a small foundry in Carbondale. He saw the greater opportunity in Scranton,[3] and got the financial backing from his family and friends to move there. Near the L.I.&C. he established a machine and foundry shop in 1856. His brother George later joined him, and together they incorporated the Dickson Manufacturing Company in 1863. In Scranton, the Dicksons built engines and boilers for the D&H and the L.I.&C.; after fulfilling these machinery contracts, their business flourished. In 1859, Thomas Dickson became coal superintendent of the D&H; four years later the Dickson Manufacturing Company expanded its capital to $800,000, bought out a smaller company, and began making railcars and locomotives. The next year, he and his brother joined several other Scranton leaders in founding the First National Bank, the largest and most prestigious financial institution in the city. In 1865 he helped Henry M. Boies, his future son-in-law, start the Moosic Powder Company. The next year he rose to vice-president of the D&H, and in 1869 became president of this regional railroad. In 1880, Thomas and George Dickson were both economic leaders and two of the wealthiest men in Scranton (as table 3.1 partially reveals). Their influence spread throughout the region and even extended into New York.[4]

Almost as prominent as immigrant Thomas Dickson was coal baron William Connell. Born in Nova Scotia in 1827 of Scottish and Canadian parents, the self-educated Connell began work as a mule driver in a coal mine near Scranton. He worked his way up through the mining ranks and got his big chance in 1856, when he moved to Scranton from Hazleton to supervise mines owned by the Susquehanna and Wyoming Valley Railroad and Coal Company. He made money at it so he bought the mines in 1870. A coal operator at last, he got backing from his brothers James and Alexander to start William Connell and Company. His career took off and in 1872 he helped start the Third National Bank of Scranton. Soon he appeared on the boards of several big Scranton companies, such as the Weston Mill Company and the Scranton Stove Works. In 1879 he was elected president of the Third National Bank. After 1880 Connell acquired more directorships and greater wealth; when he died in 1909, he left an estate of over $5 million. Like the Dicksons, Connell was a rags-to-riches immigrant who came to Scranton only after being trained elsewhere.[5]

Another immigrant coal operator was Englishman John Jermyn. Born in 1825, Jermyn came to New York at age twenty with little money and no training. He heard there were jobs in the anthracite fields, so he moved to the Lackawanna Valley and began work for the Scrantons for only seventy-five cents a day. He had talent, nerve, and tenacity, though, and by the 1850s he had become general manager for a local coal company. Since Jermyn wanted to make it as an independent coal operator, he put his money in private and joint ventures. The critical risk in his career came in 1862, when he leased some abandoned mines northeast of Scranton. Defying the skeptics, Jermyn bought new machinery and fulfilled a contract for one million tons of coal. He then tripled his contract and built the town of Jermyn near his mines. By 1880, he was the largest independent coal operator in the area; in 1884 he moved back to Scranton, where he already held directorships in the Third National Bank and the Lackawanna Valley Bank. He seems to have had an uncanny knack for selecting lucrative investments and one observor said that Jermyn was "believed to be unaffected by the times, holding his own versus all contingencies." When he died in 1902, he left an estate of $7 million. He had married another English immigrant to Scranton and reared ten children. None of Jermyn's first nine children wedded notable Scrantonians, but his youngest child, who reached marriagable age by the time Jermyn was conspicuously prominent, married a niece of George Sanderson's.[6]

Unlike the Dicksons, Connell, and Jermyn, Scotsman James Archbald migrated to America earlier in its history. Born in 1793, Archbald became a contractor in 1817 for the building of the Erie Canal. He learned his craft and later became an engineer for the D&H; he wound up as the company's mining superintendent at Carbondale. In 1851, when Carbondale became a city, Archbald was elected its first mayor, but in 1857, at the urging of George Scranton, he became general agent for the D.L.&W. and soon moved to the regional capital. The next year he became chief engineer for the railroad, a position he held until his death in 1870. His son James, born in 1838, succeeded Archbald as chief engineer and also held directorships in the Scranton Savings Bank, Third National Bank, and the Scranton Gas and Water Company. James Archbald, Jr., married a daughter of Joseph J. Albright, coal agent for the competing D&H, and Selden Scranton's uncle.[7]

Like most of Scranton's immigrant leaders, Benjamin Hughes worked in a nearby mining town (in this case, Pottsville) before coming to Scranton in the 1850s. In that city Hughes started work as a miner for the Scrantons. Then he worked for the D.L.&W. as a miner, mine foreman, and general superintendent. He led the city's Welsh community as president of the Cambrian Mutual Fire Insurance Company and the West Side Bank. In social and political life, Hughes was president of the Ivorites Society (a Welsh organization), and president of the select council of Scranton. In rising from coal miner to bank president Hughes fulfilled an immigrant dream.[8]

Three other immigrants—William Matthews, Lewis Pughe, and William Monies—qualify as economic leaders, but they were not as prominent as Connell, Jermyn, Archbald, and the Dicksons. Englishman William Matthews came to Scranton in 1866 from nearby Honesdale and, with his brothers Charles and Richard, soon established a retail firm. By 1880, the Matthews brothers held some positions of economic and social importance in Scranton. William, president of the People's Street Railway and a director in the Third National Bank, was the most conspicuous of the brothers. Charles was a director in the Scranton Savings Bank and in 1881 became president of the Scranton Glass Company.[9]

Born in 1820, Welshman Lewis Pughe migrated to Carbondale in the 1840s; there he became active in politics as treasurer, alderman, associate judge, and state legislator. Attracted to the regional center, Pughe moved to Scranton in 1868 and started a bakery and an investment firm with fellow Carbondaler William Monies, a Scottish migrant. In Scranton, Pughe again went into politics and became treasurer of the school board. He was an active businessman, too. He was on the first board of directors of the Third National Bank, and the first president of the Scranton Board of Trade. Monies, his partner, had wanderlust and went to California searching for gold. He returned to Scranton and served as its mayor and as a director of the Merchants and Mechanics Bank. As business partners, Pughe and Monies also invested outside of Scranton, in a stove company in Pittston and in a silver mine in Colorado.[10]

The only Catholic to hold two directorships in 1880 was German migrant Frederick W. Gunster. Born in 1845, Gunster came to America in the early 1850s with his father and three uncles. The four brothers started a successful cabinet, furniture, and undertaking business, and one of them became a director in the Merchants and Mechanics Bank of Scranton. Frederick had the advantage of a college education and a law degree and held directorships in the Third National Bank and the Mutual Fire Insurance Company by 1880.[11]

The immigrant penetration of Scranton's big companies contrasts sharply with the native domination in older and more slowly growing Wilkes-Barre. Most of these immigrants to Scranton started slowly but saved some capital, usually from coal investments, before moving to Scranton. Economic success, however, does not mean social acceptance. How were these successful immigrants received by the Scranton group? Two signs of social acceptance in 1880 were membership in the city's voluntary associations and social clubs, and marriage ties with the Scranton group.

First, Scranton's immigrants joined Masonic lodges and voluntary associations of all kinds. In fact, five of these nine immigrants were officers in at least one voluntary organization, even including Scranton's historical society, which often admitted only the city's oldest families. William Connell was an officer in three voluntary associations; John Jermyn was a speaker and guest of honor at the prestigious Lackawanna County Banquet to commemorate the county's inception in 1878. When the city's metropolitan club, the Scranton Club, was founded in 1895, John Jermyn, William Connell, and other immigrants were conspicuous on the list of charter members. Also, five of these nine immigrants lived in Scranton's posh residential section, near the central business district.[12]

Second, unlike in Wilkes-Barre, no established kinship group seems to have posed a social barrier to Scranton's successful immigrants. The pioneer Scrantons wanted to attract capital and talent to their city whether from immigrants or natives. Although no immigrant married into the Scranton group, many sons of immigrants did. Most of these outsiders needed a generation's time to form social ties with the native industrial group. Also several of them had married before coming to Scranton, and those who had not married still had their fortunes to make. For the daughter of an ambitious, native-born entrepreneur to have wedded an impecunious immigrant, no matter how talented, would have been a poor risk. However, many of Scranton's immigrants had moved up in the world by the time their children were of marriageable age. If the successful immigrant's son or daughter had married another successful newcomer or a relative of the Scrantons, the marriage would have been homogamous. Thus, Thomas Dickson, John Jermyn, James Archbald, and William Matthews did not intermarry with the native-born industrialists, but at least one child of each of these men did. None of William Connell's eleven children became kinsmen of the Scrantons, but at least three of his grandchildren did. In Scranton, economic success seems to have preceded and made possible social acceptance. By 1880, then, even though only three immigrant leaders had kinship ties with the Scrantons, all nine seem to have been accepted into the relatively open Scranton society.

The successful immigrants in Scranton not only reflected an open environment, they helped preserve it. Many immigrants became heavily pledged investors with a concern for urban development that matched that of the Scranton group. Since personal or group antagonisms thwarted a united commitment to growth, Scranton's economic leaders, immigrants and natives alike, tried to get along with each other. For example, immigrant Thomas Dickson mediated a dispute in 1862 between Joseph Scranton's son and banker Amos N. Meylert, both of whom sought the office of local tax collector. A concerned Dickson resolved the "struggle for the collectorship" by persuading Meylert to withdraw his candidacy and publicly support young Scranton for the office. Dickson convinced the ambitious banker that such a noble gesture would "ensure the friendly and social feelings that have heretofore existed" among local businessmen. The Yankee Scrantons returned Dickson's favor four years later: They joined him and other Scottish immigrants in publicly praising and then nominating their patriarch, James Archbald, for Congress on the Republican ticket. The ability of Scranton's heterogeneous leaders to cooperate and compromise helped urban growth and immigrant assimilation.[13]

A group of economic leaders larger than the nine immigrants consisted of ten native-born newcomers from the core and the hinterland of the Lackawanna Valley. As Scranton grew to be the largest city in northeast Pennsylvania, it drew several prominent men from Honesdale and Carbondale. These nearby townsmen, along with similar migrants from Towanda, Montrose, and Dundaff dominated Scranton's economic leadership by 1880. In the formation of its leadership, therefore, Scranton depended heavily on its hinterland, the three counties north and northeast of Scranton. As map A indicates, this geographic spread extended from north-northwest of Scranton to the south-southeast; this excludes Wilkes-Barre, which dominated the Wyoming region southwest of the Lackawanna Valley. Scranton became a magnet for nearby entrepreneurs, who used their families to help supply them with contacts, skills, and capital.[14]

At the head of the D&H canal, Honesdale sent a stream of men to the regional capital of Scranton. Honesdale had great expectations when it was founded in 1825: first, it replaced Bethany as the seat of Wayne County; second, the increasing load of coal shipped over the canal helped boost Honesdale to 1,500 people by 1834. These outward successes masked the D&H's initial ownership of half the land and all the industry in town. Perhaps more ominous, the New York owners of the D&H invested more capital in Carbondale, where they built engine, paint, and repair shops to supplement the local coal mining industry. Yet Jason Torrey, who originally owned the entire upper half of Honesdale tried to create business and growth. His kinsmen started the Honesdale Bank, the Honesdale Mill, and later the Wayne County Savings Bank. By the 1850s, though, Scranton had asserted itself as regional capital of the Lackawanna Valley. Edward Kingsbury and Benjamin Throop were among the first the come to Scranton from Honesdale; some of the Torrey group followed later.[15]

One of the most successful Honesdale migrants to Scranton was Edward W. Weston, a grandson of Jason Torrey. Weston got a country-school education in nearby Salem; then he moved to Honesdale in 1844 to learn surveying and engineering from his uncle, John Torrey. Weston worked with his uncle until 1859, when he became manager in charge of the lands and surveys of the D&H.

This job shifted Weston to Carbondale; when the D&H opened new mines in Scranton two years later, Weston moved there. In 1864, he became superintendent of all coal-mining operations for the D&H. Once in Scranton, Weston busied himself with the economic development of that city. He ran the Weston Mill Company and he was vice-president of the Dickson Manufacturing Company. On the side he was a director of the Moosic Powder Company and the local gas company. By 1880, Weston was related to Scranton's industrial pioneers through two first cousins and fellow Honesdale migrants: James H. Torrey, a lawyer and treasurer of the Lackawanna Bar Association, who married a grandniece of George Scranton's; and Thomas F. Torrey, the general sales agent for the D&H and a director of the First National Bank, who married Thomas Dickson's oldest daughter.[16]

The Weston Mill Company was the vehicle for another Honesdale migrant, Alexander W. Dickson, to enter Scranton's economic elite. In Honesdale, Dickson's father lived next door to Edward Weston and was the partner of Charles Weston (Edward's brother) in a local flour-milling company. After young Alexander finished his education in 1864, he moved to Scranton to join the Westons' new milling firm. Living with Charles Weston's family, Dickson soon became general manager and director of the Weston Mill Company. He later perfected an innovation, the "roller process," that improved the quality of the flour. By 1880, Dickson had also become a member of the Scranton Board of Trade, an officer of the YMCA, and a heavy investor in two small coal companies.[17]

Another successful Honesdale migrant to Scranton—one who strikingly illustrates Scranton's centrifugal pull and the importance of family ties—was Judge Alfred Hand. The son of a merchant and bank director in Honesdale, Hand graduated from Yale and afterward went to Montrose to study law with William Jessup. When Hand arrived in 1857, William Jessup and his family were becoming deeply involved in Scranton activities. Jessup himself had become chief attorney for the D.L.&.W. in 1853. In that same year Jessup's eldest son, William H., married George Scranton's niece, Sarah Jay. Young William Jessup moved to Scranton with his brother George, a fellow lawyer who became vice-president of the Scranton City Bank. Alfred Hand, after being admitted to the bar, joined the Jessup law firm in 1860 and a year later cemented ties with the Montrose lawyers by marrying Phoebe Jessup, a daughter of his mentor and the sister of his partners. By this time, Hand moved to Scranton and soon started a new law partnership with Isaac J. Post, who was a nephew of the Jessups. The firm, Hand and Post, remained intact until 1879, when Hand was appointed judge of Pennsylvania's eleventh judicial district. By 1880, he was firmly entrenched in Scranton's commercial and industrial network, as the first president of the Third National Bank, and as a director of the People's Street Railway,

William Connell and Company, and the Dickson Manufacturing Company. He also held more social directorships and officerships than did anyone else in Scranton in 1880. When Scranton threw out the bait of economic development, they reeled in entrepreneurs from nearby towns.[18] The life of Alfred Hand is a chapter in that story.

The Honesdale migrants left behind brothers and cousins who dominated Honesdale's business elite in later years. Alfred Hand's brother Horace became a director of the Honesdale Gas Company and, later in his life, the president of the Wayne County Savings Bank. After Charles Weston left for Scranton to establish a flour mill, his uncle, John Torrey, bought the mill he left behind and added it to his vice-presidency of the Honesdale Bank. Torrey's son Edwin joined his father as a director on this financial institution. William Weston was the first and long time president of the Wayne County Savings Bank, which completed the Torrey and Weston domination of Honesdale's two banks. Finally, Benjamin Throop's brother Simon was a lawyer, businessman, and one-time burgess of Honesdale.[19]

The industrial town of Carbondale joined Honesdale in supplying Scranton with economic leaders. The careers of five of these men—immigrants Thomas Dickson, George L. Dickson, Lewis Pughe, William Monies, and James Archbald—have been described already. The remaining two, Horatio S. Pierce and William Richmond, like the others, were not born in Carbondale but they made money there before moving to nearby Scranton. Born in Cooperstown, New York, in 1816, Pierce moved in 1834 to Carbondale, where he lived for three decades as a successful merchant and later as president of the First National Bank of Carbondale. In 1865, the wealthy Pierce moved to the regional capital and immediately founded the Scranton Trust Company and Savings Bank.[20] Like so many other Carbondale migrants to Scranton, Pierce actively participated in Scranton's industrial development. By 1880, he was president of the Scranton Stove Works and a director in the Dickson Manufacturing Company and the Moosic Powder Company.

Born and educated in central Connecticut, William Richmond left at age twenty-one, for Dutchess County, New York, to work for his merchant uncle. Soon he moved to Honesdale and worked for three years for another merchant before moving to Carbondale, where he became a partner in a retail store. Buying out his partner in 1853, Richmond built the largest edifice in Carbondale; there he built coal cars for the D&H. In 1860, he founded the Elk Hill Coal Company, which mined heavily in nearby Dickson City. In 1874, Richmond moved to Scranton and by 1880 was a director of the Third National Bank. Just as Horatio Pierce remained president of Carbondale's First National Bank after moving to Scranton, so William Richmond kept economic ties with satellite

Carbondale. He was the first president of that town's Crystal Lake Water Company and a stockholder in the Carbondale Gas Company. In effect, then, Scranton had imported much of Carbondale's elite.[21]

Scranton's final economic leader from Carbondale was John B. Smith. Like Horatio Pierce and William Richmond, Smith migrated to the Lackawanna Valley from upstate New York. In Carbondale he became a mechanic for the D&H. His big chance came with the founding of the Pennsylvania Coal Company and its demand for skilled leadership. When Smith emerged as the general superintendent of the Pennsylvania Coal Company, he moved to this company's state headquarters in Dunmore. Lacking outlets for investment in Dunmore, Smith involved himself in the economic life of Scranton. There he became a director of the Scranton Trust Company and Savings Bank, the People's Street Railway, and the Dunmore Cemetery Association.[22]

The upward mobility of these Carbondalers who came to Scranton was dramatic. In the 1830s and 1840s, Carbondale had little wealth and less charm. Local businesses were few and of those that did exist, many were liquor shops. Rampaging fires sporadically leveled whole sections of town. Mining accidents and exposure to death and injury were daily features for the fluctuating population of Carbondale. Yet such uniform bleakness did not create uniform poverty. Some members of this heavily immigrant population moved up, and several of those who acquired skills and capital soon moved to Scranton. There they later became bankers, independent coal operators, stove manufacturers and, for one, the presidency of the D&H—the same coal and railroad company that dominated Carbondale to begin with.[23]

A small group of economic leaders, Asa B. Stevens, William F. Hallstead, and Lewis Watres, came to Scranton from its rural hinterland. From upstate New York, Stevens came to northeast Pennsylvania in the 1850s and became a marble cutter. Drawn to the regional capital in 1863, Stevens helped organize the Bridge Coal Company and also became secretary of the School Fund Coal Association. Before 1880, he also served as treasurer of the Miners and Mechanics Loan and Banking Association. In politics, he became the first sheriff of Lackawanna County in 1878.[24]

Moving to the Lackawanna Valley from near Philadelphia in 1835, Lewis Watres bought 400 acres of land in Blakely township, a few miles northeast of Scranton. He constructed a saw mill and became a lumberman, entrepreneur, and local justice of the peace. He welcomed coal development and in the 1840s opened one of the first mines below Carbondale. Owning land and making the shift to coal, Watres emerged as one of the wealthiest men in the Lackawanna Valley. Moving to Scranton in 1865, he became a major operator of the Green Ridge Coal Company and a director on the Scranton Savings Bank and Trust Company.[25]

TABLE 4.1.   Population and Percentage Growth of Scranton and the Surrounding Towns in Its Hinterland from 1850 to 1860

City or Town	Population		Percentage Growth
	1850	1860	
Scranton	1,000 (est.)	9,223	922.3
Towanda	1,171	1,622	27.8
Montrose	917	1,268	27.7
Carbondale	4,945	5,575	11.3
Honesdale	2,263	2,544	11.0
Dundaff	295	245	−19.0

SOURCES: J.D.B. DeBow, *The Seventh Census of the United States: 1850* (Washington, D.C., 1853), pp. 161, 173, 174. Joseph C.G. Kennedy, *Population of the United States in 1860* (Washington, D.C., 1864), pp. 416, 427, 428, 434, 436. Manuscript Census Returns, 1850, Wayne County, M-432, Roll 835.

Railroad engineer William F. Hallstead came to Scranton from a farm in nearby Benton township. The Hallsteads were one of the first families in the township, and William's father was a local justice of the peace. Young William attended local schools and, in the early 1850s, while still a teenager, he became a brakeman for the D.L.&W. Over the years he worked his way up to conductor, yard dispatcher at Scranton, assistant superintendent, and finally superintendent of the northern division (Scranton, Binghamton, and Syracuse) of the railroad. In 1880, Hallstead was appointed second vice-president and general manager of the D.L.&W.'s Hoboken to Buffalo system. He was also active in Scranton's economic life as a director of the First National Bank.[26]

Scranton's pattern of attracting industrial and human capital from its hinterland persisted and was the main factor in this regional center's leadership development by 1880. This migration can be seen as a boon to Scranton and a drain on the four small towns nearby.

The timing of the migration to Scranton was as patterned as the limited geographic range of towns that sent their prominent men. Since Scranton had surpassed Towanda, Montrose, Dundaff, and Honesdale in population by the early 1850s (see table 4.1), the influx of bankers and lawyers from these towns occurred in the mid-1850s, only after Scranton established its greater opportunity. Carbondale, on the other hand, was still larger than Scranton in the mid-1850s. So Scranton did not become attractive to successful Carbondalers until the late 1850s and 1860s, by which time Scranton's regional dominance had become apparent.

This migration also tells us something about the flow of capital in America's emerging industrial society. When wealthy migrants came to Scranton from static commercial towns, their transferred riches gave their adopted city a healthy injection of capital to fuel its industrial growth. Banks were major institutions for supplying industrial funds in the nineteenth century, and almost all of Scranton's economic leaders from nearby towns became bank presidents and directors. For example, men from Towanda and Montrose started Scranton's first two banking houses. By 1880, migrants from Honesdale, Dundaff, Carbondale, and Belvidere had also incorporated banks in Scranton. Two of these newcomers, Horatio Pierce and James Blair, had been bank presidents before coming to Scranton, and both founded banks shortly after their arrival. Newcomers, then, played an active role in supplying Scranton with precious capital.[27]

Except for the migrants from large family companies, only three of Scranton's economic leaders in 1880 came from outside the Lackawanna Valley. All three of these men were young lawyers when they came to Scranton, and they all became prominent there soon after arrival. First was Edward B. Sturges, who came to Scranton from Connecticut in 1869 with a college education and training in law. He soon became a coal operator and held directorships in the Pine Hill Coal Company and the Lackawanna Valley Bank (founded by his father-in-law, George Sanderson). Most of Sturges' economic activity occurred after 1880 when he invested heavily in coal lands, railroads, and an electric trolley.[28] Like Sturges, Edward N. Willard moved to Scranton from Connecticut. Arriving in Scranton in the mid-1850s, he became George Sanderson's law partner. After awhile Willard became an attorney for the D.L.&W. By 1880, after some wise investing, he had become president of the Scranton Savings Bank and Trust Company and owner-director of the Bridge Coal Company and the Green Ridge Coal Company.[29] Finally, George H. Catlin moved to Scranton in 1870 from New York City after marrying James Archbald's daughter. The Catlin family owned a lot of land in Vermont; they provided son George with a college education and training in law. With wealth, education, admission to the bar, and a proper marriage, Catlin became a force in Scranton's economic development soon after his arrival. By 1880, he was vice-president of the Third National Bank and a director of the Scranton Savings Bank.[30]

Scranton's final group of economic leaders in 1880 were four representatives of railroads or of large family companies. Two of them, Charles DuPont Breck and Henry Belin, Jr., represented the powder interests of E.I. DuPont de Nemours and Company. In 1859, Breck's father, William, moved to Scranton from Wilmington, Delaware, the DuPont's headquarters, and represented DuPont in Scranton until his death in 1870. Charles settled in Scranton with his father and, after being admitted to the bar, added a directorship in the Lackawanna Trust Company to his association with DuPont. In 1870, Henry Belin, Jr. arrived in Scranton as president of E.I. DuPont of Pennsylvania. As the head of DuPont powder, Belin, like Breck, fit well in Scranton's financial circles; by 1880 he had become a director of the Third National Bank.[31]

The DuPonts were not the only ones to discover a profit in selling powder to Scranton's coal and railroad companies. The Laflin, Boies and Turck Powder

Company of Saugerties, New York, saw the anthracite market and sent Henry M. Boies to Scranton in 1865 to represent the family's interests. After fulfilling the large demands for powder, Boies started his own Moosic Powder Company in 1869. In selling his product he came into frequent contact with powder buyer Thomas Dickson, president of the D&H. Their business relationship became a social one when Boies married Dickson's daughter Elizabeth in 1870. From that time until his death over thirty years later, Boies scored one triumph after another. By 1880, Boies was a director of the Third National Bank; soon afterward he would become president of his father-in-law's Dickson Manufacturing Company.[32]

Railroads were the first modern corporations. Like the powder companies, railroads wanted direct representation in industrial Scranton. When Joseph J. Albright resigned as coal agent of the D.L.&W. in 1866, his place was taken by William R. Storrs, who was transferred by the company from Buffalo to Scranton. Storrs' exalted position with the D.L.&W. immediately involved him in Scranton's economic life. By 1880 he had added a directorship in the People's Street Railway and various officerships in voluntary associations to his railroads position.[33]

The migrants from large family companies were not the only economic leaders who continued their same job after moving to Scranton. Almost all forty economic leaders practiced their trained vocations in some form when they came to Scranton. They had the skills needed to conduct the business of an industrial city. There is a close tie between the towns these newcomers came from and the skills that they had. Towanda, Montrose, Dundaff, and Honesdale, which were county seats or commerical towns, gave Scranton its bankers and lawyers. The nearby coal towns, such as Carbondale, Jermyn, and Archbald, gave Scranton a variety of industrialists: coal operators, foundry owners, railroad engineers, and two founders of anthracite stove companies. So as Scranton became a regional capital, it drew gentlemen bankers and lawyers from the commercial towns and immigrant industrialists from the coal towns.

When dozens of newcomers came to Scranton and became economic leaders, their varied investments collectively advanced their adopted city. They also added to Scranton's local control of its industries and services. Their economic success, reinforced by a network of social and kinship ties, kept them in Scranton for the rest of their lives. In other words, their businesses, their speculation in real estate and housing, their comaraderie with friends in local clubs and voluntary associations, and their intricate familial ties with other Scrantonians all rooted them to Scranton. In fact, all forty of these economic leaders spent the bulk of their lives in Scranton once they arrived. For one-half of these men this meant active involvement in the economic life of Scranton into the twentieth century. This loyalty seems to be typical of urban elites in regional centers; it helped Scranton tremendously and gave the city a stable group of residents to help guide future economic development.[34] Through their loyalty Scranton's economic leaders aided their adopted city in three significant ways.

First, Scranton's economic leaders had city loyalty; they were more likely than outsiders to start risky local industries. The Scranton family, for example, not only invested in iron and coal, they also started the city's waterworks. In the 1870s, William W. Scranton visited Europe to study new techniques in steel manufacturing. Then he returned to Scranton to begin the Scranton Steel Company, which competed with and later merged with the L.I.&C., becoming the Lackawanna Iron and Steel Company in 1881. Entrepreneur Henry M. Boies not only founded the Moosic Powder Company in the 1860s; he later started the Boies Steel Wheel Company in Scranton after inventing and patenting a technique for strengthening locomotive wheels. Finally, bank president and coal operator Horatio Pierce incorporated the Scranton Stove Company, even though it had to compete with a flourishing anthracite stove company in nearby Pittston.[35] These capitalists were committed to Scranton and they helped their city grow.

Second, Scranton's local tycoons helped the city diversify its coal and iron economy. Their entrepreneurship was needed because coal mining had only a small multiplier effect. They first showed their strength in the 1850s, when the Scranton group got the D.L.&W. to locate sizable machinery and repair shops in the home area. Scranton's local owners logically tied their city's diversification to linkages of the coal and iron industry. Lumber, for example, was essential in coal mining, so Scranton's entrepreneurs started local lumber companies: The Lackawanna Lumber Company, the Scranton Lumber Company, the Scranton and North Carolina Lumber Company, and the Scranton Wood Working Company were all founded in the 1880s. William Connell, who became a millionaire coal operator, diversified in the 1880s and founded the Lackawanna Knitting Mills Company and the Scranton Button Manufacturing Company.[36]

The third advantage of a strong local elite is that they bolster the political, civic, and social life of their community. In politics, the wealthier the city's economic leaders, the more likely they are to influence regional, state, and sometimes even federal laws that improve the economic environment in their town. George Scranton, for example, won a congressional seat in the 1850s and lobbied powerfully for a high protective tariff—a move that he thought would help his home town's nascent iron and coal industry.[37] Like other urban elites, Scranton's gentry was philanthropic: they donated the parks and library, the college, and an academy of music that gave their city beauty, recreation, talented youth, and pride. And the large houses and lavish country clubs built in posh neighborhoods by local nabobs not only employed a lot of builders. It also helped cement fragmented investors into a more cohesive elite. The social ties that were formed in swank neighborhoods linked these newcomers to Scranton as much as did their investments in real estate and industry.[38]

Such a description of leadership formation is simplistic because it implies that success came easily. It did not. An investor had to survive panics, stiff competition, labor problems, and a fluctuating demand for Scranton's exports. Often he had to have luck to be in the right place at the right time. At least five of Scranton's forty leaders went bankrupt and several others came very close. Henry Boies failed twice before finding his niche in the powder business. William Winton went bankrupt at least twice and so did Elisha Phinney—once in Dundaff and once in Scranton. Liberal bankruptcy laws allowed them both to bounce back. Strangely, the more effective the businessman, the more he seemed to court failure. The Scrantons aptly illustrate this odd trend. Even Thomas Dickson almost failed in Carbondale and was "largely in debt" his first few years in Scranton. A liberal credit system allowed the Scrantons and Dickson to survive years of debts and unpaid promissory notes. Scranton's open system gave its capitalists the right to fail as well as suceed, and they did both.[39]

Scranton's forty economic leaders, then, often had tense moments in their rise to the top. The arbitrary cutoff at the year 1880, of course, does not allow for a full investigation of the dynamic process of leadership change through the lifetimes of prominent men. If 1890 were the cut off year, instead of 1880, the list of economic leaders would be longer. It would include men who had not yet achieved full prominence in 1880: Samuel Hines, a representative of the Erie Railroad; banker William T. Smith; and J. Benjamin Dimmick, Charles Matthews, and Thomas Torrey, the last of the successful Honesdale migrants. If 1890 were used, however, death would keep out Platt, Albright, Sanderson, Dickson, Watres, and Pierce; and these were men whose leadership roles help us understand entrepreneurship in Scranton during its early industrialization. If 1870 were chosen instead of 1880, William Connell, John Jermyn, and several post-Civil War arrivals would be excluded from the elite because they were not yet prominent. Also, much of Scranton's industrial structure in 1870 was inchoate because several important banks and local companies had not yet been founded. The cutoff at 1880, then, marks a rough end to Scranton's first wave of migrants and its first phase of industrialization.[40]

Scranton's pattern of drawing most of its capital and leadership from its hinterland reflects the era when it grew. From 1850 to 1880, large companies were only beginning to require formal training; they had only started to shift personnel in a vast bureaucracy to respond to expanding markets. The transportation and communications developments of the period were only beginning

Making Up Coal Trains, a Scene in The Delaware, Lackawanna, and Western Depot Yard at Scranton, Pennsylvania

to permit large companies to invest in many regions. During these thirty years, most of Scranton's doctors, lawyers, and businessmen were trained in apprenticeship programs rather than in specialized groups in universities. Similarly, most of the engineers and chemists who worked for railroads and coal companies were trained on the job, not in a classroom or laboratory.[41]

In such a system, the Lackawanna Valley was relatively self-sufficient. The outside world seemed to be threatening only when there was a fall in demand for its exports. Naturally family and neighborhood units were strong, and it is not surprising that among economic leaders kinship ties played a major role in creating opportunity and guiding migration. The rise and fall of towns and cities in the region understandably spurred a shifting of wealth and talent to the regional capital. That's why Scranton was able to grow so fast.

After 1880, the transportation revolution increasingly broke down the autonomy of local markets. Not only did large corporations dominate primary and secondary exports. National chain stores, food processing companies, insurance companies, and multi-regional banks exploited economies of scale to set up branches throughout the country. This new "national economy" provided cheaper goods and more efficient services. But it did so at the cost of local and regional subordination to multiregional corporations throughout the nation.[42]

The trend toward specialized training in engineering, business, medicine, and law gradually formalized the process of entry into this national system. After

1880, Scranton recruited leaders from a wider geographic area. The more successful newcomers were often specialists, who were trained in universities outside the region. They were less likely to have come to Scranton because of kinships ties and more likely to have come because a corporation transferred them. These changes were gradual though; even today kinship ties, short migration, and family loyalty help explain leadership formation in cities all over America. From 1850 to 1880 Scranton had completed only its first phase of industrialization. The changes imposed by outside corporations were only beginning.[43]

5

The Two Different Worlds
of Scranton and Wilkes-Barre:
A Look at Economic Leaders
in Relatively Open and Closed Systems

Scranton and Wilkes-Barre were the largest cities in northeast Pennsylvania and capitals of two adjacent regions—the Lackawanna and Wyoming Valleys. If we could have traveled through Scranton and Wilkes-Barre in 1880 we probably would have been struck by their similarities. Both were situated on rich veins of anthracite and both had pockets of iron ore nearby. Both cities were coal mining centers: Slag heaps, underground mines, and coal dust abounded. If we looked at houses in these two cities we would have seen some splendid Victorian architecture along the River Common in Wilkes-Barre, and on Washington Street in Scranton. In other places we would have seen familes with unpronounceable ethnic names living in shanties. On our tour we might have noticed a First National Bank, a First Presbyterian Church, and a YMCA in both cities. In fact, we might pass through both cities without realizing how different they were; they were settled at different times and their leaders had different strategies for growth. The Scranton story begins in the 1840s; to understand Wilkes-Barre we have to go back to the 1660s, when the king of England doled out land in America with startling incongruity.[1]

The early settlement of the Wyoming Valley was enlivened by frantic land disputes. King Charles II sparked this turmoil when he unwittingly granted northeast Pennsylvania to two agents: the colony of Connecticut and William Penn. In 1662, Charles confirmed that the western boundary of the Connecticut colony went to the Susquehanna River; nineteen years later he granted all of present-day Pennsylvania to William Penn and his heirs. These clashing charters posed no problem until the 1750s, when land shortages made the Connecticut Yankees and the south Pennsylvanians both think about settling the disputed land. Both groups moved to formalize their claims in 1754. First, the Penns confirmed their "Full and absolute right of preemption" for all present-day Pennsylvania from nine Indian chiefs at a conclave in Albany. Apparently red men spoke with forked tongues because two days later they sold Pennsylvania's Wyoming Valley to the Connecticut Susquehanna Company. The French and Indian War soon broke out and delayed permanent settlement until 1769. In January of that year Governor John Penn commissioned Captain Amos Ogden and a group of ten men, later called Pennamites, to take possession of the Susquehanna land. They arrived and started to build a settlement one mile from present-day Wilkes-Barre. Only two weeks after their arrival, they must have rubbed their eyes in disbelief: forty Connecticut Yankees had come to claim the Wyoming Valley. Which of the groups was most startled we do not know. Both of them had a charter, both bought out the Indians, and now both groups would fight to live on the land.[2]

At first, the Pennamites were inferior in numbers but superior in wiles. They amiably asked the Yankee leaders to come over to chat about land titles; when three Yankees strolled into the Pennamite fort they were quickly arrested "in the name of the Commonwealth of Pennsylvania." They were then escorted with their thirty-seven followers sixty miles to a jail in Easton. So ended round one. But the Yankees set bail for themselves, marched back to Wyoming, and took possession of the fort. The ousted Pennamites soon returned with assorted sheriffs and magistrates. They all stormed the fort and again sent the Yankees packing for the calaboose in Easton.[3]

From 1769 to 1771, the Pennamites and Yankees played this cat and mouse game five times, each time with more men and more anger. The Yankees finally got the upper hand when they joined forces with Lazarus Stewart and his fifty "Paxton boys." Stewart was a native of Lancaster, Pennsylvania, and had already feuded with Governor Penn over Indian protection and land claims in central Pennsylvania. Penn posted a £200 reward for Stewart when he and his Paxton rangers began dispensing frontier justice to renegade Indians. Stewart and the Yankees became natural allies; when they met, the Yankees, led by Zebulon Butler, promised Stewart and his men land in the Wyoming Valley for their support against the Pennamites. The alliance worked: the Paxton men and the Yankees expelled the Pennamites from the Wyoming Valley in 1771. Governor Penn urged English General Thomas Gage to come down from New York and oust the Yankee intruders; Penn even offered a £300 reward to anyone who would capture Stewart and Butler. But none of this worked; the Yankees were entrenched and the Paxton men had a township of land.[4]

The Yankees lived a stable farming life for the next few years. They traded goods up and down the Susquehanna River; they even sent representatives to the Connecticut assembly. As leader of the Yankees, Colonel Zebulon Butler became both judge and justice of the Connecticut assembly. His cousin, Colonel Nathan Denison, was a local justice of the peace in the Wyoming Valley and also served in the Connecticut assembly. The Yankees seem to have fully accepted the Paxton men: They got their land and Lazarus Stewart held the rank of captain. One of Stewart's men, Matthias Hollenback, even became the settlement's leading merchant. He would buy goods in Philadelphia and carry them west by wagon to the Susquehanna River. Then he would put his loot into an Indian canoe and push it by hand 150 miles up river to Wilkes-Barre. He so distinguished himself in this trade that he took his place with Butler, Denison, and Stewart as leaders of the Yankee community. For five years after the eviction of the Pennamites, the Connecticut settlement grew and prospered.[5]

What the Connecticut settlers patiently created, the Indians and the government impatiently destroyed. The Yankees supported the rebels during the Revolutionary War so the Pennsylvania Tories and the British sponsored an Indian raid on Wilkes-Barre. In the "Wyoming Massacre of 1778" most of the nearly 300 settlers were killed by Indians. Hollenback, Butler, and Denison escaped but Stewart died in battle. The next blow to the Yankees came four years later when the Confederation Congress declared that Pennsylvania had rightful title to all the disputed land. This decision triggered another Yankee-Pennamite war that lasted off and on till 1799. Finally, the disputants struck a compromise: the Yankees could keep their land if they would submit to the Pennsylvania government. This solution resolved the land question and newcomers came by the hundreds to build homes and farm the land in newly formed Luzerne County, which included most of northeast Pennsylvania.[6]

Wilkes-Barre became the county seat of Luzerne County. It was the oldest town in northeast Pennsylvania and had a good location on the banks of the Susquehanna River. When Wilkes-Barre became a borough in 1806 its leaders were the same men who led the Yankee charge in the 1770s. Zebulon Butler died in 1795 but his son Lord became first president of the town council. Matthias Hollenback was the first treasurer of Luzerne County and later he was a burgess of Wilkes-Barre. He and Nathan Denison were the law of the land: they became associate judges for the Luzerne County court. Hollenback did especially well. He apparently owned 10 percent of the land in Wilkes-Barre by 1802, and also built up a remarkable mercantile business. After the Wyoming Massacre he used his credit at Philadelphia to buy merchandise and rebuild his store in Wilkes-Barre. He started with dry goods and hardware; soon he expanded into grist and saw milling and fur trading. With the profits he established branch stores all up and down the Susquehanna River. As a result "no man was better known through lower New York and all over northern Pennsylvania." The Yankee elite of the 1770s had become the Wilkes-Barre elite of the early 1800s.[7]

The sons of the founding fathers kept their families prominent in Wilkes-Barre. Nathan Denison's son George was a lawyer and entrepreneur; he was also burgess of Wilkes-Barre, president of its town council, state legislator, and a congressman. George Hollenback, son of Matthias, picked up where his father left off. George built up the Hollenback stores along the Susquehanna River and founded the Wyoming Bank in 1829. Lord Butler, Zebulon's son, was local postmaster, burgess of Wilkes-Barre, and the first president of its town council.[8]

The Wilkes-Barre elite became a closely knit group bound by marriage and kinship. The Butlers, Denisons, Hollenbacks, and Stewarts were the founding families of Wilkes-Barre: those who later flourished in Wilkes-Barre were those who married into these families. Andrew Lee, for example, was a Paxton ranger under Lazarus Stewart; Lee's two sons both married into Stewart's family. One of them, Washington Lee, also studied law under Charles Denison. In 1870, Lee was a millionaire land owner and the wealthiest man in Wilkes-Barre. John Conyngham, Garrick Mallery, and Hendrick Wright married granddaughters of Zebulon Butler. All three became lawyers: Conyngham and Mallery were prominent judges and Wright became a congressman, chairman of the Pennsylvania Democratic party, and chairman of two Democratic national conventions.[9]

The Wilkes-Barre elite created an array of social institutions that tied them even closer. Edward Davies has studied these institutions and argues that they helped give cohesiveness to the local leaders. When Wilkes-Barre became a borough in 1806, it already had a debating society and a local library company. The next year the city fathers built the Wilkes-Barre Academy. A few years later they started two important institutions: first, the Wilkes-Barre Law and Library Association, which solidified the city's position as legal and administrative center of northeast Pennsylvania; second, Masonic Lodge 61 F.&.A.M., which brought together Wilkes-Barre's leading businessmen and politicians. All members of this lodge were interrelated: they admitted only those men with kinship ties to Wilkes-Barre's founding families.[10]

From 1800 to 1850, the primary export of the Wyoming Valley shifted from agriculture to coal. The marketing of anthracite early in the century gradually transformed the economic life of northeast Pennsylvania. But it did not change the leadership structure of Wilkes-Barre. Those who made money as lawyers and merchants simply switched into coal operating, banking, and transportation. For example, in 1813 George Hollenback sent the first Wyoming Valley coal to Philadelphia; shortly thereafter, Lord Butler began trading coal to towns along the Susquehanna River. In 1820, Washington Lee discovered coal on his 1,000 acre estate; soon he shipped hundreds of tons of coal down the Susquehanna River to Baltimore.[11]

No city prospers without good transportation. The Wilkes-Barre elite used all its economic muscle and political skills to bring turnpikes, canals, and later railroads to town. In the early 1800s, the Wilkes-Barre leaders helped build turnpikes to Easton and to Mauch Chunk. Their big chance came in 1824 when the Pennsylvania legislature put up forty million dollars for public works in the state. The Wilkes-Barre kinship group went into action to get as much money as they could to make a major canal out of the Susquehanna River. George Hollenback got himself appointed to the Pennsylvania Canal Commission and sponsored the North Branch Canal, to be built from southern Pennsylvania all the way up the Susquehanna to New York. Garrick Mallery and George Denison represented Wilkes-Barre in the state legislature in 1827, and lobbied successfully for the North Branch Canal. Construction began on the canal in 1829 and was completed from Wilkes-Barre to Philadelphia in five years. The canal was a boon to Wilkes-Barre, but was a boondoggle for the state. The building and operating costs for the canal exceeded its receipts by hundreds of thousands of dollars annually. It hurt the state but helped Wilkes-Barre when the taxpayers of Pennsylvania paid for Wilkes-Barre's economic development.[12]

Guided by a small kinship group, Wilkes-Barre grew slowly from 700 people in 1820 to 2700 in 1850.[13] Yet the city fathers showed skill in state politics and in building the anthracite trade. Their cohesiveness probably helped them mobilize for urban growth. But it also fostered narrow-mindedness. They listened to those who married into their kinship group but shunned those who did not. Their insularity made them contemptuous of outsiders and closed to innovation. When George Hollenback faced George Scranton they were not merely representing rival towns; they were symbols of two different traditions and two different approaches to urban development. Wilkes-Barre was the oldest city in northeast Pennsylvania; it was a planned city in a good location. Scranton did not exist until the 1840s; its very founding was an accident. Wilkes-Barre was a rich town and its elite plowed money into coal. Scranton was short on capital yet its founders took a desperate chance on manufacturing. The Wilkes-Barre elite was based on kinship, the Scranton elite on proven talent. Over time Wilkes-Barre developed a closed system with power concentrated in a conservative elite. Scranton was relatively open, its leaders were venturesome, and economic power in the city was dispersed.

These two different cities fought each other for urban dominance. Wilkes-Barre wielded astonishing political power for a small town; state politics in Wilkes-Barre was the art of getting the Pennsylvania legislature to thwart rivals and to support public works for Wilkes-Barre. To Scrantonians state politics was a snake pit and Wilkes-Barre was the biggest viper in Pennsylvania. Wilkes-Barre hindered Scranton's moves to the legislature for large city limits, corporate charters, and a separation from Luzerne County. Yet in the long run Scranton's open and venturesome elite overcame the closed conservative leadership in Wilkes-Barre. In 1840, Wilkes-Barre was almost seventy years old and Scranton did not exist; fifteen years later Scranton was the larger city; after fifteen more years Scranton was three times the size of Wilkes-Barre. When the dust had settled two things were clear: Scranton's elite wanted to build a city and Wilkes-Barre's elite wanted to preserve its power. Scranton's entrepreneurs promoted a diversified economy, spacious city limits, an active board of trade, and the arrival of talented immigrants; their recipe for urban growth was a good one. Wilkes-Barre's economic leaders of 1880 seem to have wanted none of these four ingredients, and for good reasons: They all threatened the influence and even the survival of Wilkes-Barre's kinship group.[14]

The contrast between Scranton and Wilkes-Barre will be clearer if we systematically compare both of their economic elites. Fortunately we have the information to do this, since I've collected a mass of data on Scranton's economic leaders, and Edward Davies has done the same for Wilkes-Barre.[15]

Wilkes-Barre was a small city but it had forty-five economic leaders with two or more directorships in 1880. Most of these forty-five were interrelated; they controlled the largest banks, the major coal companies, and the railroads and trolleys in Wilkes-Barre. For example, they totally controlled the First and Second National Banks, the Wyoming Valley Coal Company, the Wilkes-Barre Coal and Iron Company, and the Delaware, Lehigh, and Wyoming Railroad. In fact, they held almost 90 percent of all positions on boards of directors in Wilkes-Barre.[16]

As Davies points out, the economic elite of Wilkes-Barre was also the city's social and political elite. Lodge 61, the Malt Club, the Cheese and Crackers Club, and the Wyoming Historical and Geological Society were major social institutions. Economic leaders started them and used them to talk business and to groom future leaders. Those outside of these clubs lost out. They might have good investment ideas, but they couldn't tap the major sources of capital in Wilkes-Barre.[17]

The Wilkes-Barre kinship group held an iron grip on local politics. They were a tiny fraction of the city's population but they dominated the local conventions of both parties. Narrow city limits seem to have helped Wilkes-Barre politicians keep a hold on local politics and groom leaders for state and federal office. In the 1870s, Hendrick Wright was the state chairman of the Democratic party, Henry Hoyt was the governor of Pennsylvania, and George Woodward was the chief justice of the state supreme court. Such political power made Wilkes-Barre

TABLE 5.1. Economic, Social, and Political Influence of Forty Economic Leaders in Scranton in 1880

	Total Organizations and Offices	Total Positions (Directorships, etc.)	Positions Held by the Forty		Positions Held by Relatives of the Forty		Total Positions Held by the Forty and Relatives	
			Number	Percentage	Number	Percentage	Number	Percentage
Economic organizations	43	205	129	63	15	7	144	70
Social organizations	21	176	55	31	45	26	100	57
Political offices	41	41	6	15	4	10	10	24

SOURCE: See Burton W. Folsom II, "Urban Networks: The Economic and Social Order of the Lackawanna and Lehigh Valleys during Early Industrialization, 1850-1880" (Ph.D. diss., University of Pittsburgh, 1976), appendixes V, VI, and VII.

the envy of every city in Pennsylvania—including Philadelphia, Pittsburgh, and Scranton. Wilkes-Barre's kinship group was an economic, social, and political elite.[18]

Power was much more diffused in Scranton than in Wilkes-Barre. No kinship group dominated Scranton life; even the authority of the Scranton family was greatly constrained. As indicated in table 5.1 economic, social, and political offices in Scranton were somewhat dispersed. Scranton's forty economic leaders held 63 percent of the seats on local boards of directors. They held most of the directorships on some of the city's largest businesses: the First National Bank, the Dickson Manufacturing Company, the Scranton Steel Company, and the Weston Mill Company. Such concentration of authority is large but it was larger in Wilkes-Barre, where forty-five economic leaders held almost 90 percent of the directorships.

Scranton had no social clubs like Lodge 61 in Wilkes-Barre. Scranton's economic leaders joined a variety of clubs and voluntary associations, as suggested in table 5.1. The YMCA, the Lackawanna Scientific and Historical Society, and the Lackawanna Bible Society were among the more visible social organizations. And they involved Scranton's top industrialists. But no club had the prestige or local importance of Lodge 61, the Malt Club, or even the historical society in Wilkes-Barre. In Wilkes-Barre, social status often preceded economic success. In Scranton, economic success was more often the result of what you did rather than who you were. So economic leaders in Scranton probably joined voluntary associations more as a public duty than as an avenue to wealth.[19]

Another feature of Scranton's social organizations in 1880 was the strong participation by relatives of economic leaders. These relatives held over one-fourth of all executive positions on the city's voluntary associations. In several cases, the relatives were the sons of economic leaders, who were entrusted with social influence instead of economic responsibility. In most cases the relatives seems to have been fulfilling a social role after making a fortuitous marriage. Whereas in Wilkes-Barre such marriages often preceded economic participation, in Scranton not many of these relatives ever wielded economic influence.[20]

Few of Scranton's economic leaders held political office in 1880. According to table 5.1, they controlled only six of the forty-one city and county political offices, while their relatives held four others. This lesser domination is, of course, still a large representation for such a small group of people, especially since they held the district attorney's office and both city controller positions. While a handful of economic leaders held some important political offices, many upwardly mobile immigrants ran successfully for election to various ward, city, and federal offices. The triumph of immigrants and unskilled laborers in local politics is not surprising; they greatly outnumbered the local industrialists. The price of having a large city in which to expand, then, was having the Irish Catholics run it. Many city fathers in Scranton recognized, with regret, that the implications of an open economic environment were an open political environment as well. The necessity of economic expansion, though, meant they had to have wide city limits and run the risks of democratic rule.[21]

When Scranton had its city limits stretched to almost twenty square miles in 1866, the Irish immediately won control of the new city government. The editor of the Scranton *Republican* decried the "Fenian victory." He asserted earlier that "everybody recognizes the attempt of our Irish votes to monopolize city government." Yet if the choice came down to having narrow city limits or having the Irish in office, most economic leaders reluctantly took the Irish. At least they were "our Irish" and not politicians in Wilkes-Barre. In the words of one observer, "It is thought better to endure the ills we have than to fly to others we know not of. . . . If the organization of city government should be delayed, for six months or a year, there is no predicting what brood of evils and disorders might be hatched."[22] In 1880, then, Scranton's businessmen developed industries and expanded their city limits, under the political supervision of Irish mayor Terence V. Powderly, the national president of the Knights of Labor.

Wilkes-Barre's age, political tradition, and social institutions all militated against its leaders creating an open political environment. The economic leaders in Wilkes-Barre preferred political control of city government to expanded city limits. They were veterans at wielding political influence in Pennsylvania for their own glory and that of their city. Through the state legislature, they had built the North Branch Canal and blocked Scranton and Hazleton from breaking off from Luzerne County. Wilkes-Barre's leaders seem to have opposed wide city limits because they feared they would be ousted by the new voters, who would have been mostly immigrants. Wilkes-Barreans, therefore, didn't incorporate their city until 1871, five years after Scranton did so, and its city boundaries only included 4.14 square miles, less than one-fourth the size of Scranton.[23]

In Wilkes-Barre, then, economic leaders were social and political leaders as well; power derived from membership in a kinship group. In Scranton authority was more fragmented; a more open system involved a variety of people in the city's economic, social, and political life. A comparison of the social characteristics of the economic leaders in Wilkes-Barre and Scranton in 1880 shows further differences in these two urban elites.

Economic leaders in Wilkes-Barre and Scranton differed in background. Most of Wilkes-Barre's men were English in origin and almost 90 percent were born in Pennsylvania, usually in the Wyoming Valley. Most economic leaders in Scranton had an English heritage too. But only two were born in the Lackawanna Valley.

Others came from almost every New England and Middle Atlantic state. Also, nine were born in five foreign countries; eleven other immigrants held a single directorship in Scranton. Such openness contrasts with the more closed atmosphere of older Wilkes-Barre. There, only two immigrants were economic leaders, and they were just barely qualified. Most immigrants didn't have the kinship ties needed to join the city's homogeneous English-stock elite.[24]

The contrast in the leaders of Wilkes-Barre and Scranton is also apparent if we look at their education and religion. Almost two-thirds of Wilkes-Barre's and one-third of Scranton's elite went to college or had training in law. As a Scranton man said, "The leading families of Wilkes-Barre are nearly all descendants of the pioneers of the Wyoming Valley and are all cultured to an enviable degree." To be educated is, in a sense, to be cultured but schooling also makes economic sense. The younger leaders in Scranton, those who had reached maturity in the rapidly industrializing 1850s, clearly perceived the economic advantages of formal training. Twelve of the fourteen born after 1834 went to college or became lawyers; only two of the twenty-six born before 1835 had college or law in their backgrounds. More than 80 percent of Wilkes-Barre's and Scranton's leaders were Episcopalians or Presbyterians, the traditional upper-class denominations. Wilkes-Barre's elite preferred the more exclusive Episcopalian church while Scranton leaders were mostly Presbyterians.[25]

Almost by definition, the economic leaders in Scranton and Wilkes-Barre were businessmen. Most were active in several occupations, and some easily combined law with coal-mining and banking. Yet there was still a difference in the two cities. Wilkes-Barre's inbred leaders strongly gravitated toward service professions such as banking and law, and they used these skills to become successful coal operators. Scranton's more self-made entrepreneurs represented a wider variety of professions and trades, but they leaned heaviest toward direct coal and iron investment. Their training ran the gamut from law and engineering to marble-cutting and milling.[26]

The economic leaders in Scranton and Wilkes-Barre seem to have established exclusive enclaves near the centers of their cities. Many wealthy bankers, lawyers, and coal barons built splendid mansions, several of which still stand, right next to each other. The elite neighborhood in Wilkes-Barre was especially conspicuous; over 90 percent of the city's economic leaders lived in a four block area along the River Common. Scranton's leaders were much more dispersed. Most lived in a six square block area that included Wyoming, Washington, Jefferson, Olive, Mulberry, and Vine Streets. A dozen others lived in suburbs in Providence, Green Ridge, Hyde Park, and Dunmore.[27]

Within Scranton's posh neighborhoods, the newcomers from Honesdale, Carbondale, and other nearby towns seem to have scattered about in no particular order. In Scranton, town of origin did not correlate with place of residence. Many prominent newcomers to Scranton did have close ties with fellow migrants from the same town. For example, former Carbondalers William Monies and Lewis Pughe were business partners in a large investment company. Former Honesdaler Edward Weston asked a fellow Honesdale migrant to Scranton, Alfred Hand, to witness the signing of his will. Finally, former Carbondalers Horatio Pierce, Edward Weston, Lewis Pughe, and William Monies all went back to Carbondale to attend the funeral of Thomas and George Dickson's father.[28]

Wilkes-Barre's and Scranton's leaders also differed in political affiliation. Almost 50 percent of the Wilkes-Barreans backed the Democratic party, while Scrantonians were over 80 percent Republican. This variation may be explained by the long Democratic tradition in Wilkes-Barre. Many of the city's antebellum gentry had been Democrats; their sons, who formed much of the 1880 elite, simply maintained their families' political tradition. As a younger city, Scranton had no such tradition; most of its 1880 leaders came to town after the founding of the Republican party. Many of these men found themselves in natural agreement with the Republican party in its business philosophy of high tariffs and its social philosophy of pietistic reform.[29]

The ages of Scranton and Wilkes-Barre and the ages of their economic leaders present a paradox. Scranton was a younger city, but most of its leaders were older than their counterparts in Wilkes-Barre in 1880. Most of Scranton's leaders had arrived in the 1850s and 1860s, when they were in their middle- to late-twenties. Few had been born in Scranton, and most had begun careers or established themselves in other areas before migrating. Almost one-half of the Wilkes-Barre elite, in contrast, had been born in or near Wilkes-Barre; many of them had made their fortunes, through business or marriage, before they reached the age of thirty. The higher median age of Scranton's leaders reflects the relatively longer time it took them to make their fortunes. By 1880, they were an older group and had only six members under the age of forty. For the youthful members of Wilkes-Barre's kinship group, the opportunity to acquire a fortune came earlier, and a dozen of them held at least two directorships by age forty.[30]

By comparing Wilkes-Barre's and Scranton's leaders we can understand why they behaved so differently. Wilkes-Barre was an older city run by old English-stock families who went to the same churches, joined the same clubs, and lived in the same neighborhood. They were all kinsmen who shared money-making schemes. On the subject of marketing and export most of them had the same idea: sell coal. Anthracite was plentiful and for a long time it had low entry costs. The demand for coal increased steadily during the 1880s and Wilkes-Barre had good transportation to New York and Philadelphia. So the decision to invest in coal was a wise one.

TABLE 5.2.   Percentage of Employees in Coal and Manufacturing in Luzerne and Lackawanna Counties in 1880

Industry	Percentage of Employees in Luzerne County	Percentage of Employees in Lackawanna County
Coal	92.2	76.2
Manufacturing	7.8	23.8
	100.0	100.0
	N = 28, 983	N = 18,250

SOURCES: Francis Walker and Charles W. Seaton, supts., *Report on the Mining Industries of the United States, 1880* (Washington, D.C., 1886), pp. 625-26; idem, *Report on the Manufacturers of the United States, 1880* (Washington, D.C., 1886), p. 177.

Once the Wilkes-Barre elite had chosen coal as their export, they saw no reason to switch. They did their job well and made the Wyoming Valley a major center for anthracite. So the leading families taught their coal trade to their children and this kept coal booming for generations. Newcomers quickly saw that credit flowed most freely in anthracite. Since the road to success was paved with coal, they saw no reason to take a detour.

This is not to imply that anthracite was a sure thing. Charles Parrish made and lost fortunes three times in coal and he was not alone. And, of course, there were ways to make money other than investing in coal. Local services such as banking, trolleys, and utilities drew lots of Wilkes-Barre capital. Real estate, too, was a perennial elite investment. But the success of the services depended on the success of the export; without a strong export there would be no people to demand local services. So Wilkes-Barre chose to stake its future almost solely on coal. Some went bankrupt but others made a steady profit. After generations of coal operating in Wilkes-Barre, it was a way of life for capitalist and worker alike.[31]

The heavy emphasis on coal production in Luzerne County is indicated in tables 5.2 and 5.3. Only three manufacturing companies existed in Wilkes-Barre in 1880, and these seem mostly to have produced coal machinery for a local market. Certainly Wilkes-Barre had a demand for manufactured goods. Yet outsiders had founded two of these three companies, all of which proved to be so feeble that the Dickson Manufacturing Company in Scranton built a branch operation in Wilkes-Barre. Most Wilkes-Barreans didn't seem to care: by 1880 they hadn't even set up a board of trade.[32] Members of Wilkes-Barre's old families no doubt believed their exclusive clubs were better than an inclusive board of trade. And in these clubs they were among old friends. They didn't need to worry about hearing new ideas or meeting with immigrants.

The decision of Wilkes-Barre's capitalists to concentrate on coal and local services was both conservative and profitable. During the 1800s, they made the

TABLE 5.3.   Percentage of Value of Coal and Manufacturing Production in Luzerne and Lackawanna Counties in 1880

Industry	Percentage of Value of Product in Luzerne County	Percentage of Value of Product in Lackawanna County
Coal	80.2	41.8
Manufacturing	19.8	58.2
	100.0	100.0
	N = $22,227,384	N - $18,374,429

SOURCES: Francis Walker and Charles W. Seaton, supts., *Report on the Mining Industries of the United States, 1880* (Washington, D.C., 1886), pp. 625-26; idem, *Report on the Manufacturers of the United States, 1880* (Washington, D.C., 1886), p. 177.

Wyoming Valley the world's largest producer of anthracite. Their reliance on coal was rational but harmful to their city in the long run. The national market for anthracite began shrinking in the 1920s and Wilkes-Barreans couldn't revive it. Nor could they easily change to something else.[33]

Both the Lackawanna Valley and the adjacent Wyoming region had coal in abundance and iron ore in small amounts. Even though their natural resources were similar, the capitalists in Wilkes-Barre and Scranton made different choices for investment. While Wilkes-Barre tied its future to coal, Scranton forged a diversified economy. It was a younger city and never had an old elite or restrictive institutions to guide local money into coal. In fact, the Scranton family started their city by using available ore to make nails and rails. They incorporated the L.I.&C. and it became the largest exporter in northeast Pennsylvania; other people came to town to invest in iron and Scranton's reputation was established as the manufacturing center of northeast Pennsylvania.[34]

Iron and steel production required much higher levels of capital for entry than did coal. The irony is that Wilkes-Barre's wealthy old families were better able to afford the iron investment than were Scranton's newcomers. One Scranton writer said in 1875 that Wilkes-Barre's "aggregate of individual wealth . . . exceeds any city or town in Northern Pennsylvania." The wealth recorded in the manuscript census of 1870 confirms this opinion: Wilkes-Barre had forty-one men with over $100,000, and Scranton had only thirty-three. Furthermore, the iron deposits in Montour County were close to Wilkes-Barre; to reach Scranton, they had to be shipped up the Susquehanna River right by the coal barons' houses! Since Wilkes-Barre's capitalists virtually ignored manufacturing, several outsiders came to town to exploit the coal and iron. By the mid-1860s, though, the only successful manufacturing company in Wilkes-Barre was the small Vulcan Iron Works; but it was partially outside controlled and one of its officers even lived in Scranton.[35]

While Wilkes-Barre stuck with coal, Scranton exported both coal and iron products. In 1880, Scranton's L.I.&.C. and Dickson Manufacturing Company were each larger than all the manufacturing companies in Wilkes-Barre combined. Also present in Scranton was the Green Ridge Iron Works, the Scranton City Foundry, the Scranton Brass and File Works, and the Lackawanna Carriage Works. Scranton leaders also invested in local services and industries related to coal and iron. In the services, Edward Weston covered the whole Lackawanna Valley with his Weston Mill Company; the Stowers Pork Packing and Provision Company sold meat products throughout the Lackawanna and Wyoming regions. In the industries related to coal and iron, Scrantonians operated two local powder companies by 1880; one of them, the Moosic Powder Company, sold in the region and the other, E.I. du Pont de Nemours of Pennsylvania, sold throughout the state. Lumber was important in coal mining and several Scrantonians founded lumber companies in the 1880s.[36]

Scranton's capitalists were eclectic; they experimented with a lot of investments and some of them failed. For example, the Lackawanna Railroad, the Greenwood Coal Company, the Scranton Frear Stone and Manufacturing Company, the Scranton Silver Mining Company, and the Second National Bank had all folded by 1880. In some fields the results were mixed. Two local stove works failed, for example, before the Scranton Stove Company succeeded. Amidst a welter of investments Scranton completed its first stage of industrialization with the proven talent to export both iron and coal products.[37]

As Scranton became a center for manufacturing it brought together many capitalists who were willing to take different types of risks. This made for a combination of inventiveness and creative entrepreneurship. For example, Henry Boies founded the successful Moosic Powder Company; then he perfected a gunpowder cartridge that reduced the death and injury resulting from carelessness in mining explosions. Boies seemed to court risky ventures, and failed twice before coming to Scranton. Once he made his fortune in powder, the credit lines were open and he went to work inventing a flexible steel wheel for locomotives. He started the Boies Steel Wheel Company in 1888 to manufacture his patented invention. A lot of Scranton's immigrants became accustomed to risk and took remarkable chances. For example, John Jermyn sunk his life savings into coal mines that no one else wanted. He "had confidence both in the mines and himself" and he went on to build an empire.[38]

By the 1880s, Scranton had the entrepreneurs, the inventors, and the capital to launch another stage of rapid economic development. As usual, iron and steel were in the forefront. In that decade Scranton men started the Green Ridge Iron Foundry, the Dunmore Iron and Steel Company, and the Scranton Forging Company. Soon afterward local capitalists also started the Scranton Fire Brick

Manufacturing Company, the Scranton Jar and Stopper Company, and the Scranton Glass Company. Some of these enterprises required little capital for entry; capitalists in Wilkes-Barre could easily have started them in their own city if they had wanted to. The Scranton Glass Company, for example, was first capitalized at only $15,000; and it earned so much that its capital stock expanded tenfold in only ten years.[39]

In the 1880s, some venturesome Scrantonians brought added capital to their city by investing in other regions. The Lackawanna Valley was too small to hold their entrepreneurial energy. The immigrant team of William Monies and Lewis Pughe, for example, built stoves in Pittston, mined silver in Colorado, and searched for gold in California. Other Scranton men founded two unlikely enterprises: the Scranton Gold and Silver Company in Montana and the Stephens Tin Mining, Milling, and Manufacturing Company in South Dakota. Edward Fuller made a fortune in salt and became president of the International Salt Company. Finally, millionaire James Blair invested in railroads that stretched across the Midwest. Scranton's capitalists seemed always ready to take chances as they speculated in a welter of industries throughout the nation.[40]

If gold had been discovered in 1880 in the Moosic Mountains between Scranton and Wilkes-Barre, here is my vision of what the two different elites would do. Scranton leaders would rush to the mountains with picks and shovels. Some would try to invent a Geiger counter that could find gold; others, more sober, would invent mining equipment, build rail lines up the mountains, or sell food to the miners. The board of trade would try to incorporate the mountain into Scranton's city limits; if this failed they would give a tax incentive to anyone who would pave Main Street with gold. In Wilkes-Barre, this frantic behavior would be viewed with both confidence and contempt. Their leaders would take the next train (or carriage) to Harrisburg and try to work through the state legislature to prohibit the chartering of any gold company in Scranton. Then they might produce old land claims and allege that the Moosic Mountains were actually property of the old founding families (and their descendants, of course) through the Susquehanna Company's treaty with the Indians in 1754. Wilkes-Barreans would try to win in the courtroom what Scrantonians would try to win with picks and shovels.

Comparing Scranton and Wilkes-Barre shows more than how elites influence economic development. It shows how a city's age, its growth rate, and its social institutions can shape the social mobility of its economic leaders. Wilkes-Barre was an older city with an exclusive elite that cloaked its power in an array of clubs. Scranton was a younger more open city. It grew more rapidly than Wilkes-Barre and had more opportunity for upward mobility into its elite.

Other studies also show a correlation between rapid city growth and rapid social mobility. For example, Warren, Pennsylvania, and Paterson, New Jersey, the subjects of separate studies,[41] were like Scranton in their high growth rates and fluid social mobility. In the 1870s, newcomers to Warren apparently seized the initiative from the old settlers, as they did in Scranton, and changed the export to oil. In both cities this change created lots of opportunities. In Warren, these newcomers, as a group, were more upwardly mobile than the old settlers were; in Scranton many of its newcomers became part of the city's economic elite. Paterson, a textile center, had a population boom from 1840 to 1880 similar to that in Scranton. And in both of these cities many rags-to-riches immigrants walked their streets. Scranton, Warren, and Paterson seem to tell this story: an open environment and a rapid growth rate make for a fluid social structure with high social mobility at all levels. If this is true, then the American dream of going from "rags to riches" was a myth or a reality depending on where you lived.

In the Lackawanna and Wyoming regions two different elites had two different ideas about economic development. Scranton and Wilkes-Barre had similar coal and iron resources and similar access to outside markets. Yet their local elites chose different investment strategies. Wilkes-Barre was an old city and most of its economic leaders came from old families. They were homogeneous in social background and they formed restrictive social clubs to make sure their city's leaders stayed that way. Forming a large kinship network, they began exporting coal and their combined investments made the Wyoming Valley the largest coal-producing region in the anthracite fields. In the adjacent Lackawanna region, the younger city of Scranton had the same potential in coal, but its entrepreneurs were more varied in background and outlook. The city was a child of the industrial revolution. It had no old families or exclusive clubs to channel wealth into coal. The Scranton family started with nails and rails and from then on a motley bunch of capitalists risked money on a variety of industries: powder, coal, and railroads were the more sensible ones; salt, tin mining, and button making were more remarkable. Yet the diverse businessmen in Scranton imposed an order on their city's economic development through the local board of trade. The variety of different investments in Scranton helped give it a more rapid growth rate and a more complex infrastructure than that in Wilkes-Barre. Ultimately, Scranton's more diversified economy helped it withstand the removal of the city's first and largest enterprise, the Lackawanna Iron and Steel Company in the early 1900s, and the sudden collapse of the coal industry in the 1920s.

6

The Rise of an Urban Network
in the Lackawanna Valley

Scranton's entrepreneurs not only directed the future of their city, they shaped the growth of their region as well. In fact, from 1850 to 1880 Scranton forged an urban network in the Lackawanna Valley. While this was happening capitalists in New York City were dominating key iron, coal, and railroad industries in the Lackawanna Valley. The relationship among New York City, Scranton, and the small towns nearby was one of economic dominance and subordinance. The three-level hierarchy, illustrated in figure 1, helps to explain this pattern of dominance and subordinance.

Right from the start, the New Yorkers only invested in the big railroads and coal companies in the Lackawanna Valley. By 1880, these captains of industry had gained a majority of stock in Scranton's first and largest industries, the L.I.&C. and the D.L.&W. The smaller industries and services were less manageable from New York, and their smaller volume of business held little charm for the adventurous capitalists in the nation's largest city. These barons of Wall Street had visions of national markets. They preferred to speculate in transportation and primary exports in newly-developing regions, and their investments crept westward throughout the nineteenth century.[1]

Despite the presence of New Yorkers, Scranton's entrepreneurs were tenacious; in 1880, they still controlled much of their city's future. For example, Scranton men held directorships on the L.I.&C. and D.L.&W., and local boy Thomas Dickson was president of the D&H. The Dickson Manufacturing Company, the Scranton Steel Company, and John Jermyn's coal company still competed well in national markets. Even when outside capital became necessary, Scrantonians never relinquished local ownership without a fight. But they were caught in the squeeze of having to invest heavily in coal and iron technology for their export to remain competitive in national and world

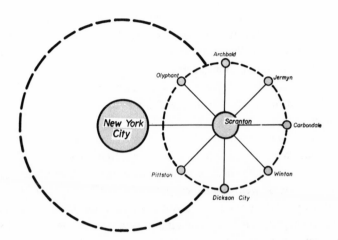

Figure 1.   Urban Dominance and Subordinance in the Lackawanna Valley

markets. Since local Scranton men had a hard time raising the capital, they had two choices: seek capital outside the region, and submit to outside control, or refuse to expand, and thereby preside over the death of their city's main export.[2] As the region's coal, iron, and rail industries grew in size, then, their ownership usually shifted to the wealthier corporate investors in New York City.

New York may have dominated Scranton but Scranton dominated the other coal towns in the Lackawanna Valley. Scranton drew its capital and leadership from commercial towns to the north and east; and by 1880, Scrantonians dominated all the coal towns in the core of the region. These subordinate coal towns included Carbondale, the five towns between Carbondale and Scranton, and Pittston, which bordered the Lackawanna and Wyoming Valleys. In these seven towns, Scranton investors developed local coal land, but others owned banks and services.

The town of Carbondale, the "Pioneer City," provides the first and best example of outside domination from Scranton and New York City. By 1880 Carbondale had gone through two stages. Until the 1850s it was the only industrial town in the Lackawanna Valley. Its existence had always been tied to the mining done by the D&H, so even when it was the regional hub, outside domination stymied local development. Carbondale's second stage, its fall from the top in the Lackawanna Valley, was more dramatic. As the largest town in the region, Carbondale had attracted men of talent and means from northeast Pennsylvania and upstate New York. Men like James Archbald and Edward Weston, superintendents of the D&H, and merchant William Richmond, founder of the Elk Hill Coal Company, had all migrated to Carbondale from Honesdale.

Engineer Thomas Dickson, who became a foundry owner in Carbondale, his brother George Dickson, and future lawyer Alfred Darte moved to the Pioneer City from Dundaff. Horatio Pierce, Carbondale's first bank president, and D&H mechanics Charles and John B. Smith came there in the 1830s from upstate New York.[3] In the 1850s, when Carbondale began losing its regional primacy, all these leaders left for Scranton. This loss was followed by economic subordination to Scranton, at one level, and to New York City at another.

Since Carbondale was a mere branch town of the D&H, its hold on ambitious entrepreneurs must have always been weak. Opportunities were not plentiful. The D&H owned all of the coal land surrounding Carbondale and most of the urban real estate there as well. Most local enterprise revolved around the D&H, whose manufacturing interests (the sawmill, and the machinery, car repair, and paint shops) supplemented its mining interests in Carbondale. By the 1850s, the town had several stores, a foundry, three small stove enterprises, a marble business, a flour mill, and a brewery—even though coal-related fires regularly gutted large sections of the business district.[4] None of these small ventures ever grew much, but some of their owners succeeded in a big way after they left Carbondale. Lured by greater economic opportunity elsewhere in the region, Carbondale's wealth and talent migrated in two large waves.

The first wave left Carbondale to work for the Pennsylvania Coal Company, which began building a railroad from Hawley to Pittston in 1849 to compete with the D&H. This railroad could not lure the wealthiest Carbondalers because it was smaller than the D&H. Instead, it attracted the town's secondary leaders, the skilled mechanics and foremen of the D&H, who assumed comparable or better positions with the new railroad. These migrants included Scotsmen Andrew Bryden and William Law, who became co-superintendents of the Pennsylvania Coal Company's mines in Pittston; small businessman James McMillan, who joined them in Pittston; and John B. Smith, who left for Dunmore and soon became state president of the Pennsylvania Coal Company. Also leaving Carbondale in this wave were coal operator Edward Jones and his business associates George Simpson and James J. Williams, who moved to Archbald and invested in Scranton.[5] This group showed much talent, but they were not rich when they left Carbondale so their loss did not seriously affect that city's meager investment punch.

It was the second wave of emigration that devastated Carbondale. In it Carbondale lost its wealthiest and most talented men to Scranton—a paralyzing blow that insured Carbondale's future stagnation. This emigration began in the mid-1850s, only after Scranton began to emerge as the regional capital of the Lackawanna Valley. In the regional center these men could be where the action was. They could exploit greater opportunities in business and real estate. The wealthy Carbondalers who came to Scranton moved quickly to the top level of economic leadership in the largest city in northeastern Pennsylvania. Scranton's rise and Carbondale's fall, then, were closely related (see table 6.1).[6]

The emigration of Carbondalers was part of Scranton's centralization of talent in the Lackawanna Valley. The decision of entrepreneurs in the Lackawanna Valley to settle in Scranton at least kept the talent inside the region. After all, they could have gone to New York City, and some in fact did before Scranton emerged. Charles T. Pierson, for example, had established the largest independent foundry in Carbondale in 1833. In 1852, before Scranton showed its regional dominance, Pierson sold his foundry to Thomas Dickson and left for New York City to become a merchant. Pierson returned to Carbondale in 1856 and suddenly began speculating in coal land around rapidly growing Scranton. Convinced of Scranton's potential, Pierson gave strong financial backing to Dickson to go there to build a new foundry. Shortly after Dickson made the big move, Pierson joined him as a business partner in the foundry and as a next door neighbor on Scranton's elegant Washington Street.[7]

Even Wilkes-Barre, the regional center in the adjacent Wyoming Valley, benefited from Carbondale's displacement as regional hub. Four members of Carbondale's emaciated professional elite ended up in Wilkes-Barre. These four migrants included Alfred Darte, Jr. and Alfred Darte III, the son and grandson of one of Carbondale's first lawyers; Alexander Farnham, another lawyer who was the son of one of Carbondale's few physicians; and John S. Law, the vice-president of Carbondale's largest bank. As in the migration to Scranton, those Carbondalers moving to Wilkes-Barre appear to have transferred their wealth and status intact and then exploited the greater opportunity in the larger city. John S. Law, for example, the wealthiest of the prolific Law family in Carbondale, helped start the First National Bank there. His relatives, primarily skilled employees of the D&H, left Carbondale for Pittston and the Pennsylvania Coal Company in the first migration around 1850. Leaving in the second wave, banker Law migrated to the established city of Wilkes-Barre, and soon achieved a higher position, president of the Second Miner's Bank of Wilkes-Barre. Eventually, he moved to New York City.[8] Such was a pattern of mobility in the northern anthracite coal fields.

The exodus of Carbondale's elite to Scranton and Wilkes-Barre may reveal even more about the differences in the two regional capitals. As indicated in chapter 5, Wilkes-Barre recruited its economic leaders from among those with social standing in the community—those who were members of a kinship group and two social clubs. Economic leaders in the younger city of Scranton were usually upwardly mobile immigrants or businessmen from small towns nearby. The Carbondale emigration to Scranton and Wilkes-Barre illustrates this contrast

TABLE 6.1. Population and Percentage Growth of Scranton, Wilkes-Barre, Carbondale, and Pittston from 1850 to 1880

City	1850 Population	1860 Population	1860 Percentage Growth	1870 Population	1870 Percentage Growth	1880 Population	1880 Percentage Growth
Scranton	1,000 (est.)	9,223	922.3	35,092	280	45,850	31
Wilkes-Barre	2,723	4,253	56	10,174	139	23,339	129
Carbondale	4,945	5,575	13	6,393	15	7,714	21
Pittston	4,094	3,682	-10	6,760	87	7,472	11

SOURCES: J.D.B. DeBow, *The Seventh Census of the United States: 1850* (Washington, D.C., 1853), pp. 173, 174; Joseph C.G. Kennedy, *Population of the United States in 1860* (Washington, D.C., 1864), pp. 427, 428; Francis A. Walker, *The Statistics of the Population of the United States, 1870* (Washington, D.C., 1872), pp. 251, 252; Francis A. Walker and Charles W. Seaton, *Statistics of the Population of the United States, 1880* (Washington, D.C., 1883), pp. 312. 314.

in leadership. These four prominent Carbondalers who went to Wilkes-Barre had a claim to social standing; all were professionally trained and all had, in highly skilled occupations, fathers who had migrated to Carbondale early in its development. None of the eight prominent men who went to Scranton was a trained professional, and none had a wealthy father in or out of Carbondale. In fact, few of these men had fathers anywhere near the Lackawanna Valley, since five of the eight were immigrants. Whether by accident or design, Carbondale's emigrants followed a clear pattern in their choice of destinations.

The mobility of wealth and talent in the Lackawanna Valley tells us nothing about the mobility of groups below the top level. Granted, the view from the top shows clearly that several men grew wealthy in Carbondale and wealthier in Scranton. This tells us nothing, however, about the mobility of mule drivers, mechanics, unskilled workmen or others. It is possible, but improbable, that various unskilled workers who migrated from Carbondale to Scranton fared worse, as groups, than those who remained in Carbondale or migrated elsewhere.[9] Whether the case, many businessmen in Carbondale struck it rich after moving to Scranton.

After importing much of Carbondale's elite, Scranton dominated the older town's internal services. In 1880, Scranton men were presidents of the D&H and both local banks in Carbondale. Scranton leaders also held directorships and potential control over Carbondale's gas and water companies.[10] For the most part, Carbondale's economic subjugation fits the model in figure 1. Investors in New York City, the multiregional center, controlled most of Carbondale's export; entrepreneurs in Scranton, the regional capital, dominated Carbondale's major services; local Carbondalers owned only those businesses and stores too small to attract outside capital.

These circumstances doomed Carbondale to a permanent position as a small coal town. Few leaders emerged to fill the vacuum caused by the exit of so much talent. Those who remained were either leg men for the D&H, which meant limited local wealth and innovation, or relatives of Scrantonians, which potentially meant more capital migration. Even independent manufacturer Eli E. Hendrick, whose "large and beautiful grounds" eventually became "the finest residence in the city," was dependent on the outside world. He left Carbondale twice to invest in oil production in western Pennsylvania. In his first venture, Hendrick was a victim of stock manipulation in New York City; in the second he sold his oil refinery to Standard Oil. Returning to Carbondale in the 1870s, Hendrick became a local banker (for a bank owned in Scranton) and started a small manufacturing company.[11]

It's hard to exaggerate the harm done to Carbondale, when the few leaders there left town. Some of them had received schooling or apprenticeships in

Carbondale. After being trained in Carbondale, they emigrated and then used their skills to develop larger cities nearby. Scranton, for instance, received a select group of talented entrepreneurs without bearing the costs of their education or training. Furthermore, when these leaders migrated, they transferred loyalty and investment skills to their new home town. Thomas and George Dickson, for example, both grew up in Carbondale and spent all of their adolescence and early adulthood there. During this time they went to school in Carbondale, they married local girls, and they got their first jobs there from the D&H and from a local foundry. In their wills, however, they left the bulk of their fortunes to family and institutions in Scranton and left no money in Carbondale. Before moving to Scranton, Horatio Pierce lived for thirty-two years in Carbondale; there he learned banking, business, and coal operating. His will, however, disclosed far greater benevolence toward Scranton and a plea to his grandson in Brooklyn to come to Scranton and take control of his Lackawanna Coal Company.[12]

Shortly after the departure of Carbondale's leaders, a local resident wrote a book and analyzed Carbondale's defeat to Scranton. He noted the "plain" buildings, "constructed . . . for utility only" in the company town of Carbondale. He compared them to those in "other towns, much younger" where men "have built not for the present merely, but for the future, giving their towns the appearance of thrift and permanence, and of their intending *to stay* (his emphasis), and abide by the interests of their town, and cherish it as a home." Reflecting on cities with "elegant and costly buildings," he observed that "capitalists are attracted to them as 'go ahead towns,' and have helped to swell the tide of success. As a consequence, real estate and rents advance at rapid rates." It may be, then, that Scranton's "elegant and costly buildings" reflected the long-term commitment of its entrepreneurs. When other people in the Lackawanna Valley saw these buildings, they knew that Scranton was the city the big investors were gambling on.[13]

Carbondale, of course, was not the only town to send leaders to Scranton. Many entrepreneurs from commercial towns in the hinterland of the Lackawanna Valley migrated to Scranton also. Scranton men, however, chose to specialize in industry and did not invest in any of these towns not mining coal. Honesdale, for example, sent many leaders to Scranton but no one in Scranton was a director in a Honesdale company in 1880.[14] By 1880, then, Scranton's entrepreneurs had become industrial leaders and were investing only in industrial enterprises in the region.

Carbondale was only one of several towns in the Lackawanna Valley under outside domination from New York City and Scranton. After the region's initial coal development, entrepreneurs created a string of towns and villages, as map C indicates, from Carbondale to Pittston. These mining patches eventually came

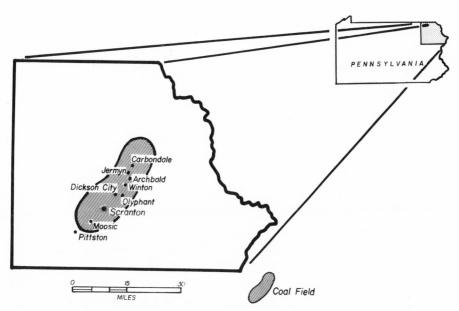

Map C.   Cities and Towns in the Lackawanna Valley in 1880

under outside control, and none of them ever had many people. Most of these towns existed merely to export coal, which generated few services beyond company housing and company stores (see table 6.2). In most of these seven towns, local coal operators started the first coal company. By 1880, though, all locals except for William Richmond, John Jermyn, and Edward Jones and his partners had sold out to the D&H. Richmond owned the Elk Hill Coal Company in Dickson City; Jermyn owned all of the mines in Jermyn; and Jones and his partners controlled small enterprises in Archbald and Olyphant. With the centralization of talent, Richmond, Jermyn, and one of Jones' partners moved to Scranton—which strengthened that city's hold over the region's coal towns.

While sharing the domination of coal with New York City, Scranton came to own most of those few services that the larger towns supported. In Jermyn, for example, coal baron John Jermyn owned the local flour mill. He also became the first treasurer of the town's savings and loan association and almost single-handedly financed the building of the Episcopalian and Methodist churches. He even paid part of the Methodist minister's salary. Henry M. Boies of Scranton owned the powder mills in Jermyn and absorbed them into his Moosic Powder Company, which he directed from his main office in Scranton.[15]

In the town of Archbald, the pattern of domination by outsiders was similar. By 1880, James J. Williams was the president of the town's only incorporated service, the Archbald Water Company. Williams and local coal operator Edward Jones, the wealthiest men in Archbald, seem to have reinvested much of their

TABLE 6.2.   Owners of Industries and Services of All Incorporated Towns (Except Carbondale and Pittston) in the Lackawanna Valley in 1880

Incorporated Town	Primary Export	Owner(s) of Primary Export	Other Export or Incorporated Services	Owner or President
Archbald	Coal	D&H, Edward Jones, and George Simpson	Archbald Water Company	James J. Williams
Jermyn	Coal	John Jermyn	Jermyn Steam Flouring Mills; Rushdale Powder Company	John Jermyn
Olyphant	Coal	D&H	– –	– –
Dickson City	Coal	William Richmond	– –	– –
Winton	Coal	Edward Jones and George Filler	– –	– –

SOURCE: W.W. Munsell and Company, *History of Luzerne, Lackawanna, and Wyoming Counties, Pennsylvania, with Illustrations and Biographical Sketches of Some of Their Prominent Men and Pioneers* (New York, 1880), pp. 462-72.

profit in the Merchants and Mechanics Bank in Scranton. Jones kept an office in Scranton, and Williams moved there permanently in the late 1880s so that he could better coordinate his Scranton investments. In the regional capital, Williams took his place among economic leaders as the president of the Merchants and Mechanics Bank and vice-president of the Wilson Lumber Company.[16]

In a real sense these towns and villages never had a chance to develop. In some towns the export was originally controlled by New Yorkers from the D&H. Other towns had local owners at first, but most of them soon sold out to a company in New York or in Scranton. The few local coal operators who survived seem to have invested local profits in Scranton and then moved there. Whatever the pattern, the small towns usually lost local autonomy to outsiders.

The power of New York City and Scranton also extended westward to Pittston, a town on the border between the Lackawanna and Wyoming Valleys. The Pennsylvania Coal Company, part of New York's Erie Railroad, established Pittston when it began coal production in 1849. Like Carbondale, Pittston was both a coal town and a company town right from its founding. Unlike other Lackawanna Valley towns, though, Pittston was located between the two regional capitals of Wilkes Barre and Scranton. Both of these cities shaped Pittston's development.[17]

The Pennsylvania Coal Company was the key to Pittston's growth. By 1880, this New York company had constructed eight coal breakers in Pittston and became the largest employer in the town. In fact, since there were few internal services, the coal miners and their families were almost all the people in town.

Pittston's early population burst was misleading, though; it did not mark the rise of a new major city. With outsiders in charge of coal operation, no local entrepreneur emerged to give the city investment punch. The regional capital of Wilkes-Barre was not much larger than Pittston in 1870; yet in that year Wilkes-Barre had ten times as many people worth at least $100,000 as Pittston did. Pittston had the people but not the capital and its growth stagnated (see table 6.1).[18]

During the 1850 to 1880 period, entrepreneurs from Scranton and Wilkes-Barre viewed Pittston's urbanization with interest. New Yorkers only wanted Pittston's coal, so investors in Scranton and Wilkes-Barre started the Pittston Bank, the town's first bank, in 1857. Eight years later it merged with the locally owned First National Bank. Although Pittston gained control of its bank, it soon lost local control over its only secondary export, a stove company. Founded by a Pittstonian in 1867, the stove company became important only after William Monies and Lewis Pughe of Scranton gained control of it in the late 1860s. Fully involving Scranton, Monies and Pughe commissioned Scranton's Dickson Manufacturing Company to build a 45-horsepower engine and boilers for their enterprise. By 1880, the Pittston Stove Company was producing 4,000 stoves yearly, the largest number anywhere in the anthracite area, and was annually netting $75,000 for its Scranton owners.[19]

Pittston's leaders tried hard to develop and keep local industries. Recognizing the town's regional subordination, one booster observed that "for some reason the town and its interests have stood still, while Scranton on the north and Wilkes-Barre on the south have made gigantic strides onward and upward." Another critic described Scranton as "the lobster town of the universe, projecting a claw here, a mandible there and feelers to the right and left reaching over stretches of farming lands, swamps, streams, forests, and glens, but holding under each outstretched tentacle a town, a hamlet, a few mining shanties, but all containing the grand desideratum of cities—human population." Fearing the "tentacles" of regional "lobsters," a Pittston merchant stressed the need "to bestir ourselves or see our borough gobbled up by some of our enterprising neighbors."[20]

Pittston never grew much but its local elite was loyal and did give the town some economic stability. By 1880, locals owned two banks, a small knitting factory, and a terra cotta works. This small burst of local entrepreneurship in Pittston contrasts with the leadership migration in Carbondale—and Pittston had surpassed Carbondale in population by 1880.[21]

Two distinct social groups formed much of Pittston's small economic leadership in 1880. First were the immigrants, primarily Scottish, who had come to Pittston from Carbondale around 1850 to work for the newly-founded

Pennsylvania Coal Company. Their emigration from Carbondale signaled the Pioneer City's decline in regional influence. In Pittston, this group controlled the local managerial positions in the Pennsylvania Coal Company; they also held directorships on the Miner's Savings Bank. The second social group included English-stock entrepreneurs from nearby Wilkes-Barre. In fact, they were kinsmen of Wilkes-Barre's economic leaders. They were often merchants, lawyers, and independent coal operators whose work had nothing to do with the Pennsylvania Coal Company. Separating themselves from the Carbondale immigrants, this Wilkes-Barre group held the presidencies and most of the directorships in both the First National Bank of Pittston and the People's Savings Bank. They also controlled the presidencies of the Pittston Ferry Bridge Company and the Pittston Knitting Company. These two groups of leaders gave Pittston the economic elite that Carbondale lost and that the other small Lackawanna towns never had.[22]

The model pictured in figure 1, then, helps explain the pattern of urban relationships among New York City, Scranton, and the small coal towns in the Lackawanna Valley. Yet these urban relationships were dynamic as some towns mushroomed into cities and others stagnated and shrank. Once these patterns of urban development were set, they were hard, but not impossible to break.

Two activities are typical of economic life in the Lackawanna Valley: first, capital and talent flowed from the small towns to the regional center to the multiregional center; second, the multiregional centers sought dominance through the development and expansion of corporations. Scranton, for example, attracted industrial and human capital from its regional hinterland. Then Scranton, in turn, lost control of its local coal and railroad companies to big investors in New York City.[23]

In a recent essay, Rowland Berthoff tried to tell the story of the Pennsylvania anthracite regions.[24] Using newspapers, correspondence, and company records, Berthoff thought he had discovered a completely fragmented society. Within the anthracite towns, "community ties were weak."[25] Urban growth appeared to be random, and there was "no regular order"[26] to the development of new towns and cities. The elements of a social structure were present, Berthoff concluded, but the cohesiveness of a stable social order was absent. So the society was completely atomistic. The mobility and change generated by "the industrial revolutionaries" had produced in the anthracite regions "an American social disorder almost without parallel in the modern world."[27]

The economic leaders in Wilkes-Barre and Scranton, in Berthoff's view, contributed to this "social disorder" by their lack of strong institutions. In fact, the social institutions that did exist "fail[ed] to achieve any encompassing order, [and] only furthered the social disorganization which the Industrial

Revolution wrought in the anthracite region." The leaders in both cities were, Berthoff insisted, "severely middle class." With the centralization of decision-making and its upward flow to New York City in the railroad and coal industries, Scranton and Wilkes-Barre were, in fact, "headless societies." They had no "arrogant elite . . . to impose an order on the region."[28]

Berthoff expands this model of social disorder to include America as a whole in the nineteenth century, which he surmises "was an epoch of enormous migration, immigration, and social mobility, during which the recently established social order became badly disorganized and in fact disorderly."[29]

By failing to systematically reconstruct the social order of the anthracite regions, Berthoff merely records some contemporary impressions. He fails to separate the general patterns of anthracite life from the particular facts reported in local newspapers. For at least two centuries, the maudlin among us have been lamenting the disintegration of society. Industrialization did fragment America into an array of social and economic groups. But the social order was not destroyed. Stabilizing influences abounded in the Lackawanna Valley. Voluntary associations and social institutions of all types—singing societies, ethnic lodges, churches, and boards of trade among others—provided unifying threads of order and continuity in the midst of rapid social change.[30]

In the Lackawanna Valley, one generation of industrialization transformed thinly-settled farmland into an urban sprawl tied to coal and manufacturing. Yet in the midst of this change there was stability. Scranton was not a "headless" chaotic city. The elite there, from the founding family to the leaders of the board of trade, were aggressive. They imposed openness on their city's economy; they centralized talent within their region; and they shaped an urban network with their investments. The cities and towns in the region were not disparate pieces of an unsolvable puzzle. They were part of a pattern of economic dominance and subordinance among the multiregional city of New York, the regional capital of Scranton, and the seven dependent coal towns nearby. The urbanizing Lackawanna Valley had formed a new social order.

7

Like Fathers, Unlike Sons:
The Fragmentation of Scranton's
Early Economic Leadership, 1800-1920

Scranton's open economic system continued to work after 1880. Its leaders further strengthened and diversified their city's iron and coal base. From 1880 to 1900 Scranton's population more than doubled from 45,000 to 102,000. Scranton had become the third largest city in Pennsylvania, and the thirty-seventh largest city in the nation.[1] And all of this was accomplished during the lifetimes of the city's founding fathers. So as Scranton entered the twentieth century, its people had even greater expectations of the future.

Beneath this optimism new problems had emerged that would soon test the ingenuity of Scranton's next generation of leaders. First, improvements in transportation, communication, and technology were creating a new entity, the national corporation. These new and bigger businesses were cutting costs, eliminating competition, and trading goods from coast to coast. The Lackawanna Iron and Steel Company, Scranton's first and largest company, was just one of several local industries facing stiff national competition. Would Scranton's local businesses survive and prosper in this competitive environment? Second, these nationwide markets posed a special threat to anthracite coal. Coal was Scranton's reason for existence: its link with the past and its tie to the future. Yet the fuel market was more competitive than ever. Bituminous coal and wood had been perennial threats, and by 1900 electricity, heating oil, and natural gas appeared on the market. Would Scranton be able to keep its main export competitive in national and world markets? Third, Scranton would face these problems with a new generation of leaders. Would these leaders inherit the unity and openness of the founding fathers? And would the talent emerge (perhaps from the children of the 1880 leaders) to keep local industry strong?

96

In 1880 these problems seemed remote. Scranton was still a mecca for nearby entrepreneurs. Its leaders were riding high—determined to protect their precious coal, and then diversify from it. For example, in the 1880s Scranton confronted the loss of anthracite as a fuel to make steel. The board of trade (later the chamber of commerce) countered by trying to discover new uses for Scranton coal, and promoted anthracite in a variety of grades and sizes to cater to different demands ranging from industrial to home heating use. So the creation of new markets more than offset the loss of old ones. One new market was the use of anthracite as a fuel for local industries started in the 1880s. These included companies to manufacture glass, trolley engines, locomotive wheels, carriages, and nuts and bolts.[2]

In the late 1800s, then, the inventiveness of Scranton's entrepreneurs persisted. One of the most successful innovations in the city's history was the development of an international correspondence school. This scheme was hatched after 1885, the year that the Pennsylvania legislature passed a law requiring mine foremen to pass an elaborate exam that tested their knowledge of coal mining procedures and regulations. Other states soon followed Pennsylvania by creating similar laws. Before these bills passed, mining expert Thomas J. Foster of Scranton wrote *The Colliery Engineer*, which described in detail Pennsylvania's mining code. With the new mining codes in force Foster found himself swamped with requests for information on coal mining. Foster sensed an opportunity and began a correspondence school in Scranton in 1891 to teach the technicalities of coal mining to aspiring mine foremen all over the world. A Scranton firm published Foster's textbook, and in 1901 the school and the publishing house combined to become a single large corporation, International Textbook Company. Foster and Scranton's leading industrialists ran the company. Once they showed that people wanted formal instruction on coal mining, they developed courses and textbooks on other subjects. By the 1920s, International Textbook Company was capitalized at ten million dollars; it had educated over three million students by mail; and it employed over 3,200 persons.[3]

Another innovation that succeeded in Scranton was Charles S. Woolworth's operation and perfection of the five-and-ten-cent store. Born in upstate New York, Woolworth, his brother Frank, and partner Fred M. Kirby experimented in the late 1870s with the opening of specialty stores featuring largely five-and-ten-cent merchandise. Shoppers were often skeptical of the first stores opened in Harrisburg, Lancaster, and York, Pennsylvania. In 1880, however, when Charles Woolworth set up a five-and-ten-cent store in Scranton, the idea caught on. The sales in Scranton were a modest $9,000 the first year but the Woolworths had laid the foundation for an empire, and Charles had found himself a new home in

Scranton. A decade of brisk sales in Scranton encouraged Woolworth to start branch stores in New York and Maine in the 1890s. By 1920, after rapid expansion, the Woolworth company was a major American corporation, and Charles Woolworth of Scranton was chairman of its board of directors. Woolworth blended right into Scranton's economic elite; he also held directorships on the First National Bank, the International Textbook Company, and the Scranton Gas and Water Company.[4]

The introduction of electricity in the 1880s brought out the best in Scranton's entrepreneurs. They didn't produce Thomas Edison but they did have James Wightman, who designed and built one of the first motors to run trolley cars by electricity. In 1884, Scranton had become one of the first cities in the nation to have an electric trolley system. Sensing opportunity, Wightman started his own company in Scranton to manufacture trolley engines on a large scale. Other Scrantonians tried to adapt electricity to coal mining. In 1894 they founded the Scranton Electric Construction Company, which perfected and manufactured electrical apparatus (*e.g.* mechanical drills, locomotive hoists, and mining pumps) for use throughout the anthracite coal fields. In the 1920s, Frederick J. Platt, a grandson of one of Scranton's founding fathers, was president of this multiregional company.[5]

The textile industry became another source of diversification and innovation in Scranton from 1880 to 1920. As in other industries, expansion in textiles resulted from both the attraction of talented newcomers to Scranton and the initiatives of local entrepreneurs. In the former case, the Sauquoit Silk Manufacturing Company and the Klots Throwing Company helped make Scranton second only to Paterson, New Jersey, in silk production. Local economic leaders William Connell and Henry Belin, Jr., branched into textiles after they had succeeded in coal operating and gunpower manufacturing. Connell founded the Lackawanna Knitting Mills Company and the Scranton Button Manufacturing Company; Henry Belin helped to organize the Scranton Lace Company. Largely as a result of these local efforts, Scranton led the nation in the manufacturing of lace products, such as table cloths and curtains, and composition buttons.[6]

Two final industries in Scranton reflected creativity and local entrepreneurship: a company that produced steel locomotive wheels and one that manufactured salt. The development of a flexible steel locomotive wheel was the brainstorm of inventor Henry Boies. After obtaining three patents in 1888, he founded the Boies Steel Wheel Company to manufacture and distribute his product. Scranton's connection with salt production was the work of Edward L. Fuller, a nephew of economic leader George Fuller. Edward Fuller's early investments were in coal and railroads, and he became one of the largest coal operators in the anthracite coal fields. He pursued a secondary interest, his presidency of the Avery Rock Salt Mining Company, and after several mergers Fuller became president of the International Salt Company in the early 1900s.[7]

Scranton did not emerge inevitably as a center for manufacturing trolley motors, locomotive wheels, lace curtains, textbooks, or salt. Nor was there any particular reason why Scranton should have become a major headquarters for an international correspondence school, or the think tank for directing a chain of five-and-ten-cent stores. Other cities throughout America had good enough location and transportation to have been sites for these industries. Even the operation and distribution of electrical mining equipment could have been done in Wilkes-Barre, or in anthracite towns other than Scranton. A key to Scranton's success seems to have been the presence of aggressive entrepreneurs, who had a philosophy of openness and a commitment to growth. As the spiral of growth in industries, services, and population persisted, the city of Scranton, which was founded on a hunch, officially became one of the forty largest cities in the country in 1900.

In Scranton's boom-town atmosphere, few could imagine that the bubble would burst one generation later. Yet by the 1920s, Scranton endured a series of crippling setbacks that reduced its roaring industrial expansion to a whimper. First, the New York owners of the L.I.&S., Scranton's first and largest industry, removed their entire corporation to Buffalo in 1901. Eager to exploit the Lake Superior ores, and fearing competition from U.S. Steel, the New Yorkers sacrificed their rolling mills and blast furnaces in Scranton to gain the locational advantages of iron production on the Great Lakes seaport of Buffalo. Scrantonians fought courageously against the move, but for decades they had lacked decisive representation on the corporation's board of directors. The problems of outside ownership for urban development were suddenly apparent to the startled thousands of local steel workers who had to choose between going to Buffalo or finding jobs elsewhere.[8]

Scranton's aggressive entrepreneurs countered this first threat to their city's urbanization with bold declarations of future expansion. Mobilizing behind their board of trade, Scranton businessmen campaigned for ten days in 1908 to raise one million dollars for future industrial development in Scranton. For ten days the board of trade distributed booster buttons, advertised in newspapers, and held rallies. When the cheering stopped the board of trade had raised $1.25 million, which was placed in an Industrial Development Corporation to attract new industries to Scranton. This concentration of capital under centralized direction helped Scranton's businessmen compete in America's new national markets, where accelerated competition upped the stakes for players of the industrial game.[9]

During this bleak period in Scranton's history, the board of trade helped cushion the city's shock of losing its largest corporation. Scranton's population still grew, albeit at a slower rate, to 137,000 persons by 1920. But the worst was yet to come. Changes in the national fuel market in the 1920s triggered the decline of Scranton's anthracite coal; this calamity had region-wide repercussions and proved to be insurmountable. Anthracite had long been Scranton's primary export; in 1920 alone over 30,000 Scrantonians labored in the various phases of mining, cutting, and loading this valuable resource for distribution throughout the nation. For almost one hundred years American consumers were a receptive market for anthracite, and capitalists in Scranton and New York ripped open the Lackawanna Valley to supply this demand. When oil and natural gas emerged in the late 1800s, Scranton's board of trade widely advertised their plentiful and cheap supplies of smokeless anthracite coal. Coal operators carefully marketed different sizes and grades of anthracite, including powdered coal, to conform to different industrial and home-heating preferences. Recognizing the precariousness of the fuel market, William W. Scranton in 1878 warned his peers at a local banquet that diversification would protect the local economy against the possible decline of anthracite. Finally, in the 1920s, after generations of brisk sales, anthracite lost its competitive advantages. Mining the deeper coal deposits increased the costs of providing this fuel to consumers. Finally, a series of strikes in that decade made Lackawanna coal "unreliable." So the producers of heating oil and natural gas seized their chance to increase their share of the market. Since most consumers in the 1920s preferred turning dials to shoveling coal to heat their houses, Scranton lost its primary export.[10]

The decline of coal reverberated throughout Scranton's economy. Companies had to shut down or lay off hundreds of men. Venture capital dissipated and the decline in local income threatened merchants with falling revenue and real estate values. The industries related to coal, especially the railroads, also suffered greatly. Railroads in Scranton employed over five thousand men in the 1920s in shipping, building, and repair work. The cutbacks in shipping coal, possibly combined with the competition to railroads from other carriers, meant stagnation for another major employer in Scranton.[11]

Many Scrantonians thought their city would prosper forever; instead their problems were only beginning. Independent of the demise of Scranton's coal trade, but shortly after it, the local textile industry almost collapsed. The introduction of synthetic clothing after World War I, and the failure of Scranton's entrepreneurs to adjust to it, triggered the reduced demand for Scranton's textiles. The onslaught of the Great Depression in 1929 further shrank the market for expensive silk and lace products. During the first third of the twentieth century, then, Scranton witnessed the departure of its largest industry, the collapse of its primary export, the decline of its secondary export, and the stagnation of its transportation industry. All of this happened just in time for the nationwide depression in the 1930s. This threatened the rest of Scranton's industries and services. The 1940 census reported the first decennial loss of population in Scranton's history, and succeeding decades continued this trend.[12]

Scranton's economic leaders of the 1920s were not able to reverse the changes that stunned their city. Their world differed from that of their forefathers in several ways. Not only were consumers turning away from coal, but new large-scale corporations created a national survival of the fittest as well. In 1880, Scranton supplied goods, except for coal and transportation, to local and regional markets with little threat from larger outside corporations. By 1920, however, improved transportation, communication, and technology enlarged the world of business. Mergers and consolidations in many industries meant that big businesses everywhere severely challenged local Scranton companies. In 1880, for example, three of Scranton's largest enterprises, the Dickson Manufacturing Company, the Moosic Powder Company, and the Stowers Pork Packing and Provision Company, dominated markets in the Lackawanna Valley for locomotives, gunpowder, and meat products. By 1920, in the face of competition from national corporations, these companies disappeared and were replaced by Allis-Chalmers, DuPont, and Swift. Scrantonians lost out to larger outside companies. As a result, Milwaukee, Wilmington, and Chicago—not Scranton—became the national corporate headquarters for these industries.[13]

The creation of a national economy intensified patterns of dominance and subordinance within the Lackawanna Valley. In 1880, Scrantonians owned many local and regional industries while New Yorkers controlled transportation and coal. In the more national economy of the 1920s, Scranton surrendered local ownership in its utilities, its flour milling, and even partially in its banking. In head to head competition, corporations in New York and other cities in the country frequently undersold their Scranton competitors. The larger the industry, the greater seems to have been the competition from outside. Economies of scale made corporate growth necessary, outside competition inevitable, and eventual absorption a reality for many companies in America. Those cities, usually multiregional centers, that were the headquarters for the surviving corporations, stood the best chance of attracting the largest population and gaining the concurrent advantages.[14]

Some Scranton men met the challenge of the 1920s and proved themselves capable of directing companies from local to regional to national dominance. Charles S. Woolworth, Paul Belin, Edward Fuller, and Ralph W. Weeks of Scranton became presidents of multimillion dollar corporations that produced dry goods, lace, salt, and textbooks for markets throughout the country. Many other exporters in Scranton were not so able. They were absorbed or shut down when faced with stiff outside competition. For example, Henry Boies, president in the 1880s of the Moosic Powder Company, the Boies Steel Wheel Company, and the Dickson Manufacturing Company, could not bring any of these regional enterprises into the twentieth century. Boies, like other entrepreneurs in Scranton, showed a knack for starting profitable local enterprises. He just couldn't (for whatever reasons) make the tough transition to producing in larger markets against bigger competitors.[15]

Perhaps the failure of so many exporters in Scranton was inevitable. Following a wave of mergers in the early 1900s, four or five corporations dominated most of the national market in oil refining, steel, meat packing, and many other industries. With such intense competition, Scranton's enterprises could hardly have expected to win very often. Furthermore, even though many Scranton companies could not compete in national markets, the mere success of International Textbook Company alone gave the city over 3,000 workers. One major success, then, could compensate for several failures. Also, Scranton, as the largest city in the coal fields, became a logical branch office for several corporations. The Great Atlantic and Pacific Tea Company, for example, established a warehouse and plant in Scranton in 1890; by the 1920s, it employed 400 persons there and did a lively trade with local banks. The rise of large-scale corporations, then, had a mixed impact on Scranton's growth.[16]

The patterns of dominance and subordinance in the Lackawanna Valley reflected the national concentration of industry. The three levels of dominance that existed in 1880 had intensified in 1920. Corporations in New York, and other multiregional centers, supervised much of the economic life in the regional capital of Scranton. At the same time, both Scranton and New York usually coordinated economic development in the small regional towns. A few coal companies in New York and Scranton persisted in their ownership of almost all the coal land and railroads in the Lackawanna Valley. Scranton continued its ownership of many services in nearby towns, and extended its ownership of utilities outside of the coal fields into Susquehanna County.[17]

The example of the gas and water industry in Scranton is an excellent illustration of these patterns of dominance and subordinance. The Scranton family founded the Scranton Gas and Water Company in 1854 as a mere sidelight to their ownership in the L.I.&C. After New Yorkers gained control of the L.I.&C. in 1872 and absorbed the Scranton Steel Company in 1891, the founding family turned their attention, and their capital, to developing their utility company. In 1905, after demonstrating economies of scale, the Scrantons absorbed the smaller Carbondale gas and water system, which supplied Carbondale, Jermyn,

Mayfield, Forest City, and Vandling. The next year the Scranton Gas and Water Company bought out the local companies in Providence, Dunmore, Blakely, Olyphant, and Archbald. With the gas and water service in much of the Lackawanna Valley centralized, William Scranton and his family were once again in charge of a multimillion dollar corporation. In the 1920s, however, capitalists in New York tried to centralize a variety of regional utility systems and bought out the Scranton Gas and Water Company for $28 million. In the Lackawanna Valley, then, the gas and water industry started with many small local companies; then they were centralized into one regional company in Scranton; finally a multiregional utility corporation in New York bought out the Scranton firm.[18]

The business adventures of three generations of Scrantons—Joseph, William, and Worthington—highlight the interplay between local autonomy and New York domination. Joseph H. Scranton was president of the L.I.&C., the city's first and largest industry, from 1858 until his death in 1872. During these years the New York influence increased so much that Joseph's son William could not succeed his father as company president. Young William was restless as a mere local manager so he studied the new Bessemer process in Europe and returned to start his own Scranton Steel Company in 1881. The city's low tax on new industries gave him an edge over the larger L.I.&C., but the older company won the competition and absorbed his enterprise in 1891. A decade later, the New York owners moved the entire operation to Buffalo. Ousted from the steel industry, William Scranton and his son Worthington converted the local gas and water company to a centralized regional concern; by 1906 they were supplying utilities to ten cities in the Lackawanna Valley. Their growth again could not outpace the competitive pressures from New York; in 1928 Worthington Scranton sold this large regional firm to the Federal Water Service Corporation of New York.[19] In three generations, then, the Scrantons of Scranton lost three multimillion dollar corporations to capitalists in New York.

These three generations of Scrantons tell us something else about their city from 1880 to 1920; it had a new set of economic leaders. Gone were the founding fathers who created an industry, built up a city, and opened their doors to talented newcomers. Gone also were the forty economic leaders who guided Scranton in 1880. These forty industrialists tried to pass the torch of entrepreneurship to their sons, sons-in-law, and even grandsons. But they would not be carrying it in 1920.[20]

As the mainsprings of industrial revolution, these forty capitalists had much to give their children. Blessed by the luck of the draw, these fortunate offspring could choose almost any career, with the security that only wealth can bring. Raised in Victorian mansions rife with servants, they often had doting parents to give them private school education, college if they wanted, or specialized training in engineering or industry. If these children didn't prosper they could fall back on hefty inheritances. And, as they matured, they could take advantage of Scranton's thriving marketplace to make even more money. By 1920, the sons of Scranton's 1880 leaders had ample opportunity to succeed their fathers as the pacesetters of Scranton's business world.

Yet they did not. Few went hungry, but most could not come close to matching their fathers' achievements. Only nine of the forty economic leaders in 1880 had even one son, son-in-law, or grandson who forty years later was an officer of even one corporation in Scranton. In short, the fathers and sons provide a stunning contrast. In 1880, the fathers were the presidents of all the banks and all the major industries in the city. Only two small companies eluded their executive grasp. Forty years later, in the midst of boundless growth, the sons lagged hopelessly behind. They were the presidents of only five of Scranton's twenty-one banks. Surveying their conquests, they did hold the top rank in the local lace mill, the gas and water company, the button company, a mammoth coal company, an insurance company, a mining supply company, and a cemetary association. Granted, these firms were important. Yet, the fact remains that only a minority of the sons followed their parents as economic leaders in the Scranton of 1920.[21]

In some ways the meager record of these sons seems astonishing. Not only were they showered with education, training, and wealth, but their fathers, by definition, operated almost every company in Scranton—many of which could be handed down almost intact to their children. By accident of birth, the children of Scranton's 1880 elite had the chance to expand the city their fathers had created. Yet fewer than one of every four economic leaders of 1880 had even one descendant who was a company officer in the city in 1920.[22]

Part of the reason for this startling breakdown lies in the general problem of family continuity. All forty of Scranton's economic leaders of 1880 were married; but one had no children and another five had all daughters. In none of these last cases did the daughters marry men who vaulted into economic prominence. So the corporate influence of six families ended through a lack of male heirs. At the other extreme, seven of the forty families had trouble preserving their fortunes because they had eight or more children. These leaders could certainly afford large families. But the costs of rearing and educating so many children dwindled the family's resources and, at inheritance time, splintered the family wealth into small pieces.[23]

Some families lost their local influence because their sons left Scranton for opportunities elsewhere. By educating sons and daughters "back east" and taking vacations outside of Scranton in the summer, many of Scranton's early industrial leaders created psychological mobility in their children and made it easier for them to leave Scranton for business opportunities in other cities. James Archbald and Clarence B. Sturges, for example, made investments in the southern anthracite fields and moved there to oversee them. Studying medicine at the University of Pennsylvania, Alfred Hand, Jr., became a physician and practiced his profession in Philadelphia. Daughters vacationing outside of Scranton often met men from other cities; when marriages resulted, the daughters usually went to their husbands' home towns. John Jermyn's daughter Susan, for example, married bank president R.A. Downey of Oswego, New York, and moved there with him. These examples were rare, though, and for the most part the new generation did not in any way carry on the economic leadership of their fathers.[24]

The nature of corporate recruitment after 1880 also helped scatter venturesome sons. The emerging national corporations, with their networks for upward mobility, shifted Scranton men around the country. Cousins John J. Albright and Joseph A. Archbald, for example, moved to Buffalo as employees of the D.L.&W. Thomas Torrey, the son-in-law of Thomas Dickson, worked for the rival D&H in New York City. The Belin family had members who moved to Wilmington, Delaware, to work for their DuPont cousins in the powder industry. Corporate migration became a prominent feature in Scranton after the 1880s.[25]

The fragmentation of some of Scranton's larger family fortunes seems remarkable. For example, brothers Thomas and George Dickson became presidents of a national railroad, the largest manufacturing company in northeast Pennsylvania, an iron company in New York, the vice-president of the largest bank in Scranton, and directors on a variety of large companies. Yet only one of Thomas Dickson's three sons went into business, and under his leadership the Dickson Manufacturing Company went out of business. George Dickson's only child, Walter, became a mere salesman and held no corporate influence. The four sons of multimillionaire James Blair were nonentities. Only one of Blair's sons appears to have been gainfully employed, and his job was that of assistant cashier in his father's bank.[26]

Some of the sons of Scranton's early industrialists literally squandered fortunes. Economic leader Benjamin Throop became a millionaire by investing in real estate, banks, and utilities. His surviving son had, at best, modest business skills, and when he and his wife died prematurely in 1894, the eighty-three-year-old Throop undertook the task of rearing his only grandchild, five-year-old Benjamin, Jr. The elder Throop died shortly thereafter, but young "Benny" inherited a ten-million-dollar fortune. Young Throop married into the Connell family, and having no financial worries, he began raising German shepherd dogs. He served in World War I but by that time his wife had divorced him, and he seems to have lost any interest that he might have had in gainful employment or in the city of Scranton. During the 1920s, like a character from an F. Scott Fitzgerald novel, he spent most of his time in Paris indulging champagne tastes in cars and women. He married a French movie star and traveled widely during their marriage. Throop died in 1935, in his mid-forties, of undisclosed stomach ailments after apparently dissipating his grandfather's entire fortune.[27]

Throop was a rare but not unique example of dissolution. Given the tradition of partible inheritance, many of the sons of economic leaders knew that they would never have to work and so they became men of leisure with no business interests. For example, James Blair's son Austin was "a gentleman of leisure [with] [n]o[thing] to do except fish and hunt." According to a credit agent "his fa[ther], James Blair, is a millionaire and supports him [and] lets him have a fine residence rent free and supplies him with funds when required."

Without strong parental guidance, a slothful life was understandably attractive to these scions of wealth. Owing to the genetic improbability that Scranton's 1880 elite would produce only children like themselves, with a knack for business, the fragmentation of economic leadership should not surprise us. Edmund B. Jermyn's taste for horseracing—this son of the multimillionaire coal operator apparently "never missed a day's [horse] racing at Honesdale or at Goshen, N.Y."—becomes understandable. The son grew up under different conditions with different options in life from those that were available to his rags-to-riches father.[28]

Parental guidance surely must have been important in perpetuating economic leadership over generations. Yet it is hard to measure under any conditions and impossible to test without interviews. The Throop and Blair families may provide clues to one possible relationship between parental guidance and the breakdown of family economic leadership over this. On the one hand, all of Benny Throop's parents and grandparents died before he was eight years old, so he had no familial pressure to become a businessman and pass on the family fortune. The four sons of James Blair, on the other hand, had a long-lived father who personally directed many of his enterprises until his death at age ninety. The elder Blair outlived two of his sons and the other two had passed middle age by the time they were independent of paternal control. By living so long and holding on so tightly to his investments, Blair may have deprived his sons of a chance to wield economic influence in Scranton. The role of varied parental supervision, the lack of business talent, the quest for leisure, corporate mobility, and the problems of family continuity in general all seem to have combined to fragment the Scranton economic elite of 1880.[29]

Of course, not all of Scranton's early industrialists had downwardly mobile sons. Nine of the forty top capitalists in the Scranton of 1880 passed the torch of leadership from father to son in 1920. In any randomly selected group of forty families, however, some would produce sons, or have sons-in-law, with a flair for business. Probably, though, nine of forty randomly chosen families would not have corporate officers as sons. This merely shows that industrial leaders are much more likely than other groups in the population to father corporate officers. It does not show continuity of economic leadership because more than three-fourths of the industrial families of 1880 in Scranton failed to continue a line of corporate succession in the following generation.[30]

The conspicuous prominence of these nine second- and third-generation leaders in Scranton in 1920 creates a superficial impression of solid elite continuity over time. In that year Charles Weston, Paul Belin, and Worthington Scranton were presidents of the First National Bank, the Scranton Lace Mill, and the Scranton Gas and Water Company, just as their fathers had been thirty years earlier. A few sons and sons-in-law of John Jermyn and William Connell represented their families prosperous coal and banking investments in 1920. As the president of two banks, a water company, and a newspaper, Louis A. Watres in 1920 had actually surpassed the economic influence of his father in Scranton. The visible success of these men obscures the lesser achievements of many other Scranton sons.[31]

In short, the rare successes of the sons of Scranton's 1880 gentry dotted a larger landscape of failure. For example, James Linen, a nephew of Thomas and George Dickson, married James Blair's daughter Anna in 1869. Blair and the two Dicksons held three of the five directorships of the First National Bank in 1880, and in 1891 Linen became president of the bank for a twenty-two year stretch. To the casual observer, such an occurrence illustrates overpowering elite continuity. If one looks at all eight sons of Blair and the two Dicksons, however, a sharply etched picture of failure clearly emerges. Seven of their eight sons never darkened the door of a corporate boardroom; under the eighth the Dickson Manufacturing Company disintegrated. Continuity from father to son may actually have been the undoing of the business. Furthermore, H.A. Coursen, like bank president James Linen, married a daughter of James Blair, yet Coursen remained a small retailer with no apparent economic influence. In the city of Scranton, at least, the scions of power were not the men their fathers were. Before historians can assert the continuity of economic leadership or family wealth, they must study all the children of the rich and not just the conspicuous successes.[32]

As this fragmentation of Scranton's early industrial elite suggests, the executives who guided Scranton's economy in 1920 were largely a new group of leaders. The remnants of the first generation of the city's industrialists were only a small component in Scranton's economic elite of 1920. Two other elements included native-born newcomers from towns in Pennsylvania and New York, and many upwardly mobile first- and second-generation European immigrants. The arrivals from nearby towns included several from the Lackawanna Valley, such as Charles Welles from Dundaff, J. Benjamin Dimmick from Honesdale, the Pecks from Peckville, and the Dales from Daleville. The emergence of a more national economy by 1920 had broadened Scranton's recruiting base; thus, Charles Woolworth came to Scranton from Watertown, New York, to make his fortune in five-and-ten-cent stores. Immigrants, too, shared in Scranton's prosperity. Ethnic leaders appeared who understood American customs and who started banks and other ventures in Scranton. The South Side Bank, for example, was dominated by Germans, the West Side Bank by Welsh, the Merchants and Mechanics Bank by Irish, and the Bosak State Bank by Czechs. In manufacturing, German-stock immigrants controlled the Scranton Nut and Bolt Company in 1920.[33]

These ethnic leaders were often spurned by Scranton's early industrial families. Andrew J. Casey and Michael Bosak, leaders of the Irish and the Czech communities in Scranton in 1920, are typical examples. Born in Ireland, Casey and his brother migrated to Scranton as young men in the 1860s. Unlike the Scranton industrial elite of the time, the Caseys were Catholics, Democrats, and partners in the liquor trade. Andrew Casey, in fact, spent much of his youth as a wholesale liquor dealer. In 1897, he became the first treasurer and later the president of the Penn Central Brewing Company, a consolidation of fourteen breweries in the state. Casey also operated banks in Scranton and Carbondale and, with his brother, he built a mammoth hotel in Scranton. He belonged to the Chamber of Commerce and he devoted time to various ethnic lodges and Catholic organizations. Michael Bosak came to America from Czechoslovakia in his teens in 1886, and began work as a breaker boy in a Hazleton coal field. After seven years he had saved enough to move to Olyphant as a merchant. Demonstrating talent and receiving family support, Bosak soon became president of two banks in Olyphant and moved to Scranton to start another. An aggressive entrepreneur, Bosak also founded the Bosak Realty Company, the Bosak Manufacturing Company, and a bank in Wilkes-Barre. Like Casey, Bosak was an active Catholic and Democrat. Both of these immigrants easily surpassed the trifling accomplishments of most of the sons of the 1880 WASP elite, yet neither was welcome at the Scranton Club, the city's plush metropolitan club.[34] The rise of ethnic leaders to displace the older fragmenting elite illustrates the churning mobility both upward and downward in the rapidly industrializing city of Scranton.

The examples of Casey and Bosak also help to show the fragmentation in Scranton's 1920 economic elite. It was larger, more heterogeneous, and more divided than the elite of 1880. The 1880 leaders also had upwardly mobile immigrants among them, but they were primarily British protestants who assimilated easily into the city's early industrial network. Guided by the Scranton group, the town's early business leaders seem to have sublimated ethnic and religious rivalries for an overriding commitment to urban and economic development. Recruiting urban leadership on the basis of talent, the Scranton group had marital and business ties with various English and Scottish migrants. In promoting wide city boundaries, the Scranton group reluctantly but assuredly sacrificed political leadership to the majority of Irish Catholics in the enlarged city. The early Scranton businessmen formed the unifying board of trade, instead of divisive ethnic institutions. They made this organization the cornerstone of a planned program of industrial recruitment and urban expansion, and they installed a Welshman as its first president.[35] Separate churches and masonic lodges existed in early Scranton, but their rivalries did not supersede the city's larger commitment to urban growth.

The conscious decision of an urban elite to sublimate economic and social tensions to economic development may seem inevitable, but it is not. In economic terms, city growth does mean rising land values and ringing cash registers. But it also means the arrival of business competitors and they are not so welcome. Population expansion and a large influx of foreign immigrants also changed the structure of local urban society. These foreigners had different customs and values from the businessmen who brought them to Scranton. This pot of semimeltable ethnic and religious groups, as American historians have recently discovered, brewed political trouble in America during the late nineteenth and early twentieth centuries. The social issues of immigration restriction, alien suffrage, woman suffrage, and prohibition mobilized immigrants and natives alike. Native Protestants often advocated immigration restriction, woman suffrage, and prohibition while Catholics and nonpuritans opposed these pietistic reforms. The resolution of these social reforms, to many Americans, was more important than having a growing city or a healthy pocketbook. When urban reformers banned the saloon, for example, they sacrificed local breweries and all the jobs that went with them. When they restricted immigration they halted the supply of new industrial workers to their city. The ability of Scranton's early economic leaders to consciously promote growth instead of becoming fragmented over social issues, is remarkable.[36]

The Scranton elite in 1920 did not seem to share the strong commitment to urban growth that their predecessors had. To be sure the chamber of commerce, a unifying institution, was strong and it apparently welcomed the membership of immigrant businessmen. Other institutions had emerged since 1880, however, that fragmented Scranton's population. These included exclusive social clubs, social reform associations, ethnic and religious organizations, and labor unions. These institutions actually thrived on the diversity and separateness within Scranton's population. They promoted values that often conflicted with those of urban expansion and economic development. In the 1890s, Scranton's first generation of economic leaders and their friends separated themselves socially from the other ethnic groups in the city, including many of the upwardly mobile economic leaders, by creating the Scranton Club, the Scranton Country Club, and debutante balls. In the same spirit, economic leaders Henry Boies, Edward Sturges, and Edward Fuller founded the Scranton Municipal League in 1900. The League's goal was to centralize political power in a strong mayor and a city council elected at-large, a maneuver that would have obliterated ethnic political influence. Other "social reformers" in Scranton supported the American Protective Association (an anti-Catholic group), the Immigration Restriction League, and the Anti-Saloon League. Recoiling from hostility in a strange new world, Scranton's immigrants separated into a variety of ethnic communities, each with its own church and social organizations to preserve its values and heritage. The Polish National Alliance and the Knights of Columbus, for example, stressed loyalty to ethnicity and religion, not loyalty to Scranton. The founding of St. Thomas College in 1888 and Marywood College in 1915 reflected a large and continuing financial commitment from Irish Catholics to preserve and transmit their cultural heritage to succeeding generations. Finally, the rise of strong labor unions in Scranton by the 1920s indicated the increasing ability of some urban laborers to exact group economic benefits from the city's mainstay industries. All of these institutions served a function, and no doubt provided happiness and comfort to many members. The point is that they helped fragment Scranton's population, and they seem to have hindered mobilization for urban development in the crucial decade of the 1920s.[37]

A good example of the change in attitude in Scranton toward urban development is the dispute over the annexation of Dunmore. By the early 1900s, the spacious urban boundary perceptively established by the city fathers had filled in with people. Connecting with Scranton on the east were 20,000 people in the legally separate borough of Dunmore. The Scranton Chamber of Commerce strongly advocated the absorption of Dunmore to increase local population and to eliminate overlapping urban services. This would lower the costs of city government for the consolidated city. In 1912, Scranton's mayor, who favored annexation, appointed as city solicitor Philipp V. Mattes, a Republican grandson of one of the founders of Scranton. Mattes had the same zest for city growth that his grandfather had, so he eagerly tried to line up support in the city council for Scranton's expansion. The city council ultimately vetoed the mayor's annexation bill, according to Mattes, because the five Republican diehards feared the personal political consequences of adding the Democratic majority in Dunmore to the balanced vote in the city of Scranton. The Republican Mattes urged the Republican councilmen to reconsider but they would not. Their loyalty to party and their desire for office outweighed their concern for Scranton. This Republican attitude toward Scranton's growth in 1912 contrasts sharply with the Republican attitude in 1866. In that year Scranton Republicans fought in the state legislature for wide boundaries for their industrial city. They knew full well that if they won their political fight with the legislature they would be ousted by the very people they absorbed. And indeed the Democratic majority in the newly incorporated land helped elect Democrats in Scranton's next local election. In 1912 the Republican councilmen did not want Scranton to grow. After they defeated the annexation of Dunmore, the chamber of commerce successfully promoted a law to divest the city council of its power to veto the mayor. By this time, though, the threatened officeholders in Dunmore "marshalled their troops and defeated annexation" in a referendum in Dunmore. Scranton's expansion had been permanently thwarted.[38]

The reality of an increasingly fragmented elite in Scranton by the 1920s assumed importance when the anthracite coal industry collapsed in that decade. Scranton's economic leaders were not so capable of mobilizing for counteraction as they once were. When the market for anthracite coke disappeared in the 1880s, Scranton's coal operators and its board of trade helped create new uses for anthracite by marketing it in different sizes and grades. In 1901, when the city's first and largest industry moved to Buffalo, influential Scrantonians tried to stop the move legally. When this failed, the board of trade roused the local citizenry to contribute over one million dollars to bring new industries to town. By the 1920s, though, when the entire outside market for anthracite coal was threatened, Scranton's economic and political leaders showed no such unity of purpose. To protect their city, they needed to find new exports or form a strategy for pricing and promoting the qualities of anthracite against those of the cleaner and increasingly cheaper fuels of natural gas and heating oil. Perhaps the obstacles to the success of such a campaign would ultimately have been insurmountable. Nonetheless, few seem to have tried. No citywide effort was launched to save the export that employed 35,000 Scrantonians.[39]

Nero is alleged to have fiddled while Rome burned; Scrantonians merely fiddled around while their city's export collapsed. In 1924 and 1926, for example, Scranton suffered two long coal strikes. Local labor leaders and coal miners apparently valued higher wages more than job security or protecting their city's primary export. The coal operators themselves (many of whom were New Yorkers) were no help either. As a group they lacked ingenuity in losing a market they had so long dominated. Some were downright destructive. In an effort to discover more coal, for example, some operators tunnelled dangerously underneath the city of Scranton. Several mine cave-ins during the 1920s and 1930s risked lives, damaged property, and made Scranton a perilous place to live.

With anthracite in decline the chamber of commerce mounted no vigorous crusade to raise money or to find new exports. Money seemed to be spent on everything but protecting local industry. In the late 1920s, businessmen in Scranton willingly raised money to build a posh country club outside the city; yet they showed no matching desire to build industries inside the city. As the coal production subsided during these years, other Scrantonians spent untold thousands of dollars constructing an enormous Masonic temple downtown. The local Irish Catholics vigorously financed St. Thomas and Marywood Colleges, but many of their parishioners needed jobs when the mines closed. In 1926 local Methodists finished construction of an ornate church in downtown Scranton almost overlooking the D.L.&W. station, where coal traffic was declining sharply. Depression followed on the heels of the collapse of the anthracite industry. Every census report after 1930 has recorded another decline in Scranton's population.[40]

The collapse of an export was unique to Scranton in the 1920s. But the expansion of corporations and the increased fragmentation of economic leadership may be central to cities and regions throughout America in the early twentieth century. Such trends do not necessarily result in urban stagnation. In the Lehigh Valley, in fact, there was a reversed pattern of initial ethnic conflict and eventual city growth.

8

Bold Guys Finish First: Ethnic Groups, Entrepreneurs, and Cities in the Lehigh Valley, 1800–1920

Capital and talent were centralized in Scranton after a dedicated group of city-builders came into a thinly settled region. Not all industrialists had the luxury of entering such an empty region. The Lehigh Valley, a three-county iron and steel producing region south of the Lackawanna region, was older and had several towns established before it industrialized. Comparing these two regions helps to show the close connection between entrepreneurship and city growth.

The Lehigh Valley both resembles and differs from its Lackawanna neighbor. Both began industrializing from extractive industries around 1840, and both had an active multiregional center nearby. The Lehigh Valley, however, was first settled in the early 1700s by various ethnocultural groups: Lutheran Germans, Moravians, and Scotch-Irish presbyterians. This dramatically contrasts with the later settlement of the Lackawanna region by New Englanders. Also, the abundance of iron ore and the dearth of coal in the Lehigh Valley gave it a raw material base almost reversed from that of the Lackawanna region.[1]

As a hinterland of Philadelphia, the Lehigh Valley underwent settlement beginning in the early 1700s. The incoming settlers began mixed farming and marketed their produce down the Lehigh and Delaware Rivers to Philadelphia. At first, Philadelphia supplied urban services through itinerant merchants, but the settlers formed small towns in the mid-1700s as trading and service centers.[2]

From the earliest settlement, the Lehigh Valley had a potpourri of cultural groups. A sprinkling of Quakers and other English migrants was swamped by three waves of incoming Germans, beginning around 1700. A few small groups of Scotch-Irish formed enclaves in the region as early as the 1720s. Finally, a large colony of Moravians settled the central Lehigh Valley in the 1740s. These Europeans had their reasons for leaving their homeland. Foremost among them was the post-Reformation religious conflicts that wracked the European continent in the 1600s and 1700s. Many Europeans had fought and refought the Reformation for too many generations. They grew tired of religious wars and ethnic hostilities so they came to America. Yet when they arrived in the Lehigh Valley in the 1700s they often reenacted these religious disputes.[3]

The Germans were the largest and easily the most diverse of the groups migrating to the Lehigh Valley. William Penn offered cheap land to the Germans and an early trickle of them into the region was followed by several large waves of Lutheran and Reformed Germans. These Rhinelanders formed separate ethnic communities with many social institutions to preserve their different cultures. German schools and churches especially helped them maintain traditions and transfer values to future generations. German-language newspapers helped promote the idea of an ethnic community. Singing societies, agricultural fairs, and even different food and dress shaped a way of life among these Pennsylvania Germans.[4]

A colony of Moravians, a religious group from central Czechoslovakia, began migrating to the Lehigh Valley in 1741. They soon formed the towns of Bethlehem and Nazareth. In fact, these towns were exclusively Moravian for a century after they were founded. Led by Count Nicholas von Zinzindorf, these Moravians ordered their social, economic, and political life around a set of religious doctrines involving devotionalism and personal piety. Zinzindorf claimed personal access to God and developed a loosely structured set of ideas on salvation, the celebration of Christ, and work. Like other Protestant denominations, the Moravians stressed religious feeling and experience more than specific doctrine and liturgy. The first generation of Moravians created a communal economic system called a "General Economy," where everyone worked without personal profit for the church and community. The Moravians segregated their communes by age and sex; each commune worked and worshiped together. Moravians gave most of their labor to the community in return for food, clothing, and shelter.[5]

Unlike the Germans, Scotch-Irish, and Quakers, the first generation of Moravians in America ignored market forces and spent their money and time on missionary work to convert their neighbors. Skilled Moravian craftsmen were especially useful as missionaries: they would display their labor and dispense their gospel. Count Zinzindorf, however, clearly separated zeal for God from zeal for mammon. He publicly denounced capital accumulation, which he saw as contradictory to Moravian principles. Zinzindorf and other Moravians believed that factories and profits would weaken religious institutions and ethnic ties.

They feared that if the Moravians adopted a market economy their craftsmen might want private profit more than public service. So most first-generation Moravians seem to have accepted Zinzindorf's explanation that making profits occurred "assuredly not under divine providence, but under the direction of Satan."[6]

The various ethnocultural groups in the Lehigh Valley lived in frequent tension with each other. According to one account, the Scotch-Irish had "fighting proclivities and their antipathy towards German settlers caused inharmonious conditions with the peace-loving Moravians." Much of this conflict originated in religious perspective. The Moravians were more evangelical than the Presbyterian Scotch-Irish and the Lutheran and Reformed Germans. Over several generations, these ethnic groups also disagreed on what to do about war, taxes, and schools. For example, the Germans and Scotch-Irish believed in Indian removal, the Moravians in Indian conversion. The Germans supported the Fries Rebellion, a tax revolt in the 1790s, and the Moravians opposed it. The Scotch-Irish favored a Pennsylvania law passed in the 1830s to give state aid to common schools, but many Germans, and probably most Moravians, fought it because it would separate religion from education.[7]

How much these cultural tensions hampered economic development is hard to know. They certainly made the ethnic groups distrust one another. An economic historian who has studied this problem insists that ethnic clannishness led to shortages of credit in the region. That ethnic merchants sometimes distrusted outsiders is clear from the surviving records of a Quaker merchant: he "proposed to sell to none but Friends." Trading within ethnic groups was understandable, but in economic terms it made for shortages of some goods and surpluses of others. It further promoted a conservatism that prevented the formation of capital for large projects.[8]

The ethnic clannishness in the Lehigh Valley fragmented urban development right from the start. Bethlehem and Nazareth became exclusive Moravian communities, and they refused to permit outsiders to live in their towns. Directly west of Bethlehem on the Lehigh River was Allentown, "perhaps the most intensely German city in the state." The older town of Easton, at the junction of the Lehigh and Delaware Rivers, was a center for the Scotch-Irish in the Lehigh Valley. As an active trading center, Easton also attracted some Germans and fallen Moravians.[9] These ethnic towns existed apart from each other and by 1800 they had begun their separate patterns of growth.

During the first half of the 1800s, the Lehigh Valley slowly began to industrialize. Local German, Moravian, and Scotch-Irish leaders in Allentown, Bethlehem, and Easton made money in farming and in the river trade; then they started small banks, waterworks, and iron concerns. Not all their money went into economic development. They also supported churches and schools to pre-serve and glorify their religious heritages. The Moravians, for example, esta-blished a large church, an academy, the Moravian College and Theological Seminary, and the Moravian Female Seminary; these costly institutions were the center of their community life. The German Lutherans in Allentown were not to be outdone; they started an academy, a male seminary, and a ladies seminary to get their message across. Finally, the Scotch-Irish Presbyterians in Easton established two schools: an academy and Lafayette College. To build, maintain, and staff these schools absorbed a lot of scarce capital that might have gone into new industries. To have one was almost assuredly to do without the other. In the end, these ethnic groups built their schools and let Philadel-phians initiate the canals and iron companies in the region.[10]

Philadelphians spearheaded industrial growth in the Lehigh Valley in the 1820s with the founding of the Lehigh Coal and Navigation Company (here-after L.C.&N.). They were responding to a demand for a cheap fuel, because prices for timber and charcoal had climbed during the War of 1812. They formed the L.C.&N. to investigate the possibility of exporting anthracite down the Lehigh and Delaware rivers to Philadelphia. After surveying the region, the L.C.&N. leaders chose a coal deposit above ground at a place named Summit Hill; in 1820 they shipped the first coal to skeptical buyers in Philadelphia. The town of Mauch Chunk, nine miles downstream from Summit Hill, developed as a service and export center on the Lehigh River.[11]

Throughout the 1820s, coal tonnage from the Summit Hill mines increased; and, as the demand for services also expanded, Mauch Chunk steadily grew. The Philadelphia market obligingly boomed when anthracite became competitive with other fuels. In 1827, the L.C.&N. leaders increased production by building a gravity railroad, the first in the anthracite fields, from Summit Hill to Mauch Chunk. By 1831, they had also invested heavily to widen and deepen the erratic and meandering Lehigh River.[12] They needed to make these railroad and canal improvements to offset the locational advantages of coal exporting down the nearby Schuylkill River, which was more navigable than the Lehigh and also closer to Philadelphia.[13]

The railroad and canal improvements insured the expansion of the Lehigh Valley, the competitiveness of the nearby coal, and the increase in coal trade through Mauch Chunk. Like Carbondale, Mauch Chunk began as a company town. Mauch Chunk, though, was not on top of valuable coal, so it developed as a shipping center and not as the site of extraction. With coal deposits lying in the craggy terrain north and west of Mauch Chunk, and iron ore south and east, the L.C.&N. merely bought some of the coal land and put their headquarters nearby in Mauch Chunk. With so much coal and iron land nearby, and with so little of it under outside domination, the migrants to Mauch Chunk had more opportu-

Mauch Chunk, Pennsylvania

nities to create local industry than did Carbondale's population. Newcomers to Mauch Chunk serviced the L.C.&N. as coal shippers and boat builders; but many of these migrants branched into local enterprises and became small manufacturers or coal operators. They also developed the town's services, such as the gas and water company, two banks, several stores, and a hotel. Mauch Chunk would ultimately end up like Carbondale, but not because the Lehigh Valley town didn't have locally owned industry.[14]

The mountainous terrain gave Mauch Chunk a gorgeous location; but the steep slopes confined the town's expansion to less than two square miles. These mountains, then, imposed physical limits on the town's growth. Writing in the 1880s, one observer noted that "although nature challenged man's admiration here [in Mauch Chunk], she did not invite him to become a resident. . . . She promised here only the beauties and the majesty of the mountains, and the wealth in her treasure vaults as the means of making countless comfortable houses elsewhere." The author observed that, as the photograph suggests, "the houses [on Main Street] are built without dooryards upon the street, and impinge upon the base of the mountains on either side. . . . Almost every foot of available building ground is occupied."[15]

Such a restriction on one small town usually doesn't mean much for regional economic development. Not so with Mauch Chunk. That town formed an aggressive economic elite that made Mauch Chunk the center of industrial development in the Lehigh Valley. While ethnic groups squabbled in Allentown, Bethlehem, and Easton, the industrialists in Mauch Chunk tried to build a large empire in a tiny town.

Since Mauch Chunk was founded as an L.C.&N. town, the first waves of prominent settlers, often nearby Germans, were the company's employees. These migrants came to Mauch Chunk in the 1820s and early 1830s; they included chief bookkeeper John Ruddle, chief engineer Edwin Douglas, company storekeeper Asa L. Foster, railroad boss Isaac Salkeld, blacksmith Daniel Bertsch, contractor William Butler, and carpenter George Belford. Other prominent migrants were merchant John Leisenring and hotelkeeper John Lentz. Leisenring's son, John, Jr., became the L.C.&N.'s chief engineer. John Leisenring's grandson, Edward, became the president of the L.C.&N. in the 1890s. Most of these early migrants had little education and they often came to Mauch Chunk from areas nearby. In Mauch Chunk, many of these men became kinsmen; in fact, we can call them the "Leisenring group."[16]

The formation of Mauch Chunk's elite entered a second phase in the early 1830s, after completion of a gravity railroad and the Lehigh Canal. These technological improvements created more coal traffic on the Lehigh River and more population growth for Mauch Chunk. Boatmen, miners, repairmen, and carpenters all came to find jobs. Among these men was a group of New Englanders, who made money as boatmen, independent coal operators, and merchants. Separating themselves from the German settlers and the L.C.&N., these Yankees formed a second social group in Mauch Chunk. The strong tie between entrepreneurship and kinship in this second group can best be explained through a brief sketch of its leader, Asa Packer.

Born in Mystic, Connecticut, in 1805, Packer migrated as a youth to his cousin's farm in Susquehanna County, Pennsylvania. In addition to farming, Packer also developed carpentry skills and spent a year as an artisan in New York City. In 1833, back in Susquehanna County, he learned of the need for boatmen on the Lehigh Canal. He soon migrated to Mauch Chunk with his brother Robert and his brother-in-law James Blakslee. Asa Packer and Blakslee ran coal boats for others and soon commanded their own boat; they also used their carpentry skills to build and sell canal boats. Packer invested wisely and moved into coal operating in the 1840s. Here he made his fortune. Rewarding his kinsmen, he helped his brothers, a nephew, a nephew-in-law, two brothers-in-law, and a son-in-law become merchants and coal operators. This group included fellow Yankees Robert W. Packer, Harry Wilbur, Elisha P. Wilbur, Charles O. Skeer, James Blakslee, and Garret Linderman. By 1850, Packer was easily the wealthiest man in Mauch Chunk; his best years, when he organized a regional railroad, were yet to come.[17]

By 1850, at the outset of the development of the iron industry, the wealthy Packer and Leisenring groups had given Mauch Chunk the potential to become the regional capital of the Lehigh Valley. These entrepreneurs had enough wealth to finance local industry; furthermore, they had an industrial orientation that contrasted with the religious emphasis in the older towns of Allentown, Bethlehem, an Easton. While leaders in these older towns lavished capital on

religious and educational institutions, the bulk of the capital in Mauch Chunk
was invested in iron and coal production and in transportation to outside markets.[18] The chance for Mauch Chunk capital to move into regional transportation came in the 1840s, when the L.C.&N. had the usual problems of flooding in
the summer and freezing in the winter. Since the L.C.&N. had a monopoly on
canal transportation in the Lehigh Valley, some capitalists talked about the need
for a railroad.[19]

The building of canals and railroads was big business: locals usually needed
help from outside entrepreneurs in multiregional centers. New Yorkers started
the D&H in the Lackawanna Valley, for example, and Philadelphians started the
L.C.&N. in the Lehigh Valley. Outside dominance also appeared in the Lehigh
Valley when a group of investors, led by Philadelphian Edward R. Biddle, got
the state legislature to give them a railroad charter in 1846; they immediately
began selling stock for a rail line through the region. [20]

Building the Lehigh Valley line was so risky that its backers couldn't sell
enough shares for the multimillion-dollar project to begin. In 1851, just before
its five-year charter was to expire, Asa Packer, who had already invested in the
enterprise, bought most of the outstanding stock and determined to build a
profitable rail line himself. Packer got help from his friends and kinsmen so he
confidently agreed to finance a forty-six-mile stretch from Mauch Chunk to
Easton. Originally chartered as the Delaware, Lehigh, Schuylkill, and Susquehanna Railroad, its name was soon shortened to the Lehigh Valley Railroad;
Packer appointed as chief engineer Robert Sayre, then an engineer for the competing L.C.&N.[21]

Under Packer's direction, the Lehigh Valley Railroad became a major regional
line. Packer completed the Mauch Chunk-to-Easton line in 1855, and leased
rolling stock from the Central Railroad of New Jersey (where John Taylor
Johnston, fellow director of the Lehigh Valley Railroad, was president). For
traffic Packer used coal shipments from his own Packer, Carter, and Company, from his coal-operating relatives, and from his friends around Mauch
Chunk. Packer expanded the Lehigh Valley Railroad by constructing independent lines north and west into adjacent coal markets, testing their profitability, and then consolidating them into the Lehigh Valley system. By 1866,
this railroad was a 161-mile network that carried more than twice the coal
and freight of its competitor, the L.C.&N. In 1868, the Lehigh Valley Railroad's stock was over $16 million, a mammoth figure; and the multimillionaire
Packer had become one of the wealthiest men in Pennsylvania, a presidential
candidate, and a folk hero for miles around.[22]

Constructing a railroad through the mountainous Lehigh Valley in the 1850s
required courage, vision, capital, and credit. In completing this task, Packer

had to play politics with other carriers, plan the most efficient right of way, and negotiate bond sales in tight money markets. While doing this he had to face unexpected setbacks—a sudden rise in the cost of materials, a cholera epidemic among the construction crew, and the sudden closing of lines of credit. The atmosphere in the Lehigh Valley must have been electric as Asa Packer sunk his entire personal fortune into building a regional railroad. Packer's empire, like that of the early Scrantons, was necessarily fragile and the agent for the R.G. Dun Company recorded the delicate maneuvering. On Christmas day, 1855, he "heard it rumored a few days ago that he [Packer] had failed and immediately heard it contradicted." Packer had become "very much in debt" and was "laboring under great financial difficulty," but he escaped temporarily by advancing railroad stock to his creditors. Almost two months later the Dun agent recorded that "no suits [have been] brought as yet. Whether he will get through we can't say." Just five days later Packer was "somewhat relieved from embarrassment" but five months later "his paper [was] protested" and the indomitable Packer maneuvered again to satisfy nervous creditors. Finally, three years later, in 1859, the agent proclaimed that Packer's "credit is now beyond question." Like the Scrantons a decade earlier, Packer had "reached beyond familiar horizons" and the Lehigh Valley had a locally owned railroad.[23]

Packer's completing of the Lehigh Valley line made Mauch Chunk the industrial center of the Lehigh Valley. As the regional center for a canal and a railroad, Mauch Chunk had an industrial orientation that separated it from the larger ethnic towns of Allentown, Bethlehem, and Easton. Mauch Chunk's wealthy and aggressive elite separated it from Carbondale, the first industrial town in the Lackawanna Valley. In fact, Mauch Chunk's elite in 1870, as indicated in table 8.1 recorded more wealth than did that of any other town in the Lehigh Valley; indeed it may have had the highest mean per capita income of any city in the nation. If only the surrounding mountains had given Mauch Chunk more room to expand it surely would have become the regional capital of the Lehigh Valley.

After the 1850s, Mauch Chunk's elite, the Packer and Leisenring groups, extended their regional investments in iron, coal, and railroads. Asa Packer and his kinsmen, of course, controlled the Lehigh Valley Railroad. Garret B. Linderman and Charles O. Skeer, sons-in-law of Asa Packer, were among the wealthiest independent coal operators in the anthracite area. James Blakslee, Packer's brother-in-law, was president of the Montrose Railroad. In the Leisenring group, John Leisenring, Jr., was the president of a coal company and two iron companies in Virginia and Tennessee; he also held directorships on powerful regional companies such as the L.C.&N. and the Central Railroad of New Jersey. His son Edward became president of the L.C.&N. Fisher Hazard, an

TABLE 8.1.   Number of Families Holding Different Amounts of Real and
Personal Wealth in Five Lehigh Valley Cities According to the Federal Manuscript Census of 1870

Real and Personal Wealth	Number of Families in			
	Easton	Allentown	Bethlehem	Mauch Chunk
Over $ 50,000	85	76	21	24
Over $ 100,000	32	21	11	9
Over $ 200,000	8	2	4	5
Over $ 300,000	3	1	1	4
Over $ 400,000	0	0	1	3
Over $ 500,000	0	0	1	3
Over $ 1,000,000	0	0	0	1
Over $10,000,000	0	0	0	1
Total wealth of those holding over $50,000	$8,300,000	$7,100,000	$2,500,000	$13,700,000

SOURCES: Manuscript Census Returns, Nineth Census of the United States, 1870,
Lehigh County: Microfilm Series M-593, Rolls 1362, 1363; Northhampton County: Microfilm Series M-593, Rolls 1381, 1382; Carbon County: Microfilm Series M-593, Roll 1320.

associate of Leisenring's, founded a small manufacturing company in Wilkes-
Barre and was a director on the L.C.&N. Finally, the Packer and Leisenring
groups combined to control the iron exports in nearby Lehighton, Weissport,
and Parryville.[24]

In local economic development, Mauch Chunk's two social groups divided
the town's industries and services. There must have been some rivalry among
these men. In industry, the Packer group dominated the Lehigh Valley Railroad
while the Leisenring group associated with the rival L.C.&N. In services, the
Leisenring crowd dominated the First National Bank, while the Packer group
controlled the younger Linderman National Bank. In utilities, members of both
groups ran the gas, water, and electric companies. In religion and politics Yankee
Asa Packer and his kinsmen were Episcopalians and usually Democrats; John
Leisenring and his relatives were often Presbyterians and Republicans.[25]

The economic problem for both groups of capitalists in Mauch Chunk still
remained: How could they spur economic development in a town that could
not expand? By remaining in Mauch Chunk an entrepreneur limited his range of
local enterprises and sacrificed the large gains to be made in real estate elsewhere. He also jeopardized his outside investments because communication
lags could result from living away from them. Yet social ties and tradition
militated against his emigration. And where and when would he go? Not surprisingly, the two social groups in Mauch Chunk resolved the problem in different ways. Because of the large amounts of capital involved, their decisions
influenced the future urbanization of the Lehigh Valley.

While the Mauch Chunk entrepreneurs contemplated relocation, the Lehigh Valley emerged as a potential center for iron manufacturing. Allentown and Bethlehem had ore deposits nearby, and in the 1830s the L.C.&N. scouted the Lehigh Valley looking for a site for an iron factory. The Philadelphia leaders of the L.C.&N. had a big stake in the future of the Lehigh Valley, so they offered land and free transportation on their canal to anyone who could erect an iron furnace and run it for three months with anthracite.[26] A flurry of tinkerers tried to win the L.C.&N.'s prize: they futilely built contraptions to smelt the local iron with the abundant anthracite to the northwest. In 1839, the L.C.&N. finally imported Welshman David Thomas of the Ynescedwin Iron Company. In South Wales, Thomas had used local anthracite deposits to make iron; in America, he explored the Lehigh Valley and chose Catasaqua, a village five miles west of Allentown on the Lehigh River, as his site for an anthracite blast furnace. After some trial and error, he smelted the ore and won the L.C.&N. prize. He was America's first person to make iron from anthracite; he preceded the Scrantons by over a year. In Catasaqua, Thomas became superintendent of the Lehigh Crane Iron Company, which the L.C.&N. directors had founded and were controlling from Philadelphia. Since the Lehigh Crane Iron Company made steady profits during the 1840s, entrepreneurs in the region thought about making anthracite iron.[27]

Though slower than the Philadelphians, Allentown's more conservative investors did see possibilities of profit and city growth in iron production. In 1845, several Allentown businessmen held a meeting "for forming a company to erect an anthracite furnace for the manufacture of iron for production at or near Allentown." In a resolution, the group "considered [it] of vast importance to this community that an anthracite furnace for the manufacture of iron should be established among us." Then they tried to sell $40,000 worth of stock. Five years earlier the Scrantons tried the same thing even though they had less money and no city to draw on for support. Unlike the Scrantons, the Lutherans in Allentown never took the risk; they never raised the needed capital.[28]

Allentown's businessmen may have been cautious, but Philadelphia's weren't: Bevan and Humphries, a Philadelphia shipping firm, sent Samuel Lewis to the Lehigh Valley in 1845 to pick a site to build an iron furnace on. Lewis, after some investigation, chose Allentown, "his decision being induced by the close proximity of ore beds and transportation facilitated by the canal." Heeding Lewis' advice, Bevan and Humphries bought land in Allentown in 1846 and hired Philadelphia foundrymen and engine-builders to make equipment for iron production. Later that year they were making pig-iron. In 1851, Bevan and Humphries sold the iron works to the Allentown Iron Company, a new concern with both Philadelphia and Allentown men on the board of directors. This new company rechanneled some of the profits into Allentown's local economy; as a local writer observed that "the works when running at full capacity have employed a very large number of men, and have been a potent factor in Allentown's prosperity." Outsiders continued to invest in Allentown iron and by 1880 Allentown had four iron companies; local capitalists controlled only one of them and held part interest in the other three. The largest concern, the Roberts Iron Company, employed about 1,200 people and was owned almost entirely in Philadelphia and Hazleton.[29]

Despite outside ownership, iron and steel production boosted Allentown's growth. Unlike Carbondale, Allentown was no company town; its capitalists owned some of the export and most of the local services. Allentown's iron industry helped the city grow, as table 8.2 indicates, by giving jobs to thousands of natives and newcomers. These workers created demands for housing, food, clothing, and other local services, mostly owned by the local German-stock leaders. They were willing to risk investing in the small services but not the large iron export. As the site of four iron industries, however, Allentown surpassed Easton in 1880 as the largest city in the Lehigh Valley.[30]

The leaders in both Allentown and Easton were cautious. After they neglected their region's iron, they forfeited their region's railroad. In 1846, businessmen in Allentown and Easton tried "to effect an organization to open books for stock subscription" for the Lehigh Valley Railroad; but they couldn't raise the money and Asa Packer had to take it over. From 1840 to 1880, capitalists in these towns seemed afraid to start an industry. Yet they were much wealthier than their counterparts in Scranton. It's hard to tell whether Allentown and Easton men were just conservative or whether they were so heavily committed to helping local churches and schools that they had little extra for industry. Whatever the case, their lack of initiative kept their cities from integrating the Lehigh Valley into an urban network the way Scranton did in the Lackawanna Valley.[31]

Easton was the oldest city in the Lehigh Valley and was also the largest for over a century. The data in table 8.1 show there was a lot of wealth in Easton. Yet its proximity to Philadelphia, its satisfying role as an entrepôt for Philadelphia trade, and its strong financial commitment to Lafayette College helped sap its entrepreneurial strength. Situated at the junction of the Lehigh and Delaware Rivers, Easton enjoyed locational advantages similar to those of Pittsburgh. But Philadelphia's location, a mere fifty miles down the Delaware River, helped frustrate Easton's ambitions. Philadelphia became a multi-regional center, while Easton became a shipping point for coal down the Lehigh River and farm products down the Delaware River. As an entrepôt, Easton developed

TABLE 8.2. Population and Percentage Growth of Mauch Chunk, Allentown, Bethlehem, and Easton from 1850 to 1880

City	1850 Population	1860		1870		1880	
		Population	Percentage Growth	Population	Percentage Growth	Population	Percentage Growth
Mauch Chunk[a]	2,557	4,841	89	5,426	12	5,605	3.3
Allentown[b]	4,343	8,025	85	13,884	73	18,063	30
Bethlehem[c]	1,516	2,866	89	8,068	182	10,118	25
Easton[d]	8,761	11,068	26	14,154	27.9	16,458	16

SOURCES: J.D.B. DeBow, *The Seventh Census of the United States: 1850* (Washington, D.C., 1853), pp. 163, 173, 177; Joseph C.G. Kennedy, *Population of the United States in 1860* (Washington, D.C., 1864), pp. 418, 427, 430-31; Francis A. Walker, *The Statistics of the Population of the United States, 1870* (Washington, D.C. 1872), pp. 246, 251, 253; Francis A. Walker and Charles W. Seaton, *Statistics of the Population of the United States, 1880* (Washington, D.C., 1883), pp. 309, 313, 315.

[a] includes East Mauch Chunk in 1860, 1870, and 1880
[b] includes East Allentown in 1850
[c] includes South Bethlehem in 1870 and 1880
[d] includes South Easton in 1850, 1860, 1870, 1880

a large and conservative middle class: they were tied to Philadelphia shipping and to local services, not to industrial development.[32]

Even when Easton got rail transportation, it still avoided industry. It merely became a terminal rail point for the Morris Canal, the Central Railroad of New Jersey, the Lehigh Valley Railroad, the Lehigh and Susquehanna Railroad, and the Easton and Northern Railroad. Easton leaders may have shunned manufacturing, which was always a high risk, because they made their money in safer investments in shipping and commerce. In other cities, leaders were not so cautious. Capitalists in Boston, for example, built iron factories at nearby Glendon and South Easton; Philadelphians established the Andover Iron Company in Phillipsburg, New Jersey, just across the river from Easton. By 1880, Easton had no significant export, despite the town's good location between the Pennsylvania and New Jersey ore beds. Easton didn't even have a board of trade.[33]

Prominent men in Easton simply may not have wanted to transform their town from a shipping to an industrial center. The Scotch-Irish, especially, seem to have preferred supporting Lafayette College to starting local industries. The consequences of this industrial apathy, however, were economic stagnation for the whole town. During the 1880s, one writer decried the "lack of enterprise in Easton, its capital seeking investment elsewhere." He concluded that "growth in [the] building of dwellings . . . [and] industries of various kinds suffered."[34]

As an old city, Easton, like Wilkes-Barre, had great political power. Wilkes-Barreans used their influence to attract industries and repel rival cities. Easton's politicians, by contrast, seem to have done almost nothing for their city. For example, U.S. Senator Richard Brodhead, a Democrat from Easton, sponsored a bill to establish a government iron foundry, but he wanted it at South Bethlehem, not at Easton. Bank president David Wagener, Easton's wealthiest citizen, was also a wheelhorse in the state Democratic party; but he apparently used none of his national and state contacts to serve Easton's industrial development. James M. Porter was a lawyer in Easton and the brother of a Pennsylvania governor; yet he seems to have spent most of his time at Lafayette College, as a teacher and president of its board of trustees. He helped coax millionaire Ario Pardee, a fellow Presbyterian, into giving $500,000 to Lafayette College, but Porter attracted no money for Easton's industry. The Dun credit reporter observed that Porter "never was a lover of money. $ is consequently sometimes up, $ then down again." Lacking "$" for local industry, Easton's urban-economic development was usually down again. The combination, then, of Philadelphia dominance, satisfaction as middlemen in trade, and the financial commitment to Lafayette College prevented Easton men from shaping urbanization in the Lehigh Valley.[35]

West of Easton, the Moravians in Bethlehem remained restrictive for several generations. Yet they were divided and pressured by the quickened pace of life in America. From the time of their settlement in the 1740s, the more traditional Moravians tried to keep their community exclusive and self-sufficient. But by the early 1800s, the modernists among the Moravians were rejecting the ideas of self-sufficiency and economic isolation. They wanted efficiency for Moravian business and capital accumulation for economic growth. This new economic plan, of course, threatened Bethlehem's unity of church and state, the dominance of the church and the authority of its officials in the economic and political life of the community. To promote economic growth in Bethlehem, then, the Moravian cosmopolitans had to delimit the role of religion in temporal affairs.[36]

The divided Moravians became part of modern America in the 1840s. The keys to their modernization were three dramatic institutional changes in their community. First, they got rid of the town's communal economic system (the "General Economy"); this led to a wage system and more private ownership of land. The second change was to end segregation by age and sex; this led to nuclear families living in single-family houses. With nuclear families, a wage system, and private ownership of land, the Moravians could encourage entrepreneurship, build factories, and create rapid economic growth. The third change was to introduce political democracy to Bethlehem; the town ended the drawing of lots to determine Christ's choice for the political direction of the community. These changes meant that the Moravian church had relaxed its grip on the political and economic life of Bethlehem; it even broke with the Moravian church in German. In 1844, the church sanctioned the public election of a burgess and nine councilmen. Shortly thereafter, Moravian officials sold church lands to non-Moravians, a practice that ended Bethlehem's history as an exclusively religious community.[37]

The selling of this Moravian land south of the Lehigh River led to a quirk of history: the rapid creation of a new industrial city, South Bethlehem. It all began when Charles Luckenbach, a Moravian bank president, sold 103 acres of Moravian land to Easton speculator Charles Brodhead in 1854. Brodhead hoped to make money on his land by exploiting the iron ore in the region. In fact, he first hoped to start an iron foundry on his property with government money. A distant kinsmen of Asa Packer's, Brodhead also hoped that his land would be the terminal point for the Lehigh Valley and the Northern Pennsylvania railroads. So he lobbied with capitalists in the region and with politicians in Washington hoping they would use his land to build on.[38]

Most congressmen didn't favor federal support for the economic development of South Bethlehem, so Brodhead turned to private sources. He soon persuaded Moravian August Wolle, an owner of nearby iron mines to locate a blast furnace in South Bethlehem. In 1857, Brodhead helped Wolle draft the charter for the Bethlehem Rolling Mills and Iron Company; these two became the first subscribers to the stock. In 1860, when the firm incorporated as the Bethlehem Iron Company, Brodhead's wealthiest kinsman, Asa Packer, became a member of its first board of directors. In 1861, the company began building a modern blast furnace.[39]

Meanwhile, the Packer group in Mauch Chunk committed itself to developing real estate in South Bethlehem. Beginning in 1854, Packer and his colleagues gradually bought thirty-five acres of land in South Bethlehem for a terminus for their Lehigh Valley Railroad. They also speculated in land and bought houses in the new town of South Bethlehem. Brodhead must have been delighted because South Bethlehem flourished after Bethlehem Iron, the Lehigh Valley Railroad, and a flow of Yankee entrepreneurs came to town. The Civil War interrupted Bethlehem Iron's progress, but in 1863 the rolling of iron rails began exclusively for Asa Packer's Lehigh Valley Railroad. As Packer's demand for iron and, later, steel rails increased, so did Bethlehem Iron's prosperity. This company built new furnaces in the 1860s, adopted the Bessemer and open-hearth processes in the 1870s, and became a multimillion dollar company second in the region only to the Lehigh Valley Railroad.[40]

Packer's decision to make South Bethlehem a central headquarters for the Lehigh Valley Railroad also became a catalyst for the town's industrial development. His reasons for choosing South Bethlehem rather than another site are not clear. Early in the selection process, Robert Sayre, the chief engineer for the railroad, commended the newly opened land as a good location for a depot; he promoted it further as "the proper point" for the railroad's water supply. Sayre then invested in South Bethlehem real estate, so he had a stake in persuading Packer to industrialize South Bethlehem. Other members of the Packer group followed Sayre to South Bethlehem, and they undoubtedly helped bring Packer capital to the area. Whatever the motivation for settlement, after the mid-1850s the new town of South Bethlehem had a marketable export and regional transportation in Bethlehem Iron and the Lehigh Valley Railroad.[41]

The Packer group's decision to invest in a new city, South Bethlehem, tells us something about the apathy of other urban leaders in the region. The capitalists in Allentown, as the railroad's annual reports suggest, didn't even try to get either the Lehigh Valley Railroad or the Northern Pennsylvania Railroad to establish headquarters in Allentown. Such entrepreneurial neglect is striking because Allentown was centrally located and was easily the largest town in the vicinity. It helps to show the conservatism of Allentown's German-stock elite, whose lethargy contrasts with the opportunism of leaders in Scranton. We must suspend our critical faculties to imagine the Scranton group or the Scranton

Board of Trade letting a multimillionaire like Asa Packer wander about the Lackawanna Valley in search of a promised land for his capital investments. Yet in the Lehigh Valley, the Yankee Episcopalians and the German Lutherans preferred to look at each other from opposite sides of the Lehigh River, safely ensconced in separate boroughs.[42]

Packer's affection for South Bethlehem kindled similar zeal from his friends and kinsmen in Mauch Chunk. From 1858 to 1870, four leading families in the Packer group, the Wilburs, Sayres, Lindermans, and Cleavers, migrated twenty-five miles down the Lehigh River to resettle in South Bethlehem. They all helped operate the Lehigh Valley Railroad and Bethlehem Iron and they lived in Fountain Hill, a borough adjacent to South Bethlehem. There they built mansions and secured wealth from their real estate holdings as well as from their industrial investments. They also transferred their Democratic party allegiance and their Episcopalian church affiliation to South Bethlehem. By the 1880s, as table 8.3 illustrates, Brodhead and the Mauch Chunk migrants had become interrelated time and again through the marriages of their offspring. To a much lesser extent they also intermarried with other prominent South Bethlehem residents and with other successful newcomers.[43]

By 1880, other Mauch Chunk relatives of these four families had followed their more successful kinsmen to South Bethlehem and swelled the numbers of the Packer group there. Elisha Wilbur's brother Warren came with him to South Bethlehem and there worked for Harry Packer's Schrader Coal Company. Warren Wilbur's son-in-law, Robert Lockhart, also came to South Bethlehem, where he became a director of the Pennsylvania and New York Canal and Railroad Company, a branch of the Lehigh Valley Railroad. Also from Mauch Chunk came Elisha Wilbur's brother-in-law, Merit Abbott, who helped start the South Bethlehem Shovel Works. His son Robert established a foundry in South Bethlehem with fellow Mauch Chunk migrant Ira Cortright. James Blakslee, Asa Packer's brother-in-law, had a son who came to South Bethlehem and became a general car agent for the Lehigh Valley Railroad. After the death of coal operator Charles Skeer in Mauch Chunk, his widow, an adopted daughter of Asa Packer's, came to South Bethlehem to live. Even Packer's son Robert moved to South Bethlehem, but he later left for Bradford County to direct the northern branch of his father's Lehigh Valley Railroad. The exodus of so many Yankees from Mauch Chunk made South Bethlehem distinct; the Yankees there differed from the Moravians in Bethlehem, the Germans in Allentown, and the Scotch-Irish in Easton.[44]

The Packer group, in South Bethlehem, ran Bethlehem Iron and the Lehigh Valley Railroad. But other towns also benefitted because people living in Allentown, Bethlehem, and other places worked in these two industries. Their pres-

TABLE 8.3.   Social Data on the Group Coherence of Seven Mauch Chunk Migrants to Bethlehem

Migrant to Bethlehem	Number of Children	Children Known to Have Survived to Adulthood	Children Married to a Packer or One of the Seven's Family	Children Married to Executive of Lehigh Valley Railroad or Lehigh University
Garret B. Linderman[b]	8	4	4	0
Robert H. Sayre[c]	11	5	2	1
Elisha P. Wilbur[b]	8	8	3	1
Albert N. Cleaver[b]	0	0	0	0
Charles Broadhead[a]	3	1	1	0
William H. Sayre	9	4	2	0
William H. Sayre II	3	1	0	0
	42	23	12	2

SOURCES: Jordan et al., *Lehigh Valley* 1: 209-12, 229-32, 234-37; Jordan et al., *Encyclopedia of Pennsylvania Biography*, 1: 215-16; Atlantic Publishing and Engraving Company, *Encyclopedia of Contemporary Biography*, 1: 240-43, and 2: 11-14; Chapman Publishing Company, *Portrait and Biographical Record of Lehigh, Northampton, and Carbon Counties*, pp. 161, 810, 813; William J. Heller, ed., *History of Northampton County, Pennsylvania, and the Grand Valley of the Lehigh*, 3 vols. (Boston and New York, 1920), 3:594-95; Joseph M. Levering, *A History of Bethlehem, Pennsylvania, 1741-1892 with Some Account of Its Founders and Their Early Activity in America* (Bethlehem, Pa., 1903), p. 738.

ence created a demand for increased services. Businessmen in Allentown and Bethlehem helped supply these services so their cities directly grew because of South Bethlehem's industries. Still, the towns remained legally separated and the Yankees seemed to like it that way. In fact, they actively contributed to the separateness of the Lehigh Valley's cultural groups.[45]

Like the ethnic groups around them, Asa Packer and his kinsmen lavished capital on exclusive schools and churches. The most important of these was Packer's creation in 1866 of Lehigh University, an institution to train future engineers. He had long wanted to develop an engineering school in the Lehigh Valley, but he conspicuously avoided support for Presbyterian Lafayette College in Easton. Instead, Packer gave fifty-seven acres of land and $1.5 million for yet another regional university; later he gave about $3 million more. The Episcopal bishop of the Pennsylvania diocese was made president of the University's board of trustees. Several Lehigh University buildings, such as Packer Hall, Packer Memorial Church, Linderman Hall, Sayre Observatory, Wilbur Power House, and Wilbur Engineering Laboratory show the Packer group's personal and financial commitment to their new institution. On the one hand, the presence of a university gave South Bethlehem youthful consumers, new ideas, and national recognition. It also created jobs for builders and teachers. On the other hand, the building, maintaining, and staffing of such an institution required a steady and heavy commitment of capital, especially since Packer insisted on giving all students free tuition. Despite the infusion of millions of Packer's dollars, Lehigh University ran into financial trouble less than three decades after its founding. The Packer group must have been proud, though, that their Yankee university outclassed all the others in the region in physical splendor and educational pretention.[46]

Having the pleasures of wealth, and fearing the proximity of strangers, the Packer nabobs created an array of new schools and churches in their exclusive Fountain Hill neighborhood. The first of these was the Episcopal church of the Nativity, a pro-Cathedral near the Lehigh River that towered over the other churches to the north. A second institution was Bishopthorpe School for Girls, established under the auspices of the Episcopal Church. On the board of trustees, several members of the Packer group were joined by the rector of the local Episcopal church and the assistant Episcopal bishop of central Pennsylvania. As one writer has noted, "Bethlehem already had a Young Ladies Seminary with an enviable reputation for high quality. . . . But the . . . entrepreneurs were not Moravians and wanted a school of their own." Another institution, funded by hundreds of thousands of Packer dollars, was St. Luke's Hospital. This hospital received some support from Moravians and Episcopalians in Allentown, but the members of the Packer group were the main benefactors. They later added the Sayre Pavilion, the Wilbur Pavilion, and the Lockhart Pavilion for Women to the hospital.[47]

This flurry of Yankee activity did not go unnoticed by the Lutheran and Reformed Germans in Allentown. In 1867, shortly after Asa Packer began building Lehigh University, the Lutherans in Allentown founded Muhlenberg College. Referring to this decision, one man said that "it was felt by many that a college under Lutheran management was needed, should be established, and could be maintained. The institution, therefore, is a church school." Not to be outclassed, the Reformed Germans founded the Allentown Female College that same year. By 1870, then, the youth of the Lehigh Valley could choose higher education from among two colleges in Allentown, two Moravian colleges in Bethlehem, Lehigh University in South Bethlehem, and Lafayette College in Easton. At this same time the Lackawanna Valley didn't have a single college; yet Scranton was larger than Allentown, the two Bethlehems, and Easton combined.[48]

The many colleges and private schools in the Lehigh Valley drained local money that could have been used for economic development. Having one college probably made good economic sense; having five colleges in eight square miles was astonishing duplication. Yet these institutions were important to the different cultural groups and dominated life in their towns. They were expensive, however, and the competition to support them seems to have been more intense than the competition to support industries. In South Bethlehem, Lehigh University depended on the multimillion-dollar contributions of Episcopalian Asa Packer; Lafayette College in Easton got help from wealthy Presbyterians from Hazleton, Scranton, and New York City. Allentown's leaders, lacking the wealth of their counterparts in South Bethlehem, appealed to Lutherans throughout the country for aid to prop up Muhlenberg College.[49]

Schools and industries tied the Packer group to South Bethlehem and so did local services. In 1867, Elisha Wilbur founded his own bank and also became the first president of the South Bethlehem Gas and Water Company. William and Robert Sayre joined him on the board of directors of the utility company; so did H. Stanley Goodwin, the general superintendent of the Lehigh Valley Railroad and later a relative of the Packer group. The benefits of connecting South Bethlehem and Bethlehem, as economic if not political units, prompted Robert Sayre and Elisha Wilbur to help form the New Street Bridge Company. In 1872, Garret Linderman founded his own bank and also the Cold Spring Water Company in Bethlehem. As the bank's president, he made kinsman Albert Cleaver his first cashier and later the bank's vice-president. Cousin Charles Brodhead also remained active as the president of the Bethlehem Railroad Company and co-incorporator of the Monocacy Iron and Steel Company.[50]

Expanding local services was secondary to the development of Bethlehem

Iron and the Lehigh Valley Railroad. The strong local influence on Bethlehem Iron was apparent when Garret Linderman, Elisha Wilbur, Albert Cleaver, and Robert Sayre all became directors of this company shortly after they came to South Bethlehem. Linderman and Cleaver, in fact, became the General Manager and Treasurer of Bethlehem Iron. Elisha Wilbur became president of the Lehigh Valley Railroad in 1884 and was joined on its board of directors by kinsmen Garret Linderman and Robert Sayre of South Bethlehem, James Blakslee of Mauch Chunk, and Robert Lamberton, the president of Lehigh University.[51] The Yankee's transformation of South Bethlehem from farmland to industrial city was under way.

South Bethlehem's wealthy founders were also active in the political life of their new town. Elisha Wilbur was a member of its first borough council in 1865; he later became the city's burgess, mayor, and treasurer. H. Stanley Goodwin, superintendent of the Lehigh Valley Railroad, was the burgess of South Bethlehem for over twenty years.[52]

In Scranton, the Scranton group opened their city to outsiders; in South Bethlehem, the Packer group insulated themselves from outsiders. The Packer group wanted separate neighborhoods, and incorporated their residences into the tiny borough of Fountain Hill, separate from South Bethlehem. Isolated in their enclave, the Packer group showed an astonishing pattern of endogamy (see table 8.3). Most of them married within their group. Two married officials with the Lehigh Valley Railroad or Lehigh University, and none of these Yankees married Moravians to the north.

The endogamy of the Packer group helps to show the distinctiveness of the different ethnic groups in the region. The possibilities of marrying German Lutherans in Allentown, Moravians in Bethlehem, or Scotch-Irish Presbyterians in Easton were simply not realistic alternatives for these Yankees. They preferred to live, socialize, and marry within their group. To the west were the Germans in Allentown, to the north were Moravians, and to the east were the immigrants in South Bethlehem, who labored in the iron and railroad industries. We have several accounts of the grand parties in the exquisite mansions in Fountain Hill; but the guest list was small and was more likely to include relatives from Mauch Chunk than neighbors in Allentown, Bethlehem, or Easton.[53]

The urban fragmentation in the Lehigh Valley revealed a lot of duplication of institutions and overlapping of services. The existence of five colleges and three academies within eight miles of each other is the most striking example, but is not the only one. For example, each of the boroughs in the central Lehigh Valley supported separate political bureaucracies, fire departments, water works, and even separate road building crews. Furthermore, restricted by their proximity to one another, these cities could hardly expand. Boards of trade formed much more slowly than in Scranton, and during the 1890s fragmentation increased even more with the creation of the separate boroughs of West Bethlehem and South Allentown. Such urban dispersion reflected the presence of different social and religious groups; each one wanted to pass on its values to succeeding generations through a strong set of social institutions.[54]

The fragmented urbanization in the Lehigh Valley contrasts with what happened elsewhere. In the Lackawanna region, the multiregional center of New York, the regional capital of Scranton, and the seven subordinate coal towns all had separate functions. Because entrepreneurs, capital, and cities were more dispersed in the Lehigh Valley, its pattern of urban dominance and subordinance was different. Philadelphia, like New York to the north, started the first export and transportation companies in the Lehigh Valley. But no single city centralized entrepreneurs and capital in the region the way Scranton did in the Lackawanna region. Entrepreneurs in South Bethlehem, Bethlehem, Allentown, Easton, Mauch Chunk, and even Catasaqua had separate investments in iron companies and railroads throughout their region by 1880. The Lehigh Valley, then, had a multiregional center, several coregional centers, and several subordinate town.[55]

Philadelphia industrialists, like their counterparts in New York, invested in the export and the transportation industries of their outlying regions. In 1880, the Philadelphians controlled five iron companies in the Lehigh Valley and these were all heavily capitalized: They included three in Allentown, one in Catasaqua, and one in Phillipsburg. Philadelphians also partly owned Bethlehem Iron, the largest iron company in the region. In transportation, Philadelphians owned the L.C.&N. and held three directorships on the Lehigh Valley Railroad. They avoided the banking, small manufacturing, and services in the Lehigh Valley. As multiregional capitalists, they merely owned, or partly controlled, most of the biggest iron companies, canals, and railroads in the Lehigh region.

By the 1820s, multiregional centers were becoming an important part of industrial America as big city entrepreneurs began to transform their rural hinterland into satellite regions.[56] Canals and railroads were the key to this new economic order: they broke down the autonomy of interior regions and brought them into a national market system. With the completion of the Erie Canal in 1825, New York City became a multiregional center and Philadelphia, Boston, and Baltimore soon followed. Philadelphians started by bringing the Schuylkill coal region into their economic system. The Lehigh Valley soon followed as several Philadelphia companies, and one from as far away as Boston started iron foundries in Lehigh Valley towns in the 1840s and 1850s.

Just as Philadelphia tried to dominate exports in its interior regions, so it drew entrepreneurs from these regions during its early industrialization: Thomas

Dolan, a textile and public utilities titan; Samuel S. White, a dental manu-factuer; Thomas A. Scott, a president of the Pennsylvania Railroad; Richard D. Wood, an iron manufacturer; and Henry H. Houston, a railroad and real estate investor. The eventual migration of the Leisenring group from Mauch Chunk to Philadelphia also fits this pattern. Unlike mere regional centers, Philadelphia exerted a magnetic pull for entrepreneurs throughout America. For example, oil investors Joseph N. Pew and William L. Elkins brought fortunes to Phila-delphia from the Pennsylvania oil fields. Alexander J. Cassatt, a president of the Pennsylvania Railroad, came to the multiregional center from Pittsburgh. Iron industrialist Samuel V. Merrick and public utilities mogul Clarence Geist trekked to Philadelphia from remote towns in Maine and Indiana. Furthermore, Phila-delphia's increasing size almost guaranteed that it would produce large numbers of entrepreneurs locally.[57]

An illustration of the pull of the multiregional center is the migration of the Leisenring group from Mauch Chunk to Philadelphia. Like the Packer kinsmen, the Leisenrings eventually left Mauch Chunk for a city with a future. While in Mauch Chunk, the father and son team of John and Edward Leisenring owned iron companies in Virginia and Tennessee, and held directorships on two power-ful railroads in the Lehigh Valleys, the L.C.&N. and the Central Railroad of New Jersey. When young Edward became president of the L.C.&N. in 1893, he made the big move to Philadelphia. There, Leisenring bought a mansion formerly owned by Philadelphia gentleman Anthony J. Drexel on Philadelphia's Main Line. Leisenring's brother-in-law, John S. Wentz, later moved into the new family mansion and invested with Leisenring in coal and cement. Both men's sons, Edward Leisenring, Jr. and Daniel Wentz, lived in Philadelphia and kept on investing their family fortunes in Philadelphia's economic network. Their admission into the Philadelphia Club, the most exclusive social organization in the city, shows that they were social as well as economic leaders.[58]

Also from Mauch Chunk to Philadelphia came Leisenring cohorts Harry Cort-wright and Lafayette Lentz, Jr. Both men came from third generation Mauch Chunk families, both had economic or social ties with the Leisenrings, and both went to school in Philadelphia. In the multiregional center, Cortwright ran his family's Cortwright Coal Company while Lentz mainly invested in the coal and cement companies run by the Leisenrings. In Philadelphia, Lentz remained president of the Mauch Chunk Heat, Power, and Electric Light Company. In their social lives, Cortwright and Lentz joined the Philadelphia Country Club. So the Leisenrings, Cortwright, and Lentz seem to have transferred both wealth and status from a small town in the Lehigh Valley to the nearby multiregional center.[59]

Not all of the Leisenring capital left Mauch Chunk. As in the Packer group, a few Leisenring kinsmen remained there to control local industries and services. John Leisenring's son-in-law, Mahlon S. Kemmerer, lived next door to rival Asa Packer in Mauch Chunk and was president of the Mauch Chunk National Bank. John Leisenring's brother, Alexander, also stayed in Mauch Chunk and was president of the town's First National Bank.[60] Yet the migration of most Packers and Leisenrings from Mauch Chunk to South Bethlehem and Philadelphia ended Mauch Chunk's once powerful influence.

By 1920, Mauch Chunk was just another subordinate town in the Lehigh Valley, along with Coplay, Macungie, Catasaqua, Hokendauqua, Parryville, Lehighton, and Weissport. Lacking merchants, small businessmen, and entrepreneurs, these small towns stagnated because they couldn't raise the local capital to support an export. These towns were like the subordinate coal towns in the Lackawanna Valley: they all lacked local entrepreneurs. Of these Lehigh Valley towns, only Catasaqua ever developed multiple industries and local manufacturing. That was because Welshman David Thomas, superintendent of the Lehigh Crane Iron Company, raised capital from among fellow Welshmen and outside investors. Even Thomas, though, contributed to urban fragmentation in the region: he started an iron company three miles up the Lehigh River in Hokendauqua instead of in his home town.[61]

Describing dominance and subordinance doesn't fully reveal the competitiveness of the cities and towns in the Lehigh Valley. Local interests feuded even in the building of regional railroads. For example, the leaders of the L.C.&N. lobbied in the Pennsylvania legislature against the proposed Lehigh Valley Railroad. Most towns along the Lehigh River stood to benefit from a railroad, so Allentown politicians challenged the L.C.&N. in the state legislature in the 1840s and helped get a railroad charter, the future Lehigh Valley Railroad. However, when David Thomas of Catasaqua sought a similar charter to build the Catasaqua and Fogelsville Railroad, Allentown politicians objected. Taking an interest in beautification, they argued that such a railroad, which would bring iron ore directly to Catasaqua, not Allentown, would damage the farms of the Lehigh Valley. Since both the Lehigh Valley and the Catasaqua and Fogelsville railroads got chartered, most state legislators must have been responding to arguments for economic development instead of those protecting local interests. In any case, regional development in the Lehigh Valley resulted from conflict, not homogeneity.[62]

The endogamous Yankees of South Bethlehem, despite their wealth and power, rapidly disintegrated after 1880. The successful fathers couldn't produce successful sons. Asa Packer, the patriarch of the Yankees, had two sons, Robert A. and Harry, but both died young and childless in the 1880s. Albert Cleaver and Charles Skeer were also childless. Elisha Wilbur, Robert Sayre, and Garret Linderman all had sons, but they varied widely in talent. Possibly the two most successful were Rollin Wilbur, department head and director of the Lehigh Valley Railroad, and Robert Linderman, a bank president in his twenties and president of Bethlehem Iron in his thirties. Others, like Warren A. Wilbur and William H. Sayre II, had modest careers as lesser officials on the Lehigh Valley Railroad, and directors of a few small local companies. Another group included Garret B. Linderman, Jr., who went bankrupt in the 1890s, then spent time in jail, and left afterward for New Jersey. Ray Wilbur never seems to have been gainfully employed and, according to one of his relatives, he "never worked a day in his life." Still others lost economic influence because they pursued nonbusiness interests or left the Lehigh Valley. The Yankee women tended to marry within the Packer group and brought in few talented outsiders. Variations in talent and luck, then, combined with the weighty support for social institutions, helped to dissipate the colossal Yankee fortunes in just one generation after 1880.[63]

The Yankee founders of South Bethlehem were like the Yankee founders of Scranton: both groups fragmented after only one generation of industrial growth. Both groups produced presidents of regional railroads and major iron companies, but both also had members who went bankrupt, and others who lived off the family wealth instead of working to increase it. The Yankee elites in Scranton and South Bethlehem shared the same fate; but their contrasting philosophies of urban development made their impact on their cities quite different. The Scrantons settled a thinly populated region and created an open climate for economic and urban development. They secured wide city boundaries, they centralized industry and entrepreneurs within these boundaries, and they recruited future leaders from a variety of backgrounds on the basis of talent. The Packers, by contrast, entered an older region, long-settled by conflicting ethnic groups. When the Packer industrialists moved from Mauch Chunk to South Bethlehem, they were surrounded by bellicose strangers. To the Yankees *in this particular environment*, separating themselves and erecting their own schools and churches meant more to them than building a city. Safely insulated in their Fountain Hill enclave, they seem to have spent more time and money developing their various schools, churches, and hospitals than in developing their various iron and railroad industries. Whatever the case, in the 1890s, under Packer group direction, the Lehigh Valley Railroad nearly went bankrupt, and Bethlehem Iron fell helplessly behind other national steel companies. Social institutions would be their only legacy and glory.[64]

The lack of talent in the second and third generation of the Packer group must have been breath-taking. The legendary Asa Packer took sons, in-laws, and nephews alike into an array of business partnerships but the patriarch's skills could not be handed down. The credit reporter for the R.G. Dun Company observed that only "under his [Packers'] protection" was his nephew Elisha Wilbur able to succeed. The same credit agent also said that Garret Linderman "owes his position in life largely to the late Asa Packer, into whose family he married. He has taken advantage of the opportunities put in his way."[65] With no one to put opportunities in Linderman's way after Packer's death, and no one to protect Wilbur, the future of the Lehigh Valley Railroad and Bethlehem Iron became uncertain.

The fall of the Lehigh Valley Railroad from lucrative anthracite carrier to bankrupt and mismanaged line occurred under the supervision of Elisha Wilbur. When Asa Packer died in 1879, the Lehigh Valley was a profitable regional railroad and a blue chip stock on Wall Street. In his will Packer urged his descendants to operate the railroad; the deaths of his sons, Robert and Harry, left nephew Elisha P. Wilbur in charge in 1884. Wilbur was joined on the railroad's board of directors by kinsmen Garret Linderman, Robert Sayre, Robert Lamberton, and James Blakslee. Under Packer group direction the Lehigh Valley extended its track into New York, connecting Buffalo to New York City. This expansion left the railroad short of cash and equipment; instead of reducing the regular stock dividends, Wilbur leased the Lehigh Valley line to the Reading Railroad for a guaranteed five percent return on its stock. This ill-conceived strategy backfired because the Panic of 1893 ruined the Reading Railroad and left the Lehigh Valley line with no rent and little operating capital. While the Packer group contemplated a response to this turnabout, the Federal Railway Union approached Elisha Wilbur for recognition.[66]

In labor relations, Asa Packer was the first railroad owner to establish a matching pension fund for workers, but Wilbur lacked his uncle's finesse.[67] He "adamant[ly] refused to recognize the Federal Railway Union. His curt refusal . . . insured a reaction from [the] work force." When 2,500 laborers went on strike, Wilbur simply hired scabs in their places. However, "the newly hired crews, most of whom apparently had no railroad experience whatsoever, succeeded in severely damaging locomotives and equipment in short order." According to a recent historian of the Lehigh Valley line, these "disastrously inept replacement crews" caused over one million dollars damage in a series of accidents that claimed several lives and considerable property in the fires created by the collisions. Short in cash, equipment, and credibility, the Lehigh Valley line had a drop in the price of its stock. So the Packer group asked financier J.P. Morgan to help them rescue the line from bankruptcy. Morgan aid meant

Morgan control and "Elisha Wilbur, an unwelcome representative of the old order, stepped down from the presidency in July, 1897." The other members of the Packer group also resigned from the railroad's board of directors, which cut their ties with Asa Packer's creation. With one down and one to go, they turned their attention toward Bethlehem Iron.[68]

Led by Philadelphians and the Packer group, Bethlehem Iron had become intensely conservative by the 1880s. After Packer's death in 1879, the younger leaders single-mindedly produced rails even though (1) the market had become highly competitive and (2) they had the large expense of importing most of their iron ore from Cuba to South Bethlehem. They escaped a price squeeze in 1885 when, reluctantly, Bethlehem Iron shifted from making rails to making military ordnance, which commanded a higher price per ton of finished steel. Such an imaginative strategy, as one might expect, did not originate within the Packer group and they resisted it until declining profits on rails presented them with no alternative. In fact, "the directors, who had an aversion to any form of risk-taking, made this decision only after Bethlehem was virtually assured of a customer which would absorb its entire output—the United States Navy."[69]

The wise, if belated, switch from rails to forgings and armor plate possibly spared Bethlehem Iron imminent bankruptcy or absorption. In the 1880s, the intense price-cutting of Andrew Carnegie in the rail market led to the decline and fall of many other steel companies in positions similar to that of Bethlehem Iron. Given the conservatism of the Packer group by the 1880s, Bethlehem Iron was probably fortunate to have been the only bidder on its first government contract for ordnance in 1887. Other contracts were forthcoming and Bethlehem Iron "established a reputation for quality and reliability" if not for aggressiveness and efficiency. Regarding the last, its operations were so "wasteful and inefficient" that the company in 1898 hired Frederick W. Taylor, master of scientific management, to suggest ways of improving worker productivity. Yet the Packer group soon became hostile to Taylor's innovative ideas. Of one suggestion to reduce the number of workers handling raw materials, Taylor observed that the owners "did not wish me, as they said, to depopulate South Bethlehem." He further commented that "they owned all the houses in South Bethlehem and the company stores, and when they saw we [Taylor and his assistants] were cutting the labor force down to about one-fourth, they did not want it." A recent historian of Bethlehem Steel has further noted that the Packer group failed to

> adopt Taylor's other suggestions which promised to cut costs and increase productive efficiency. Those included increased job specialization, standardization of work procedures, and salary increases for key personnel (in order to avoid the wasted time and unnecessary expense of training re-

placements if the key men left the company for higher paying jobs else-where). The owners dismissed Taylor in April, 1901 . . .[70]

Surviving, then, on government contracts, Bethlehem Iron stumbled into the twentieth century—a profitable operation in spite of itself.

After 1880, the Packer group and Scranton's economic leaders shared the same fate. Neither group had the talent to make their urban industries profitable in America's increasingly national economy. Some of this failure can be explained by bad luck, some by the conservatism that afflicts sons of successful industrialists, and some by the different values that these sons held. In this last case, both the Packer and Scranton groups after 1880 seem to have cared more for their restrictive social institutions than for urban-economic development. Whereas the second generation of Scrantons lost the presidency of the L.I.&C. and the Scranton Steel Company, the second generation of Packers lost the Lehigh Valley Railroad and eventually Bethlehem Iron. The consequences of losing local ownership of the primary export soon became apparent. In 1901, the city of Scranton lost its largest industry, as New York owners moved the renamed Lackawanna Iron and Steel Company to a more cost efficient site in Buffalo.[71] South Bethlehem was a luckier city, though, and escaped a comparable fate when Charles Schwab, an imaginative entrepreneur of the highest order, took over and transformed stodgy Bethlehem Iron.

Born in Loretto, Pennsylvania in 1862, the Roman Catholic Schwab began work in the steel industry at age seventeen for a dollar a day. Rising rapidly in the Carnegie Steel Works in Pittsburgh, Schwab became Carnegie's right hand man and president of the company in 1897. When Carnegie Steel became the centerpiece of the U.S. Steel merger in 1901, the talented Schwab became the billion dollar company's first president. At U.S. Steel Schwab courted publicity and undertook controversial private business ventures, which included the purchase of Bethlehem Iron. After a lengthy lampooning by the press for his public and private behavior (not for his unquestioned managerial skills), Schwab resigned from U.S. Steel in 1904. He was angered by his public treatment (he had even been forsaken by Carnegie), and turned to his holdings in Bethlehem Iron with a determination to prove himself and "make the Bethlehem plant the greatest armor plate and gun factory in the world."[72]

Under Schwab's direction, Bethlehem Iron was transformed into a major American corporation. According to Schwab, "I backed Bethlehem with every dollar I could borrow." This backing included buying new branch plants and closing unprofitable ones, getting new contracts by selling aggressively, and reorganizing the company as Bethlehem Steel. Planning for the future, Schwab bought large tracts of land for the company east of South Bethlehem. He also bought or leased more ore land and mechanized the company's Cuban iron fields to spur production there. "Unlike the earlier owners of Bethlehem, Schwab understood the necessity of securing sources of raw materials long before these materials would be needed."[73]

After reorganization, Schwab wanted to diversify his company and challenge U.S. Steel. To do this, he began making rails and moved Bethlehem Steel away from its dependence on government contracts. Schwab adopted open hearth technology because it produced better rails than the Bessemer system did. As historian Robert Hessen notes:

> U.S. Steel, the nation's largest rail producer did not follow Schwab's lead; it would have had to replace its Bessemer facilities with open hearth equipment. Being a late starter, Bethlehem enjoyed a clear advantage; with no heavy investment in obsolete equipment to protect, it could adopt the newest and most efficient technological processes.[74]

Schwab's reorganization of the Cuban ore mines also improved Bethlehem's competitive position at the expense of U.S. Steel.

> Cuban ore was richer in iron and lower in phosphorous than was the Mesabi range ore used by U.S. Steel. It also had another advantage; it contained large amounts of nickel, so that Bethlehem could produce nickel steel at no extra cost. For a ton of iron Bethlehem's cost was $4.31; U.S. Steel's was $7.10.[75]

Schwab even made greater headway against U.S. Steel by "risking his fortune and the future of his company" in the development of structural steel. Schwab's attention here was fixed on an innovation to make steel beams directly from an ingot as a single section instead of riveting smaller beams together. Useful for constructing "buildings, bridges, or other structures," Edward Grey wrote that his invention provided "the greatest possible strength with the least dead weight and at the lowest cost." An enthusiastic Schwab wanted to market Grey's product in 1907 but tight money during the panic of that year threatened Schwab's access to credit. Announcing that "if we are going bust, we will go bust big," Schwab, like the Scrantons and Asa Packer before him, staked his fortune on a high-risk innovation. To raise the needed $5 million Schwab buttonholed several wealthy investors for large personal loans and then, through remarkable salesmanship, persuaded his major suppliers, the Lehigh Valley and the Reading Railroads, to give him credit on deliveries of the new steel. Schwab got several big contracts for the "Bethlehem beam": the Chase National Bank in New York, the Metropolitan Life Insurance Company in New York, and the opera house in Chicago were among them. This more durable and cheaper beam quickly became Schwab's "most successful innovation" and he captured a large share of the structural steel market from U.S. Steel.[76]

When the daring Schwab snatched markets from the more conservative management at U.S. Steel, he created prosperity and city growth throughout the Lehigh Valley. From 1905 to 1920, Bethlehem Steel's labor force doubled every five years. By contrast, at U.S. Steel one officer noted that "works standing idle have deteriorated . . . the men are disheartened and a certain amount of apathy exists." By the 1920s, then, the chagrined leaders at U.S. Steel secretly began making Bethlehem beams; as an official there observed, "the tonnage lost on account of competition with Bethlehem . . . is . . . ever increasing . . . we are obliged to sell at unusually low prices in order to compete." Schwab's entrepreneurship had become Bethlehem's gain and U.S. Steel's problem.[77]

Within a decade after taking over Bethlehem Steel, Schwab's aggressiveness, talent, and luck had transformed the corporation as well as the city. Even before World War I, Bethlehem Steel had become the second largest steel company in America. The *New York Times* praised Schwab's enterprise as "possibly the most efficient, profitable self-contained steel plant in the country." By 1920, Bethlehem Steel employed 20,000 persons in the central Lehigh Valley and was among the larger corporations in the world. In 1922, with unintended irony, Bethlehem Steel absorbed the Lackawanna Steel Corporation, the company that launched the Scranton experiment seventy years earlier.[78]

Schwab's innovativeness clashed with the Packer group's cautiousness right from the start. As one historian said, "many of the veteran Bethlehem executives preferred the old, pre-Taylor and pre-Schwab ways of doing things. They resented Schwab, he was an intruder." Soon after arriving in South Bethlehem, Schwab ousted the inbred Packer group from authority. In the new president's remarkable words, "I selected fifteen young men right out of the mill and made them my partners." Two of these "partners" were Eugene G. Grace, the son of a sea captain, and Archibald Johnston, a Moravian. They later became presidents of Bethlehem Steel. Unlike the Packer group, Schwab recruited executives on talent and proven ability, not on kinship.[79]

As Bethlehem Steel's land came to be measured in square miles, the problems of operating small separate boroughs became magnified. Forfeiting economies of scale, each borough provided its own modern fire fighting equipment, public schools, and good roads. The support for different colleges and academies in each borough compounded the duplication, and officials at Bethlehem Steel received the bite of large taxes without the salve of efficient services. In the 1890s Bethlehem absorbed West Bethlehem. In the early 1900s, as Bethlehem Steel expanded outside the city limits and urban consolidation gained momentum, South Bethlehem absorbed the township of Northampton Heights even though the people there "did not wish to help shoulder the big borough debt of this place."[80]

The leaders of South Bethlehem and Bethlehem created social bonds between their boroughs that they later bridged to promote unity. For example, after Schwab "took hold of Bethlehem [Steel]," Moravians rose to positions as vice-president and treasurer; concurrently, a graduate of Lehigh University had become president of Moravian College. Schwab and others strongly backed the formation of the Bethlehem Bach Choir and the Lehigh Valley Symphony Orchestra, both of which brought together talented musicians in both Bethlehems. Commenting on the advantages of combining both boroughs, one observer noted that "with a united Bethlehem under a city charter the advantages are many, the expenses should be less, receipts larger, and improvements greater and the city politically in a commanding position."[81]

Economic consolidation in the Lehigh Valley preceded the political unification of the two Bethlehems. The economies of scale in large organizations, and the absence of political restrictions against it, led to the creation in 1901 of the Bethlehem Consolidated Gas Company, which united gas service in the two boroughs. Shortly thereafter, the formation of a South Bethlehem and Allentown trolley and an Allentown and Bethlehem turnpike shows the further centralization of services in the region. The corporate leaders of economic consolidation became the political leaders of city consolidation. To unite the two Bethlehems these centralizers formed voluntary associations (the Chamber of Commerce, the Rotary Club of the Bethlehems, and the General Committee for the Consolidation of the Bethlehems). Eugene Grace, the president of Bethlehem Steel, stated in 1916 that "we are employing twenty-five thousand [people]. You would have the third largest city in Pennsylvania if we had the facilities." The next year the United States fought in World War I, which led to a consolidation of government agencies; this seemed to mobilize sentiment further in the Lehigh Valley for urban consolidation as well. Finally, after a referendum in 1918, the two Bethlehems became one city of almost eighteen square miles. The first mayor of the new city of Bethlehem was Archibald Johnston, the Moravian vice-president of Bethlehem Steel. Bethlehem at last had a more open environment and wider city limits.[82]

By 1920, the centralizing forces in the Lehigh Valley had transformed much of the earlier fragmentation. The data in table 8.4 show how Bethlehem and Allentown gained on Scranton in population. In fact, Allentown and Bethlehem emerged as coregional centers in the Lehigh Valley; Philadelphia and New York City shared multiregional dominance; and Mauch Chunk and Easton dropped to being subordinate towns.

Ethnic groups and entrepreneurs both influenced city growth in the Lehigh Valley, and they did so in different ways. Groups of Lutheran and Reformed Germans, Moravians, and Scotch-Irish Presbyterians settled the towns of Allen-

TABLE 8.4. Population and Percentage Growth of Scranton, Bethlehem, and Allentown from 1880 to 1930

City	1880 Population	1890 Population	1890 Percentage Growth	1900 Population	1900 Percentage Growth	1910 Population	1910 Percentage Growth	1920 Population	1920 Percentage Growth	1930 Population	1930 Percentage Growth
Scranton	45,850	75,215	64.0	102,026	35.6	129,867	27.3	137,783	6.1	143,433	4.1
Allentown	18,063	25,228	39.7	35,416	40.4	51,913	46.6	73,502	41.6	92,563	25.9
Bethlehem	10,118	19,823	95.9	23,999	21.1	32,810	36.7	50,358	53.5	57,892	15.0

SOURCES: *Statistical Abstract of the United States, 1942* (Washington, D.C., 1943), pp. 26, 28; *Statistical Abstract of the United States, 1923* (Washington, D.C., 1924), pp. 42, 44.

town, Bethlehem, and Easton long before industrial development became possible. These ethnic groups distrusted each other and each established separate academies, colleges, and churches in their cities to pass on their values to future generations. The scarce financial resources lavished on these institutions sapped the Lehigh Valley's capital need for economic growth; so Philadelphians made the region's first major investments in canals, railroads, and iron. So did a group of Connecticut Yankees, who got rich in Mauch Chunk when they founded the Lehigh Valley Railroad. Mountainous terrain kept Mauch Chunk from expanding so the Yankees migrated to a new city—South Bethlehem. Surrounded by conflicting ethnic groups they, too, established their own academy and college and this further fragmented city growth in the Lehigh Valley. By the 1890s, some unifying threads began to tie together the diverse social groups in the several competing towns in the region. Some businessmen promoted city consolidation because it would streamline urban services. Bethlehem Steel became a leading centralizer when Charles Schwab built it into a major national corporation. Schwab also recruited a heterogeneous group of leaders on the basis of talent, not ethnicity or family, and this further broke down ethnic loyalties in the region. The centralizers had united the two Bethlehems into one regional capital by 1920. In the Lehigh Valley, Bethlehem and Allentown became coregional centers and Philadelphia the multiregional center.

9
Conclusion

Comparing Pennsylvania's Lackawanna and Lehigh valleys helps to clarify the role of entrepreneurship in the creation of industrial America. Both regions evolved slowly until rapid development of the indigenous coal and iron ore became possible in the 1840s. The establishment of anthracite coal as a marketable fuel spurred transportation and technological improvements that linked the industrial Lackawanna and Lehigh valleys to New York City, Pennsylvania, and the outside world. Scranton and Carbondale emerged as the leading contenders for dominance in the Lackawanna Valley; Easton, Bethlehem, Allentown, and Mauch Chunk vied for industrial supremacy in the Lehigh Valley; and Wilkes-Barre triumphed early as the regional center in the adjacent Wyoming Valley.

The quality of the entrepreneurship present in the cities and towns in these three regions seems to explain urbanization more convincingly than the environmental determinism of so many social scientists. The major cities did not necessarily emerge in locations ideally suited for growth. Nor did the natural resource base of either region necessarily determine its export. In the Lackawanna Valley, for example, the Scrantons created their city in the 1840s from exports of nails and then rails, even though they had to import some of the iron ore into the region. In the Lehigh Valley, Bethlehem skyrocketed to success after 1900, when the leaders of Bethlehem Steel challenged the industrial leadership of U.S. Steel by creating new steel products from coal and iron imported into the Lehigh region. In both of these cases, superb entrepreneurship overcame the drawbacks of less-than-perfect location.

Central place theory, the cornerstone of much geographic analysis, simply cannot predict urban location in these two regions. Cities of similar sizes were not equally spaced and did not have equal market areas. In the Lackawanna Valley, urbanization was heavily concentrated in the coal producing core of the region. In fact, by 1880 a series of small coal towns had almost linked Scranton and Carbondale into a sixteen-mile stretch of continuous population. The agricultural hinterland of the region, by stark contrast, had a few widely

TABLE 9.1.   Environmental Advantages of Seven Cities in the Lackawanna, Lehigh, and Wyoming Regions

Initial Advantage and Excellent Location	Initial Advantage and Good Location	No Initial or Locational Advantage
Easton Carbondale	[a]Allentown [a]Wilkes-Barre	[a]Scranton [a]Bethlehem Mauch Chunk

[a]Regional capital

separated towns. In the Lehigh Valley, Bethlehem and Allentown became the largest cities in the region even though they were situated right next to each other on the Lehigh River. In fact, few towns formed at all in the region that were not on the Lehigh River.

Perhaps more surprising is that those settlements with initial and locational advantages were often not the ones that blossomed into large urban centers. The information in table 9.1 shows the lack of connection between early formation and eventual success. Of the first three cities in the Lackawanna, Lehigh, and Wyoming valleys, only Wilkes-Barre became a regional center. Scranton and Bethlehem had neither initial nor locational advantages, yet both cities became regional capitals. Such an outcome does not mean that strategic locations and early leads are irrelevant to city growth. It just means that cities need more than environmental advantages to become regional centers.

Another model that some geographers use relates the stage of industrial development to urban growth. In this interpretation those cities that form during an epoch of new technological innovation are said to have a decisive edge in the competition for industry and population. Those cities that evolve before an economic transformation in their regions, become committed to early technology and can't make the switch needed to become regional centers. In this view, a city that emerges during a change in its region's export has a greater chance for success than do older towns nearby. The lineup in table 9.2 shows how wrong this view is for explaining urban growth in the Lackawanna, Lehigh, and Wyoming valleys. Of the three cities that were established almost concurrently with coal and iron development, only Scranton became a regional capital. The older cities of Wilkes-Barre, Allentown, and Bethlehem grew more rapidly than did the newer industrial towns of Carbondale and Mauch Chunk. So early leads during new epochs of industrialization do not explain urbanization in the Lackawanna, Lehigh, or Wyoming region.

If not the environmental determinism of the geographers and economists, then what does explain which cities triumphed in these coal and iron regions?

TABLE 9.2.   Stage of Formation of Seven Cities in the Lackawanna, Lehigh, and Wyoming Regions

Preindustrial Towns	Industrial Towns
Easton	Mauch Chunk
[a]Wilkes-Barre	Carbondale
[a]Allentown	[a]Scranton
[a]Bethlehem	

[a]Regional capital

No single cause can explain all the complexities of regional urbanization. Yet, the varying performance of urban entrepreneurs may be the starting point to a fuller description of city growth. Entrepreneurs, both collectively and as individuals, played a decisive role in creating and preventing growth in several of the cities under investigation.

Those cities with the largest populations and the most rapid rates of growth seem to have had astonishingly venturesome economic leaders. These entrepreneurs displayed a "creative response" to urban industrial development in a variety of similar ways. First (and possibly foremost), they established and maintained local control of their primary export and protected its competitiveness in national markets. Second, they created an open environment for investing by attracting and accepting newcomer capitalists from other towns in the region. Third, they unified most entrepreneurs behind the political and economic goals of wide city limits and planned industrial growth. Fourth, they had the flexibility to adjust to the demands of new stages of industrialization. In the Lackawanna and Lehigh valleys, those urban capitalists who did these four things well created regional capitals.

Table 9.3 separates cities on a scale of entrepreneurship based on the performance of their urban elites in promoting urban-economic development. On one end of this "entrepreneurial continuum" are Scranton and Bethlehem, both of which overcame many obstacles to become regional capitals. At the other end of this scale are Carbondale and Mauch Chunk, both of which had a crippling emigration of talent and capital. In between these extremes, the performance of entrepreneurs in other towns was mixed. In Wilkes-Barre and Allentown, capitalists loyally invested in local industries, but they operated in relatively closed environments and their cautious homogeneous elites failed to respond creatively to economic opportunity.

The tenacity and talent of Scranton's founding fathers shows how capable and loyal some urban leaders can be. To become a regional capital, Scranton had to overcome mild locational disadvantages and Carbondale's head start.

TABLE 9.3.   Scale of Performance of Entrepreneurs in Seven Cities in the Lackawanna, Lehigh, and Wyoming Regions

Excellent Performance	Mixed Performance	Poor Performance
[a]Scranton (1850-1880) [a]Bethlehem (1880-1920)	[a]Wilkes-Barre [a]Allentown	Carbondale Mauch Chunk Easton

[a]Regional capital

The key to success was the Scranton family's creation of a locally owned iron industry—largely from ore imported into the region. With some imported iron the Scrantons completed the first domestic rail contract in the country. In the early years of the town's existence, the perservering Scranton group held a controlling interest in their iron works and a part interest in the first local railroad. They actively recruited other businessmen to Scranton. When the newcomers prospered so did the Scrantons, and they all plowed industrial profits into more expansion and growth. Subordinating ethnic, religious, and personal tensions as much as possible, Scranton's economic leaders achieved the political goal of planned urban expansion during their city's early industrial growth. Inventors flourished and some started companies in Scranton to market their inventions. By 1880, Scranton had wide city limits, a ten-year tax exemption for new industries, and a strong board of trade to mobilize local business for future growth.

The Scrantons defied their environment when they created a major industrial city. Unfortunately, no laws of inevitability existed to help them keep their superior urban position. Scranton began to falter in its second stage of industrialization, which roughly lasted from the 1880s to the 1920s. Many of its larger industries were absorbed by emerging corporations during these years. Scranton's early industrial elite fragmented after 1880 and the city's undivided commitment to economic growth, a force that launched this community, waned before devisive loyalties to social clubs, ethnic schools, and political parties. By the 1920s, leaders in Scranton could not mobilize local support to protect their coal industry from labor strikes and from the competition of other fuels. They also could not bring enough new industries to town to compensate for the decline of anthracite. In short, Scranton's economic leaders in 1920 could not meet the new and difficult challenges of its second stage of urban development.

Bethlehem, like Scranton in its early stages, benefited from remarkably able entrepreneurs. Unlike Scranton, Bethlehem's urban-industrial success came during the city's second stage of industrialization, from 1880 to 1920. Also unlike in Scranton, individual entrepreneurs, rather than a large group of them, spearheaded Bethlehem's economic development.

In Bethlehem, the conservatism of an older ethnically homogeneous city was eventually transformed by two spectacular entrepreneurs—Asa Packer and Charles Schwab. From the 1740s to the 1840s Bethlehem was an exclusive Moravian town literally closed to outsiders. When Asa Packer, the Connecticut Episcopalian, selected South Bethlehem as his industrial playground, the Moravians and the Packer newcomers furtively viewed one another from opposite sides of the Lehigh River. Despite occasional joint investments, the two settlements were, in the words of a contemporary, "two different worlds." The Packer group and the Moravians had remarkably endogamous marriage patterns. Much of this inbreeding must have resulted from a narrow socialization process, which restricted their contacts with outsiders. Both groups lavished millions of dollars and considerable time erecting and maintaining four colleges, among other local institutions, to promote their cultural attitudes. Giving some time to their industries the Packer group recruited leaders for Bethlehem Iron and the Lehigh Valley Railroad almost entirely from among their kinsmen. When the anointed descendants failed to match Asa Packer's competence, the future urbanization of the central Lehigh Valley was at stake.

The emergence of Charles Schwab in 1904, as president of a reorganized Bethlehem Steel, was the infusion of talent needed to unify fragmented social groups in the two boroughs for urban development. A former president of U.S. Steel, the Roman Catholic Schwab had astonishing entrepreneurial skills. He upgraded Bethlehem Steel from a small ordnance producer to a diversified international corporation surpassed in its field only by U.S. Steel. In doing this, he recruited on the basis of merit "partners" of various backgrounds right out of the factory. He countered restrictive social traditions with openness; he countered stodgy business practices with aggressiveness; he countered overlapping urban services by campaigning to consolidate the two Bethlehems. In short, Schwab and his motley band of entrepreneurs purposefully fought and overcame the exclusivity imposed by the inbred Packer group and the entrenched Moravians. The serendipitous intervention of Asa Packer and Charles Schwab, then, twice transformed Bethlehem from a small closed city into an open expanding one.

Carbondale and Mauch Chunk represent two types of towns at the extreme negative end on the scale of entrepreneurship. Here for various reasons, capitalists showed little commitment to local urban growth. In fact, both towns had a paralyzing emigration of talent that brought urban growth to a virtual standstill. In Mauch Chunk, such lack of loyalty can be explained by the physical limitations on the town's expansion. In this sense environment did shape urban development. The venture capital of the Asa Packer group could find no outlet in the mountainous surroundings of Mauch Chunk so it eventually built factories, schools, a church, and a hospital in South Bethlehem. Carbondale's fate was similar to that of Mauch Chunk, but for different reasons. As a company town of the D&H, Carbondale had outside control of its major industries right from the start. Few entrepreneurs emerged in this setting; of those who did, most eventually migrated to the regional center of Scranton, where capital invested in land or enterprise realized a greater return. Carbondale and Mauch Chunk, then, occupy positions toward the negative end of the scale of entrepreneurial performance. From the standpoint of the individual towns, its leaders can hardly do worse than taking their money and leaving. And when they did, Mauch Chunk and Carbondale, the first industrial towns in their regions, lost all hope of becoming key industrial centers.

The quality of entrepreneurship in most towns fell somewhere in between that of Scranton and Bethlehem, on one hand, and Carbondale and Mauch Chunk on the other. Wilkes-Barre is one example. It had a conservative group of economic leaders, but they were tenaciously loyal to their city. By their cautiousness they lost many chances for city growth; by their loyalty they created others. As the oldest city in the anthracite fields, Wilkes-Barre developed an indigenous business elite bound by kinship ties and by investments in real estate, urban services, and later coal. This English-stock Episcopalian elite was relatively closed to immigrant newcomers; in fact, in Wilkes-Barre's leading social club, where investment schemes were hatched, all members were kinsmen. These homogeneous capitalists did start a variety of local coal companies and these were very successful. Yet by failing to incorporate surrounding land they locked themselves into a town of less than five square miles. The old-stock elite seems to have wanted to keep their political control over a smaller city: to widen the city limits would threaten their political dominance. Finally, Wilkes-Barre's economic leaders avoided manufacturing, so this avenue of wealth was left to the younger, poorer, and more venturesome town of Scranton. Generating a modest amount of urban development in a relatively closed environment, Wilkes-Barreans had steady growth in the nineteenth century; their entrepreneurial performance was mixed.

Also falling near the center on a scale of entrepreneurship is the city of Allentown. Heavily German, Allentown seems to have had a cautious but shrewd business elite. During the 1800s, the ethnic town produced many small independent businessmen, but few millionaires. When the 1840s brought the alluring possibility of industrial conquest in iron and coal, local entrepreneurs declined to take the risk; yet they helped talk Philadelphians into establishing three iron companies in Allentown. Unlike Carbondale, Allentown had a mixture of local and outside ownership in its export industries. Also unlike in Carbondale, Allentown businessmen eagerly provided services to the increased population in the central Lehigh Valley. Yet when they took the small risks they passed up the chance to build a railroad in their industrializing region, leaving that task to the venturesome Asa Packer. When Packer scoured the Lehigh Valley for a location for his industrial projects, the relatively closed German-stock elite in Allentown apparently ignored him. They didn't even try to bring him to their city. They seemed more interested in establishing three local colleges, to preserve and transmit their cultural heritage, than in recruiting the Yankee Packer, who went to South Bethlehem instead. Allentown's ethnic entrepreneurs, then, were hardly daring; but they were not deserters either, and the abundance of small businessmen present helps explain the city's steady urbanization. For slightly different reasons, then, entrepreneurs in Allentown compare in performance with those in Wilkes-Barre.

At the negative end of the scale of entrepreneurship is Easton. By far the oldest town in the Lehigh Valley, Easton developed a very conservative business elite largely tied to the Philadelphia trade. Its location at the fork of the Delaware and Lehigh Rivers made Easton an ideal place for shipping goods to Philadelphia. As a regional service and flour milling center, Easton's predominantly Scotch-Irish merchants grew prosperous and gave their town a middle-class aura. These Scotch-Irishmen, with a sprinkling of Germans, seem to have been satisfied as merchants and middlemen; they saw no need in the 1840s to risk a switch to industrial investments. Some actually opposed the L.C.&N. coal trade flowing down the Lehigh River right into their town. They had the money and location, they lacked only the desire. Analyzing their behavior it becomes clear that they wanted to preserve and transmit their cultural values through their Presbyterian church and Lafayette University more than they wanted to invest in the urban growth of Easton. Anxious contemporaries agonized as Easton fell to second and then to third largest city in the Lehigh Valley. But the city fathers cared little about growth. The river trade brought these conservative men a comfortable livelihood and their Presbyterian-related university was a more satisfying legacy for them than any factory could have been.

These seven cities just described represent different points on a scale of entrepreneurial performance. As archetypes they show the varying strategies taken by urban elites to secure economic development. The capitalists in other towns in the Lackawanna and Lehigh valleys can also be evaluated. The failure of these other towns to become cities indicates the low performance of their few economic leaders. Dundaff, especially, with its emigration of talent and wealth resembles the negative pattern of entrepreneurship in Carbondale and Mauch Chunk. The commercial towns of Towanda, Montrose, and Honesdale also lost capitalists to Scranton, but these boroughs had well-established communities by the 1840s, so they at least survived the losses. Pittston and the coal villages between Scranton and Carbondale, like the iron towns west of Allentown, were established after the 1840s; as company towns they had few local capitalists. One minor exception is Catasaqua, an L.C.&N. community, where a local kinship group emerged and started a few small industries that led to some urban growth. Most of these company towns, however, produced few entrepreneurs, and those who did emerge usually left for the regional or multiregional center. Understandably, therefore, these towns stagnated and rate low in entrepreneurship.

The effectiveness of entrepreneurs helps explain which cities grew and which didn't in the Lackawanna and Lehigh regions. This does not mean that I want to substitute an entrepreneurial determinism of American urbanization for the environmental determinism that now exists. I merely want to say that calibre of economic leadership explains the development of cities in these two industrial regions more than environmental factors do. Both are important and they are sometimes hard to separate. Entrepreneurship and environment probably work together often, but in Scranton and South Bethlehem local entrepreneurs created regional capitals from hamlets that lacked either an early lead or a superb location. Carbondale and Easton, by contrast, never grew much; yet both were the first towns in their regions, both had excellent locations, and both had good transportation to outside markets before Scranton and South Bethlehem even existed. When entrepreneurial performance was mixed or inconclusive, as in the cases of Allentown and Wilkes-Barre, environmental factors might have been important in deciding success.

If entrepreneurs are so critical in shaping city growth, then learning how different urban elites form is a worthwhile task for historians. Defining economic leaders as those who hold positions on boards of directors may not be a perfect technique, but it is justifiable and provides clear-cut urban elites. On one hand, Wilkes-Barre and South Bethlehem had conservative elites who recruited economic leaders on the basis of kinship ties. On the other hand, nineteenth-century Scranton and early twentieth-century Bethlehem had venturesome elites and both groups usually recruited economic leaders on the basis of talent. But there is more to it than that.

The cautious leadership in Wilkes-Barre and South Bethlehem evolved in the same way. Both elites were homogeneous in social composition (heavily English-stock and Episcopalian) and both elites operated in rather closed environments. That is, both groups secluded themselves in distinctive neighborhoods, married primarily within their own group, and then recruited future urban leaders mainly on the basis of their kinship ties and their social background. Often distrustful of innovation, the Wilkes-Barre elite was slow to invest in local manufacturing and slower to create a local board of trade. Their most important social club actually required a kinship tie to a member for acceptance. Their Packer counterparts in South Bethlehem resisted marketing and organizational innovations in their management of Bethlehem Iron and the Lehigh Valley Railroad. They even shut down both of these industries and sacrificed millions of dollars in trade rather than negotiate with strikers. Not surprisingly, the Packer group lost total control of these two industries by the early 1900s. In Wilkes-Barre, the failure to diversify the local economy contributed to a dramatic loss of urban population when the anthracite industry declined after 1920.

The venturesome economic leaders in early Scranton and a consolidated Bethlehem also had much in common. Scranton's gentry was heterogeneous and included many rags-to-riches immigrants. Their families were important in establishing industry but no kinship group dominated Scranton's social or economic life. Scranton was open to businessmen of all types and success came to those who were talented and lucky, not just those with particular social backgrounds. An active board of trade helped unify the city's various entrepreneurs behind the goal of economic development. To promote growth and attract talent, the board agreed to allow all industrial newcomers a tax break, even if it meant increased local taxes and more local competition. Bethlehem Steel, under the guidance of Charles Schwab, recruited leaders in a similar way. After ousting the inbred Packer group in the early 1900s, the Roman Catholic Schwab chose fifteen partners "right out of the factory" on the basis of merit. His top henchmen included the son of a sea captain (Eugene Grace) and a Moravian (Archibald Johnston), both of whom Schwab rewarded for their proven talent, not for their social background. Scranton and Bethlehem may have been successful, then, because they were open and because they recruited leaders on their basis of merit.

The experience of Scranton and Bethlehem also shows that the quality of urban leadership in a city can change from generation to generation. Within fifteen years after the arrival of Charles Schwab in South Bethlehem, two diverse boroughs had been united and the work force at Bethlehem Steel had been more than quadrupled. In Scranton the story was reversed. The venturesome spirit that inspired the city's founders and early leaders did not persist into the 1900s. Most of the entrepreneurs of early Scranton could not hand down their creative spirits or their talents to their offspring. Few sons of Scranton's economic leaders of 1880 succeeded their fathers as corporate officers. Some led lives of leisure, others left the city, and still others went into business but lacked the talent to succeed. Various migrants to Scranton after 1880 helped to maintain some entrepreneurial energy, but apparently more talent was lost over the years than was gained. By the 1920s, Scranton simply lacked imaginative leaders with an overriding commitment to their city. They seem to have cared more about the particular welfare of their social institutions than they did for the general welfare of their coal industry and their city as a whole. Many people in Scranton took growth for granted. As one contemporary lamented, "we just never thought the coal boom would end." Whatever the case, when the coal boom did end, with labor strikes and competition from other fuels greasing its slide, Scranton joined Wilkes-Barre in a long unfamiliar stagnation.

A good way to learn what causes urbanization is to isolate a region and compare cities that grew rapidly with those that stagnated. Having done that, my conclusion is this: a splendid location helps but splendid entrepreneurs help even more—at least they did in the Lackawanna and Lehigh regions. The example of Scranton shows that keen entrepreneurship is possible, but is hard to maintain from generation to generation. The goals for a rapidly growing city—a locally owned export, an open environment for investment, and spacious urban boundaries—seem to persist but the means to achieve them (not to mention the personnel available) change over time. For a city to stay on top it needs flexible leaders with imagination and vision. No city (or country) is destined to greatness by its environmental advantages or the cultural traits of its citizens. Great cities (and countries) are created; they endure only with an abundance of talent and luck.

Notes

Introduction

1. Robert P. Thomas, "The Automobile Industry and Its Tycoon," *Explorations in Entrepreneurial History* 6 (Winter 1969): 139-57; and Harold C. Livesay, "Entrepreneurial Persistence through the Bureaucratic Age," *Business History Review* 51 (Winter 1977): 415-43.

2. Edward H. Carr, *What Is History?* (New York: Alfred A. Knopf, 1961), pp. 67, 68.

3. The quotation is from Thomas, "The Automobile Industry and Its Tycoon."

4. The classic theoretical essay here is Eric E. Lampard, "American Historians and the Study of Urbanization," *American Historical Review* 67 (October 1961): 49-61. On regional development see Robert Baldwin, "Patterns of Development in Newly Settled Regions," *Manchester School of Economics and Social Studies* 24 (May 1956): 161-79; Douglass North, "Location Theory and Regional Economic Growth," *Journal of Political Economy* 63 (1955): 243-58; Harold Innis, *The Fur Trade in Canada: An Introduction to Canadian Economic History* (New Haven, 1930); and *Problems of Staple Production in Canada* (Toronto, 1933). My operational definition of region is different from that of either North, Innis, or Baldwin, but my thinking has been strongly influenced by their varied descriptions of export and region.

5. W. David Lewis, "The Early History of the Lackawanna Iron and Coal Company: A Study in Technological Adaptation," *Pennsylvania Magazine of History and Biography* 96 (October 1972): 424-68.

6. Two recent exceptions are Roberta B. Miller, *City and Hinterland: A Case Study of Urban Growth and Regional Development* (Westport, Conn.: Greenwood Press, 1979); and Robert Doherty, *Society and Power: Five New England Towns, 1800-1860* (Amherst: University of Massachusetts Press, 1977). Two useful regional analyses of migration are Michael P. Conzen, "Local Migration Systems in Nineteenth-Century Iowa," *Geographical Review* (July 1974): 339-61; and John Modell, "The Peopling of a Working-Class Ward: Reading, Pennsylvania, 1850," *Journal of Social History* 5 (1971): 71-95.

7. The first two studies to outline systematically and test central place theory are Walter Christaller, *The Central Places of Southern Germany* (Englewood Cliffs, N.J.: Prentice-Hall, 1966); and August Lösch, *The Economics of Location* (New Haven: Yale University Press, 1954).

8. Two articles that have helped my understanding of central place theory are G. William Skinner, "Marketing and Social Structure in Rural China: Part I," *Journal of Asian Studies* 24 (November 1964): 3-43; and Carol A. Smith, "Market Articulation and Economic Stratification in Western Guatemala," *Food Research Institute Studies in Agricultural Economics, Trade and Development* 11 (1972): 203-33.

9. Brian J.L. Berry, *Geography of Market Centers and Retail Distribution* (Englewood Cliffs, N.J.: Prentice-Hall, 1967).

10. Allan Pred, *Behavior and Location: Foundations for a Geographic Dynamic Location Theory* (Lund, Sweden: Gleerup, 1967), pp. 10-11.

11. Brian J.L. Berry and William I. Garrison, "Alternate Explanation of Urban Rank-Size Relationships," *Annals of the Association of American Geographers* 48 (March 1958): 83-91; Brian J.L. Berry, "Cities as Systems within Systems of Cities," in John Friedmann and William Alonzo, *Regional Development and Planning: A Reader* (Cambridge, Mass.: MIT Press, 1964), pp. 116-37; Ronald C. Tobey, "How Urbane is the Urbanite? An Historical Model of the Urban Hierarchy and the Social Motivation of the Service Classes," *Historical Methods Newsletter* 7 (September 1974): 259-74.

12. Allan R. Pred, "Industrialization, Initial Advantage and American Metropolitan Growth," *Geographical Review* 55 (1965): 158-85; J.G. Williamson and J.A. Swanson, "The Growth of Cities in the American North East, 1820-1920," *Explorations in Entrepreneurial History* 4 (1966), supplement.

13. For a useful summary of the literature on regional economic development (by a geographer), see David Ward, *Cities and Immigrants* (New York, 1971), pp. 11-49.

14. Pred, *Behavior and Location*, p. 6.

15. Schwartz and Skinner are quoted in Frank S. Meyer, *In Defense of Freedom: A Conservative Credo* (Chicago: Henry Regnery Press, 1962), pp. 30-31.

16. Thomas, "The Automobile Industry and its Tycoon," pp. 141-42.

17. Louis Galambos, "The Emerging Organizational Synthesis in Modern American History," *Business History Review* 44 (Autumn 1970): 279-90 (the quotation is on page 288).

18. Livesay, "Entrepreneurial Persistence through the Bureaucratic Age," pp. 415-18.

19. Arthur H. Cole, *Business Enterprise in Its Social Setting* (Cambridge, Mass.: Harvard University Press, 1959), p. 28.

20. Joseph A. Schumpeter, "The Creative Response in Economic History," *Journal of Economic History* 7 (November 1947): 149-59.

21. Thomas, "The Automobile Industry and Its Tycoon," p. 142.

22. The variety of "urban rivalry" studies on cities throughout the country have established as an important theme the competition among cities for industry and population. See, for example, James W. Livingood, *The Philadelphia-Baltimore Trade Rivalry, 1780-1860* (Harrisburg, Pa.: Pennsylvania Historical and Museum Commission, 1947); Wyatt W. Belcher, *The Economic Rivalry Between St. Louis and Chicago* (New York: Columbia University Press, 1947); Richard Wade, *The Urban Frontier: The Rise of Western Cities, 1790-1830* (Cambridge, Mass.: Harvard University Press, 1959); Harry N. Scheiber, "Urban Rivalry and Internal Improvements in the Old Northwest, 1820-1860," *Ohio History* 71 (October 1962): 227-39, Constance Green, *American Cities in the Growth of the Nation* (New York: Harper and Row, 1957).

23. Historians have done several urban elite studies. These analyses usually examine the social composition and behavior of elites, but not how they shape economic development in individual cities. See, for example, E. Digby Baltzell, *Philadelphia Gentlemen* (Glencoe, Ill.: The Free Press, 1958); John N. Ingham, *The Iron Barons: A Social Analysis of an American Urban Elite 1874-1965* (Westport, Conn.: Greenwood Press, 1978); Frederic C. Jaher, "Nineteenth-Century Elites in Boston and New York," *Journal of Social History* 6 (Fall 1972): 32-77.

Chapter 1

1. Information on early agricultural life in northeast Pennsylvania is available in Emily C. Blackman, *History of Susquehanna County, Pennsylvania* (Philadelphia, 1873); H.C.

Bradsby, *History of Bradford County, Pennsylvania, with Biographical Selections* (Chicago, 1891); Alfred Mathews, *History of Wayne, Pike, and Monroe Counties of Pennsylvania* (Philadelphia, 1886); W.W. Munsell and Company, *History of Luzerne, Lackawanna, and Wyoming Counties, Pennsylvania, with Illustrations and Biographical Sketches of Some of Their Prominent Men and Pioneers* (New York, 1880); Rhamanthus M. Stocker, *Centennial History of Susquehanna County, Pennsylvania* (Philadelphia, 1887).

2. Historians have only recently recognized the importance of early American towns in integrating nearby agricultural development. See Julius Rubin, "Urban Growth and Regional Development," in David T. Gilchrist, ed., *The Growth of Seaport Cities* (Charlottesville: University Press of Virginia, 1967), pp. 3-21; James T. Lemon, *The Best Poor Man's Country: A Geographical Study of Early Southeastern Pennsylvania* (Baltimore: Johns Hopkins University Press, 1972); Richard C. Wade, *The Urban Frontier: The Rise of Western Cities, 1790-1830* (Cambridge, Mass.: Harvard University Press, 1959).

3. Stocker, *Centennial History*, pp. 265-321, 806-13; Bradsby, *History of Bradford County*, pp. 470-531; Munsell, *History of Luzerne, Lackawanna, and Wyoming Counties*, pp. 439-47; John R. Durfee, *Reminiscences of Carbondale, Dundaff, and Providence Forty Years Past* (Philadelphia, 1875), pp. 5-6.

4. In Susquehanna County, for example, see Blackman, *History of Susquehanna County*, pp. 30-48.

5. Blackman's *History of Susquehanna County* is especially useful because she details the diary entries of members of the active Post family; these diaries describe the various businesses in early Montrose and when they were established. See pp. 323-30.

6. Rubin, "Urban Growth and Regional Development."

7. Joseph A. Durrenberger, *Turnpikes: A Study of the Toll Road Movement in the Middle Atlantic States and Maryland* (Valdosta, Ga., 1931), p. 125.

8. George Johnston, *History of Cecil County, Maryland* (Baltimore: Regional Hub Publishing Company, 1881 [1967]), p. 273.

9. Joseph A. Schumpeter, *The Theory of Economic Development: An Inquiry into Profits, Capital, Credit, Interest and the Business Cycle* (Cambridge, Mass.: Harvard University Press, 1934); Arthur H. Cole, *Business Enterprise in Its Social Setting* (Cambridge, Mass.: Harvard University Press, 1959).

10. Edward J. Davies II, "The Urbanizing Region: Leadership and Urban Growth in the Anthracite Coal Regions, 1830-1885." Ph.D. diss. University of Pittsburgh, 1977.

11. Ibid.; Interview by Edward Davies with Ralph Hazletine, director of the Wyoming Valley Historical and Geological Society, October 1972.

12. Blackman, *History of Susquehanna County*, p. 24.

13. Ibid., 47; Stocker, *Centennial History*, pp. 265-321; Bradsby, *History of Bradford County*, pp. 497-531.

14. Blackman, *History of Susquehanna County*, pp. 30-31, 38-39, 41, 47, 287-93, 334-35; Stocker, *Centennial History*, pp. 298-99, 806.

15. Stocker, pp. 267-70, 298-99 (quotation on p. 267); Manuscript Census Returns, Seventh Census of the United States, 1850, Susquehanna County, Pennsylvania, National Archives Microfilm Series M-432, Roll 829.

16. Blackman, *History of Susquehanna County*, pp. 38, 42, 44-45, 157-59, 298-99, 324-26; Frederick L. Hitchcock, *History of Scranton and Its People*, 2 vols. (New York City, 1914), 1: 181-82.

17. Bradsby, *History of Bradford County*, pp. 507-8, 526-27.

18. Ibid., p. 526; Manuscript Census Returns, Seventh Census of the United States, 1850, Bradford County, Pennsylvania, National Archives Microfilm Series, M-432, Roll 756.

19. Stocker, *Centennial History*, pp. 806-12.

20. Horace Hayden, Alfred Hand, and John W. Jordan, *Genealogical and Family History of the Wyoming and Lackawanna Valleys, Pennsylvania* (New York and Chicago, 1906), 2:153-54; Blackman, *History of Susquehanna County*, pp. 392-96; Stocker, *Centennial*

History, p. 807; Joseph V. Fuller, "William Walter Phelps," in Allen Johnson and Dumas Malone, eds., *Dictionary of American Biography* (New York, 1928-1937), 14: 533-34.

21. Blackman, *History of Susquehanna County*, pp. 392-96; Stocker, *Centennial History*, pp. 806-10.

22. Blackman, *History of Susquehanna County*, pp. 393, 396; Stocker, *Centennial History*, p. 809; Durfee, *Reminiscences*, pp. 143-44.

23. Blackman, *History of Susquehanna County*, pp. 327, 395-96; Stocker, *Centennial History*, p. 806.

24. For a good description of the early Pennsylvania anthracite trade, see Samuel J. Packer, *Report of the Committee of the Senate of Pennsylvania on the Subject of Coal Trade* (Harrisburg, 1834).

25. Hudson Coal Company, *The Story of Anthracite* (New York: the Hudson Coal Company, 1932), pp. 59-72, 85-92, 103-5; Robert G. Cleland, *A History of Phelps Dodge, 1834-1950* (New York: Alfred A. Knopf, 1952), pp. 42-44; J.B. Lyon Company, *A Century of the Delaware and Hudson Company, 1823-1923* (Albany, 1925), pp. 8-80.

26. Robert G. Albion, *The Rise of New York Port 1815-1860* (New York: Charles Scribner's Sons, 1939), pp. 76-121.

27. Hudson Coal Company, *Anthracite*, pp. 59-72, 185-92; Chester L. Jones, *The Economic History of the Anthracite Tidewater Canals* (Philadelphia, 1908), pp. 74-81.

28. Hudson Coal Company, *Anthracite*, pp. 59-67; Jones, *The Anthracite Tidewater Canals*, pp. 75-79; Munsell, *History of Luzerne, Lackawanna and Wyoming Counties*, pp. 78-81, 439.

29. Hudson Coal Company, *Anthracite*, pp. 68-70; Jones, *The Anthracite Tidewater Canals*, pp. 79-81.

30. David Torrey, *Memoir of Major Jason Torrey of Bethany, Wayne County, Pennsylvania* (Scranton, 1885).

31. Ibid.; Mathews, *History of Wayne, Pike, and Monroe Counties*; Stocker, *Centennial History*; Phineas G. Goodrich, *History of Wayne County* (Honesdale, Pa., 1880).

32. Munsell, *History of Luzerne, Lackawanna and Wyoming Counties*, pp. 439, 441-43.

33. Ibid., pp. 439-43, 446-47; Durfee, *Reminiscences*, pp. 35-38.

34. The concept of "take off" into economic growth was developed by Walt W. Rostow. See Walt W. Rostow, *The Stages of Economic Growth: A Non-Communist Manifesto* (Cambridge: Cambridge University Press, 1960); and W.W. Rostow, ed., *The Economics of Take-off into Sustained Growth* (New York: St. Martin's Press, 1964).

35. Munsell, *History of Luzerne, Lackawanna and Wyoming Counties*, p. 441. For the lack of large wealth-holders in Carbondale, see Manuscript Census Returns, Seventh Census of the United States, 1850, Luzerne County, Pennsylvania, National Archives Microfilm Series, M-432, Roll 793. Wilkes-Barre had a smaller population than did Carbondale in 1850, but in that year Wilkes-Barre had sixty-one residents holding $10,000 or more in real estate and Carbondale had only one such resident, and his did not exceed $10,000.

36. Durfee, *Reminiscences, et passim*; R. G. Dun Credit Ledgers, Pennsylvania, Luzerne County, vol. 89, pp. 49, 53, 71, 89.

37. Durfee, *Reminiscences*, p. 16; Munsell, *History of Luzerne. Lackawanna and Wyoming Counties*, pp. 442-43, 446; Hitchcock, *History of Scranton* 2: 660, 22-23, 5-6; *Address to the Public by the Lackawanna Coal Mine and Navigation Company, Relative to the Proposed Canal From the Hudson to the Head Waters of the Lackawanna River* (New York, 1824).

Chapter 2

1. America's first rails were built in the 1820s and were made of wood. These were gradually supplemented by English-made iron rails during the 1830s and 1840s. A couple

of American firms experimented with making iron rails in the 1840s before the Scrantons did. But the Scrantons were the first to mass-produce notable quantities of iron rails. See W. David Lewis, "The Early History of the Lackawanna Iron and Coal Company: A Study in Technological Adaptation," *Pennsylvania Magazine of History and Biography* 96 (October 1972): 456-58; John F. Stover, *American Railroads* (Chicago: University of Chicago Press; 1961), pp. 20-29; John Moody, *The Railroad Builders* (New Haven, 1919), pp. 66-70; Peter Temin, *Iron and Steel in Nineteenth Century America* (Cambridge, Mass: M.I.T. Press 1970), pp. 109, 117.

2. Much information on the Scrantons' efforts at economic development can be gathered from the Scranton papers, known as the Edmund T. Lukens Collection (hereafter ETLC), in the Eleutherian Mills Historical Library in Wilmington, Delaware. Another smaller collection of Scranton correspondence is available in the Lackawanna Historical Society (hereafter LHS) in Scranton, Pennsylvania. The best secondary source on the Scrantons' early attempts at iron and coal development is Lewis, "The Lackawanna Iron and Coal Company."

3. The trauma of the Scrantons' early years in the Lackawanna Valley is described in the correspondence in Box 9, ETLC. For a good summary of the Scrantons from 1841-43 see Lewis, "The Lackawanna Iron and Coal Company," pp. 435-51.

4. Lewis, "The Lackawanna Iron and Coal Company."

5. John P. Gallagher, "Scranton: Industry and Politics, 1835-1885," Ph.D. diss., Catholic University, 1964, pp. 39, 57; Lewis, "The Lackawanna Iron and Coal Company," pp. 454-55; Horace Hollister, *Contributions to the History of the Lackawanna Valley* (New York, 1857), p. 166.

6. Edward Hungerford, *Men of Erie: A Story of Human Effort* (New York: Random House, 1946), pp. 76-78; Lewis, "The Lackawanna Iron and Coal Company," pp. 454-55; Hollister, *History of the Lackawanna Valley*, p. 166.

7. Edward H. Mott, *Between Ocean and the Lakes: The Story of the Erie* (New York, 1901), p. 91; Benjamin H. Throop, *A Half Century in Scranton* (Scranton, 1895), pp. 114-16.

8. David Craft, W.A. Wilcox, Alfred Hand, J. Wooldridge, *History of Scranton, Pennsylvania* (Dayton, 1891), p. 247.

9. Throop, *A Half Century in Scranton*, 114-16.

10. For the role of Albright in the Scranton enterprise, see William Henry to Selden T. Scranton, December 30, 1839, ETLC, Box 1; Joseph J. Albright to H. J. Albright, March, 1842, ETLC, Box 36; Joseph J. Albright to Selden T. Scranton, July 7 and November 9, 1850, ETLC, Box 36; William Henry to Selden T. Scranton, October 1 and 15, 1840, and February 12, March 22, and September 28, 1841, ETLC, Box 9; Joseph J. Albright to Selden T. Scranton, April 25, 1841, and February 31 [sic], 1844, ETLC, Box 9.

11. James P. Snell, *History of Sussex and Warren Counties, New Jersey* (Philadelphia, 1881), pp. 655-57. For the importance of the Blairs to the Scrantons, see George W. Scranton to Selden T. Scranton, May 30, 1845, ETLC, Box 1; George W. Scranton to Selden T. Scranton, November 26, 1846, and October 9, 1850, ETLC, Box 10; John I. Blair to Selden T. Scranton, January 1, 1847, and May 1, 1848, ETLC, Box 10.

12. Scrantons and Grant statement, probably October 1, 1843, ETLC, Box 9; John Howland to Selden T. Scranton, March 1, 1845, ETLC, Box 9; *Charter and By-Laws and Regulations of the Lackawanna Iron and Coal Company*, ETLC, Box 11; John J. Phelps to Selden T. Scranton, December 16 and 29, 1845, ETLC, Box 13.

13. In a letter to Selden Scranton, John J. Phelps asserted that "the Erie Company is managed by Connecticut businessmen—of large means, and liberal views, and they will be disposed to go for . . . the several interests of their city"; John J. Phelps to Selden T. Scranton, December 16 and 29, 1845, ETLC, Box 13; see also, Horace Hayden, Alfred Hand, and John W. Jordon, *Genealogical and Family History of the Wyoming and Lackawanna Valleys, Pennsylvania* (New York and Chicago, 1906) 2: 153-54.

14. William B. Shaw, "William Earl Dodge," Harold U. Faulkner, "Anson G. Phelps," and Joseph V. Fuller, "William Walter Phelps," in Allen Johnson and Dumas Malone, eds., *Dictionary of American Biography* (New York: Charles Scribner's Sons, 1928-1937) 5: 352-53; 14: 525-26, and 533; Lewis, "The Lackawanna Iron and Coal Company," pp. 458-59.

15. William Henry to Selden T. Scranton, February 12, March 13, and April 20, 1841, ETLC, Box 9; George W. Scranton to Phillip H. Mattes, October 17, 1845, reprinted in Frederick L. Hitchcock, *History of Scranton and Its People*, 2 vols. (New York City, 1914) 1: 36.

16. Hitchcock, *History of Scranton*, 1: 181; 2: 142-43, 308; Throop, *A Half Century in Scranton*, pp. 103–6; George W. Scranton to Selden T. Scranton, December 10, 1843, March 1 and 21, 1849, January 31, 1853, ETLC, Boxes 2, 9, and 10; George A. Fuller to Selden T. Scranton, November 24, 1863, ETLC, Box 36.

17. William Henry to Selden T. Scranton, March 8, 1840, June 8, July and August 24, 1841, ETLC, Box 9; Charles Silkman to Selden T. Scranton, March 28 and 29, 1849, ETLC, Box 13; Lewis, "The Lackawanna Iron and Coal Company," p. 442.

18. Throop, *A Half Century in Scranton*, p. 135.

19. This terminology comes from Leo Marx, *The Machine in the Garden: Technology and the Pastoral Ideal in America* (New York and London: Oxford University Press, 1964).

20. Hollister, *History of the Lackawanna Valley*, pp. 124-25.

21. Some members of this committee were upset that the North Branch Canal would not provide a feeder to connect their farming area to outside markets. Wilkes-Barre *Advocate*, December 19, 1838, in Hollister, *History of the Lackawanna Valley*, p. 105. For an additional description of the opposition to economic development, see Throop, *A Half Century in Scranton*, pp. 124-26.

22. Hollister, *History of the Lackawanna Valley*, 1869 edition, 238; William Henry to Selden T. Scranton, March 10, 1841, ETLC, Box 9; Sanford Grant to Selden T. Scranton, June 9, 1841, ETLC, Box 9.

23. Hollister, *History of the Lackawanna Valley*, 116 (Hollister's italics); Hollister, *History of the Lackawanna Valley* (1869 edition), pp. 231-32; Lewis, "The Lackawanna Iron and Coal Company," p. 454; Sanford Grant to Selden T. Scranton, June 9, 1841, ETLC, Box 9. One contemporary insisted that "the Lackawanna Iron Works, supposed to be hopelessly bankrupt, were of no account to the old settlers in their struggles for a single gleam of financial sunlight." John R. Durfee, *Reminiscenses of Carbondale, Dundaff, and Providence Forty Years Past* (Philadelphia, 1875), p. 103.

24. Samuel P. Hays, "Political Parties and the Community-Society Continuum," in William N. Chambers and Walter D. Burnham, *The American Party Systems: Stages of Political Development* (New York, London and Toronto: Oxford University Press, 1967), pp. 152-81; Lee Benson, *The Concept of Jacksonian Democracy: New York as a Test Case* (Princeton: Princeton University Press, 1961).

25. Hays, "Political Parties and the Community-Society Continuum," pp. 152-81.

26. Hollister, *History of the Lackawanna Valley*, 1869 ed., p. 252.

27. Hitchcock, *History of Scranton*, 1: 51-57.

28. Ibid.; Report of Joseph J. Albright, coal agent, May, 1852, ETLC, Box 11; Joseph H. Scranton to Selden T. Scranton, February 23, 1854, ETLC, Box 11; Charles Silkman to Selden T. Scranton, March 28, 1849, ETLC, Box 13.

29. Robert J. Casey and W.A.S. Douglas, *The Lackawanna Story: The First Hundred Years of the Delaware, Lackawanna, and Western Railroad* (New York: McGraw-Hill Book Company, 1951), pp. 32-72, 208-11; Hitchcock, *History of Scranton*, 1: 55-57.

30. Michael Meylert to Selden T. Scranton, August 3, 1853, ETLC, Box 13; William Jessup to Selden T. Scranton, February 1, 1853, ETLC, Box 13; Hayden et. al *Genealogical and Family History*, 2: 50-51, 154.

31. Hollister, *History of the Lackawanna Valley*, pp. 108, 118, 124, 133; Throop, *A Half Century in Scranton*, pp. 263-76.

32. Craft et. al., *History of Scranton*, pp. 347-50; Hitchcock, *History of Scranton*, 2: 30-31; Casey and Douglas, *The Lackawanna Story*.

33. In the Scrantons' correspondence, they frequently complain of shortages of different specialists, especially for iron manufacturing. Physician Benjamin Throop regretted the "scarcity of fresh beef, and more especially of milk. . . . There were many families who had young children, and in my daily rounds I found not a few little babies who were actually suffering." Throop, who was not one to stand still in the face of opportunity, went into the "milk business as a commercial venture." Throop, *A Half Century in Scranton*, pp. 305-8, 346.

34. Hitchcock, *History of Scranton*, 2: 132-34; W.W. Munsell, *History of Luzerne, Lackawanna, and Wyoming Counties, with Illustrations and Biographical Sketches of Some of Their Prominent Men and Pioneers* (New York, 1880), p. 436; H.C. Bradsby, *History of Bradford County, Pennsylvania, with Biographical Selections* (Chicago, 1891), p. 526; George B. Kulp, *Families of the Wyoming Valley: Biographical, Genealogical, and Historical Sketches of the Bench and Bar of Luzerne County, Pennsylvania* (Wilkes-Barre, 1885), 3: 1292.

35. Michael Meylert to Selden T. Scranton, August 3, 1853, ETLC, Box 13; Throop, *A Half Century in Scranton*; Bradsby, *History of Bradford County*, pp. 507-8, 526-27; Blackman, *History of Susquehanna County*, pp. 157-59; R.G. Dun Credit Ledgers, Pennsylvania, Luzerne County, 93: 593.

36. Hitchcock, *History of Scranton*, 2: 181-82, 220; *Scranton City Directory, 1880*; for the closeness of Fuller's ties to the Scranton family, see George A. Fuller to "Uncle Selden" Scranton, November 24, 1863, March 12, 1864, March 27, 1867, and June 18, 1878, ETLC, Box 36; R.G. Dun Credit Ledgers, Pennsylvania, Susquehanna County, vol. 178: 34.

37. Hayden et al., *Genealogical and Family History*, 2: 153-55; Rhamanthus M. Stocker, *Centennial History of Susquehanna County, Pennsylvania* (Philadelphia, 1887), pp. 806-9.

38. Hitchcock, *History of Scranton*, 1: 254-55; Chapman Publishing Company, *Portrait and Biographical Record of Lackawanna County, Pennsylvania* (New York and Chicago, 1897), pp. 119-20; Casey and Douglas, *The Lackawanna Story*, pp. 210-11.

39. Phillip Walter to Selden T. Scranton, May 19, 1852, ETLC, Box 10; for a brief description of Walter's relationship to the Scrantons, see Hitchcock, *History of Scranton* 1: 7.

40. Lewis, "The Lackawanna Iron and Coal Company," pp. 424-68; Clifford M. Zierer, "Scranton as an Urban Community," *Geographic Review* 17 (1927): 428.

Chapter 3

1. Benjamin H. Throop, *A Half Century in Scranton* (Scranton, 1895), pp. 103-4; W. David Lewis, "The Lackawanna Iron and Coal Company: A Study in Technological Adaptation," *Pennsylvania Magazine of History and Biography* 96 (October 1972): 445, 454-55; Clifford M. Zierer, "Scranton as an Urban Community," *Geographic Review* 17 (1927): 426; Frederick L. Hitchcock, *History of Scranton and Its People*, 2 vols. (New York, 1914) 1: 36; Horace Hollister, *Contributions to the History of the Lackawanna Valley* (New York, 1857), pp. 115, 121-22; Henry D. Rogers, *Report on the Geology and Mining Resources of that Part of the Lackawanna Coal Basin which Includes the Lands of the Delaware, Lackawanna, and Western Railroad Company and those of the Lackawanna Iron and Coal Company* (Boston, 1854), pp. 19-36.

2. Hitchcock, *History of Scranton*, 1: picture between pp. 60-61, 61-62; Scranton Coal Company, First Annual Meeting, November 23, 1854, Box 17, ETLC.

3. Charles Silkman to Selden T. Scranton, March 28 and 29, 1849, ETLC, Box 13; Throop, *A Half Century in Scranton*, p. 135.

4. Scranton *Republican*, March 30, 1866. Very little historical research seems to have been done on the political decisions necessary to improve urban environment for investment. An excellent description of this problem in a contemporary large city is Roy Lubove, *Twentieth-Century Pittsburgh: Government, Business and Environmental Change* (New York: John Wiley and Sons, 1969). See also Seymour J. Mandelbaum, *Boss Tweed's New York* (New York: John Wiley and Sons, 1965). My understanding of the politics of improving the urban infrastructure has been sharpened by several conversations with Lee Benson.

5. Hitchcock, *History of Scranton*, 1: 360-62; Throop, *A Half Century in Scranton*, pp. 341-44; Hollister, *History of the Lackawanna Valley*, 1857 ed., pp. 112, 118-19; Scranton *Republican*, March 30, April 13 and 27, 1866. D.M. Koon, the state representative from Providence, protested in the state legislature against the incorporation of his borough and township into Scranton. He contended that the "large and extensive farming district," which the proposed city would incorporate, "is impossible to regulate by city ordinances." In a valiant attempt to thwart Scranton's expanded boundaries, Koon submitted a petition of local Providence citizens "protest[ing] against coming in as part of this incorporated city." *The Legislative Record: Debates and Proceedings of the Pennsylvania Legislature, Session of 1866* (Harrisburg, 1866), pp. 825-26.

6. Hitchcock, *History of Scranton*, 1: 363-67; *The Legislative Record: Debates and Proceedings of the Pennsylvania Legislature, Session of 1878* (Harrisburg, 1878), pp. 420, 545, 830.

7. Hitchcock, *History of Scranton*, 1:426-34; *Report of the Scranton Board of Trade, 1886* (Scranton, 1886), pp. 43, 71-72; see also *Twenty-Fourth Annual Report of the Board of Trade, 1895* (Scranton, 1895), p. 13.

8. *Report of the Scranton Board of Trade, 1886*, pp. 71-72; Lee Benson, "Philadelphia Elites and Economic Development: Quasi-Public Innovation during the First American Organizational Revolution, 1825-1861," in Glenn Porter and William Mulligan, eds., *Working Papers from the Regional Economic History Research Center*, mimeograph, 1978.

9. Francis Walker and Charles Seaton, *Report on the Manufacturers of the United States, 1880* (Washington, D.C., 1883), pp. xxxiii, 58, 437; Throop, *A Half Century in Scranton*, pp. 298-301.

10. Richard Edwards, *Industries of Pennsylvania: Wilkes-Barre, Scranton, Pittston, Plymouth, Carbondale, Kingston* (Philadelphia, 1881), pp. 290-319 (quotation on p. 308).

11. Ibid., pp. 305, 314; Scranton Board of Trade, *Report of the Scranton Board of Trade, 1886*, p. 71; Throop, *A Half Century in Scranton*, pp. 302-4; David Craft, W. A. Wilcox, Alfred Hand, J. Wooldridge, *History of Scranton, Pennsylvania* (Dayton, 1891), pp. 284, 286-94.

12. Samuel C. Logan, *The Life of Thomas Dickson: A Memorial* (Scranton, 1888), pp. 42-43, 48-49; Luther Laflin Mills, Joseph H. Twitchell, Alfred Hand, Frederick L. Hitchcock, James H. Torrey, Eugene Smith, Edward B. Sturges, Charles H. Wells, James McLeod, and James A. Beaver, eds., *Henry Martyn Boies: Appreciations of His Life and Character* (New York, 1904), pp. 42-43, 48-49; Hitchcock, *History of Scranton*, 1: 202; 2: 53-55; Craft et al., *History of Scranton*, pp. 329-56, 261, 264-67.

13. *Scranton City Directory, 1880*.

14. Hitchcock, *History of Scranton*, 1: 453-56, 175-77, 155-60, 459, 382-86.

15. Edward J. Davies II, "Wilkes-Barre, 1870-1920: The Evolution of Urban Leadership in an Industrial Town" (unpublished seminar paper, University of Pittsburgh, 1972).

16. Historians seem to agree that elites are important, but they have provided no consensus for defining who are members of an economic elite in any city. For an array of different techniques, see Frederic Cople Jaher, "Nineteenth-Century Elites in Boston and New York," *Journal of Social History* 6 (Fall 1972): 32-77; Edward Pessen, *Riches, Class, and Power Before the Civil War* (Lexington, Mass.; Toronto, and London: D.C. Heath 1973); E. Digby Baltzell, *Philadelphia Gentlemen* (Glencoe, Ill.: The Free Press, 1958); Lee Benson, Robert Gough, Ira Harkavy, Marc Levine, and Brodie Remington, "Propositions on Economic Strata and Groups, Social Classes, Ruling Classes: A Strategic Natural Experiment, Philadelphia Economic and Prestige Elites, 1775-1860" (unpublished essay, University of Pennsylvania, 1976).

17. For a similar technique for defining economic leadership, see Lee Benson et al., "Philadelphia Economic and Prestige Elites, 1775-1860"; Davies, "The Urbanizing Region."

18. Lewis, "The Lackawanna Iron and Coal Company," pp. 434-36, 441, 452, 460; Hitchcock, *History of Scranton*, 1: 180; 2: 177-81; Horace Hayden, Alfred Hand, and John W. Jordan, *Genealogical and Family History of the Wyoming and Lackawanna Valleys, Pennsylvania* (New York and Chicago, 1906), 2:367-68, 140-43; Chapman Publishing Company, *Portrait and Biographical Record of Lackawanna County, Pennsylvania* (New York and Chicago, 1897), pp. 937-42; Manuscript Census Returns, Ninth Census of the United States, 1870, Luzerne County, Pennsylvania, National Archives Microfilm Series, M-593, Roll 1368.

19. W. David Lewis, "William Henry, Armsmaker, Ironmaster, and Railroad Speculator: A Case Study in Failure," in *Proceedings of the Business History Conference* (Fort Worth, Texas: Texas Christian University, 1973), pp. 51-94; Manuscript Census Returns, Ninth Census of the United States, 1870, Luzerne County, Pennsylvania, National Archives Microfilm Series, M-593, Roll 1368; Interview with Robert C. Mattes, director of the Lackawanna Historical Society, October 1972.

20. Hitchcock, *History of Scranton*, 2: 30-32; Hayden et al., *Genealogical and Family History*, 2: 140-43; Interview with Robert C. Mattes, director of the Lackawanna Historical Society, October 1972.

21. Hitchcock, *History of Scranton*, 1: 254-55; Chapman Publishing Company, *Portrait and Biographical Record of Lackawanna County, Pennsylvania* (New York and Chicago, 1897), pp. 119-20.

22. Hitchcock, *History of Scranton*, 1: 88-89; Chapman Publishing Company, *Portrait of Lackawanna County*, pp. 205-7.

23. Throop, *A Half Century in Scranton*, 263-76, *et passim*; Chapman Publishing Company, *Portrait of Lackawanna County*, pp. 125-27.

24. Hitchcock, *History of Scranton*, 2: 142-44; Chapman Publishing Company, *Portrait of Lackawanna County*, pp. 731-32.

25. Hitchcock, *History of Scranton*, 2: 132-34; W. W. Munsell and Company, *History of Luzerne, Lackawanna, and Wyoming Counties, Pennsylvania, with Illustrations and Geographical Sketches of Some of Their Prominent Men and Pioneers* (New York, 1880), p. 436; George B. Kulp, *Families of the Wyoming Valley: Biographical, Genealogical, and Historical Sketches of the Bench and Bar of Luzerne County, Pennsylvania* (Wilkes-Barre, 1885), 3: 1292.

26. Hitchcock, *History of Scranton*, 1: 220, 203; Dwight J. Stoddard, *Prominent Men [of] Scranton and Vicinity, Wilkes-Barre and Vicinity, Pittston, Hazleton, Carbondale, Montrose and Vicinity* (Scranton, 1906), p. xii; Hayden et al., *Genealogical and Family History*, pp. 153-56; Rhamanthus M. Stocker, *Centennial History of Susquehanna County, Pennsylvania* (Philadelphia, 1887), p. 881; Chapman Publishing Company, *Portrait of Lackawanna County*, pp. 561-62.

27. *Scranton City Directory, 1880*; Manuscript Census Returns, Ninth Census of the

United States, 1870, Luzerne County, Pennsylvania, National Archives Microfilm Series, M-593, Roll 1368.

28. *Scranton City Directory, 1880*; Hitchcock, *History of Scranton*, 1: 187; Munsell, *History of Luzerne, Lackawanna, and Wyoming Counties*, p. 438H.

29. Hitchcock, *History of Scranton*, 1: 187-90; Hayden et al., *Genealogical and Family History*, 2: 196-99.

30. Manuscript Census Returns, Ninth Census of the United States, 1870, Luzerne County, Pennsylvania, National Archives Microfilm Series, M-593, Roll 1368.

Chapter 4

1. David Ward, *Cities and Immigrants: A Geography of Change in Nineteenth Century America* (N.Y., London, and Toronto: Oxford University Press, 1971), p. 76; George E. Waring, Jr., ed., *Report on the Social Statistics of Cities*, 2 vols. (Washington, D.C., 1886), 1: 882-87.

2. Francis W. Gregory and Irene D. Neu, "The American Industrial Elite in the 1870s: Their Social Origins," in William Miller, ed., *Men in Business: Essays on the Historical Role of the Entrepreneur* (New York: Harper & Row, 1962), pp. 193-211; Herbert G. Gutman, "The Reality of the Rags-to-Riches 'Myth': The Case of the Paterson, New Jersey, Locomotive, Iron, and Machinery Manufacturers, 1830-1880," in Stephen Thernstrom and Richard Sennett, eds., *Nineteenth-Century Cities: Essays in the New Urban History* (New Haven and London: Yale University Press, 1969), pp. 98-124.

3. According to Dickson's biographer, young Thomas carefully calculated the advantages of locating in Scranton. "After a careful study of different localities, touching their advantages . . . [Dickson] concluded to establish his plant in Scranton." Inferential evidence suggests that the Scranton group encouraged Dickson's move. See Samuel C. Logan, *The Life of Thomas Dickson: A Memorial* (Scranton, 1888), pp. 49-50; and Thomas Dickson to Joseph H. Scranton, July 21, 1862, in Lackawanna Historical Society (hereafter LHS), and Dickson and Company to Joseph H. Scranton, March 15, 1862, LHS.

4. Logan, *Thomas Dickson*; Gerald M. Best, *Locomotives of the Dickson Manufacturing Company* (San Marino, California: Golden West, 1966); Chapman Publishing Company, *Portrait and Biographical Record of Lackawanna County, Pennsylvania* (New York and Chicago, 1897), pp. 502-3, 455-57; Frederick L. Hitchcock, *History of Scranton and Its People*, 2 vols. (N.Y., 1914), 1: 89-90; 2, 22-24, 37-40.

5. Hitchcock, *History of Scranton*, 2: 498-501; Chapman Publishing Company, *Portrait of Lackawanna County*, pp. 135-37.

6. Hitchcock, *History of Scranton*, 2: 277-82; R.G. Dun Credit Ledgers, Pennsylvania, Luzerne County, 93: 119.

7. George B. Kulp, *Families of the Wyoming Valley: Biographical, Genealogical, and Historical Sketches of the Bench and Bar of Luzerne County, Pennsylvania*, 3 vols. (Wilkes-Barre, 1885), 3: 1016-35; Hitchcock, *History of Scranton*, 2: 660-63.

8. Hitchcock, *History of Scranton*, 1: 215-26; Chapman Publishing Company, *Portrait of Lackawanna County*, pp. 185-86.

9. Hitchcock, *History of Scranton*, 1: 225-26; 2: 125-26; W.W. Munsell and Company, *History of Luzerne, Lackawanna, and Wyoming Counties, Pennsylvania, with Illustrations and Geographical Sketches of Some of Their Prominent Men and Pioneers* (New York, 1880), pp. 438D; *Scranton City Directory, 1876-77*.

10. Hitchcock, *History of Scranton*, 1: 211-12; Munsell, *History of Luzerne, Lackawanna, and Wyoming Counties*, pp. 438D, 392B; Chapman Publishing Company, *Por-*

trait of Lackawanna County, 706-7; *Scranton City Directory, 1876-77*; Dwight J. Stoddard, *Prominent Men [of] Scranton* (Scranton, 1906), pp. 14, 17, iv, v.

11. Chapman Publishing Company, *Portrait of Lackawanna* County, 934-35; Hitchcock, *History of Scranton*, 1: 213; Stoddard, *Prominent Men [of] Scranton*, pp. 63, xvi, 42, xi.

12. Benjamin H. Throop, *A Half Century in Scranton* (Scranton, 1895); David Craft, W.A. Wilcox, Alfred Hand, J. Wooldridge, *History of Scranton, Pennsylvania* (Dayton, Ohio, 1891)., pp. 244-45, 268, 343, 353-54; Hitchcock, *History of Scranton*, 2: 639-42; Munsell, *History of Luzerne, Lackawanna, and Wyoming Counties*, pp. 331, 407-13, 438H, 442.

13. Thomas Dickson to Joseph H. Scranton, July 21, 1862, LHS; Amos N. Meylert to Joseph H. Scranton, June 6, 1862, LHS; Scranton *Republican*, September 7, 1866.

14. The problem of city size and "its circle of influence in attracting immigrants" was first tackled by Adna F. Weber, *The Growth of Cities in the Nineteenth Century: A Study in Statistics* (Ithaca, N.Y.: Cornell University Press, 1963 [1899]), pp. 230-84 (quotation on p. 259).

15. Samuel J. Packer, *Report of the Committee of the Senate of Pennsylvania on the Subject of Coal Trade* (Harrisburg, Pa.), p. 113; Munsell, *History of Luzerne, Lackawanna, and Wyoming Counties; Alfred Mathews, History of Wayne, Pike, and Monroe Counties of Pennsylvania* (Philadelphia, 1886); David Torrey, *Memoir of Major Jason Torrey of Bethany, Wayne County, and Pennsylvania* (Scranton, 1885).

16. Torrey, *Memoir of Major Jason Torrey*, pp. 17, 27; Thomas F. Murphy, *History of the First National Bank of Scranton, Pennsylvania: 1863-1938* (Scranton: International Textile Press, 1938), pp. 69-70; Hitchcock, *History of Scranton*, 1: 91; 2: 5-7; Chapman Publishing Company, *Portrait of Lackawanna County*, pp. 931-52; Stoddard, *Prominent Men [of] Scranton*, pp. 37, x.

17. Hitchcock, *History of Scranton*, 1: 239, 40; Manuscript Census Returns, Ninth Census of the United States, 1870, Luzerne County, Pennsylvania, National Archives Microfilm Series, M-593, Roll 1365; Manuscript Census Returns, Seventh Census of the United States, 1850, Wayne County, Pennsylvania, National Archives Microfilm Series, M-432, Roll 835; Rhamanthus M. Stocker, *History of the First Presbyterian Society of Honesdale* (Honesdale, Pa., 1906), pp. 296-97; Phineas G. Goodrich, *History of Wayne County* (Honesdale, Pa., 1880), p. 362.

18. Stocker, *Centennial History*, 76-78; Hitchcock, *History of Scranton*, 2: 7-9.

19. Stocker, *History of the First Presbyterian Society;* Mathews, *History of Wayne, Pike, and Monroe Counties;* Goodrich, *History of Wayne County.*

20. Hitchcock, *History of Scranton*, 1: 202.

21. Hitchcock, *History of Scranton*, 2: 639-44; Munsell, *History of Luzerne, Lackawanna, and Wyoming Counties*, pp. 442, 446-47; Scranton *Republican*, August 4, 1884.

22. Horace Hayden, Alfred Hand, and John W. Jordan, *Genealogical and Family History of the Wyoming and Lackawanna Valleys, Pennsylvania* (N.Y. and Chicago, 1906), 2: 191-92; Hitchcock, *History of Scranton*, 1: 92; 2: 616.

23. Munsell, *History of Luzerne, Lackawanna, and Wyoming Counties.* The human impulses toward success and failure are distributed evenly among those born into wealth and poverty. It is not surprising, therefore, that both the children of the wealthy, and the offspring of impecunious immigrants, failed to perpetuate their status over time. See Stanley Lebergott, *The American Economy: Income, Wealth, and Want* (Princeton, N.J.: Princeton University Press, 1975).

24. Chapman Publishing Company, *Portrait of Lackawanna County*, pp. 255-57; Hitchcock, *History of Scranton*, 1: 212-13; Munsell, *History of Luzerne, Lackawanna, and Wyoming Counties*, p. 438F-G.

25. Hayden et al., *Genealogical and Family History*, 2: 60-61; *Scranton City Directory, 1880*; Chapman Publishing Company, *Portrait of Lackawanna County*, pp. 739, 820; Munsell, *History of Luzerne, Lackawanna, and Wyoming Counties*, p. 400; Manuscript Census Returns, Seventh Census of the United States, 1850, Luzerne County, Pennsylvania, National Archives Microfilm Series, M-432, Rolls 793 and 794.

26. Chapman Publishing Company, *Portrait of Lackawanna County*, pp. 1049-50; Hayden et al., *Genealogical and Family History*, 2:40; Hitchcock, *History of Scranton*, 1: 245; Munsell, *History of Luzerne, Lackawanna, and Wyoming Counties*, pp. 460-61.

27. The influx of capital generated in expanding cities by newcomers on the make may have been more important in the emergence of an efficient capital market in America than tariff policies or the National Banking Act of 1863, both of which also seem to have increased the flow of funds to industrial centers. Throop, *A Half Century in Scranton*, pp. 155-56n, 202-3n, 226-27, 232-33, 235; Hitchcock, *History of Scranton*, 1, 202, 254-55; 7-9; Lance Davis, "The Investment Market, 1870-1914: The Evolution of a National Market," *Journal of Economic History* 25 (September 1965): 355-99; Richard Sylla, "Federal Policy, Banking Market Structure, and Capital Mobilization in the United States, 1863-1913," *Journal of Economic History* 24 (December 1969): 657-86; and Julius Rubin, "Urban Growth and Regional Development," in David T. Gilchrist, ed. *The Growth of Seaport Cities* (Charlottesville: University Press of Virginia, 1967) pp. 3-21.

28. Hayden et al., *Genealogical and Family History*, 2: 118-20; Hitchcock, *History of Scranton*, 2: 669-72; 1: 525-26.

29. Kulp, *Families of the Wyoming Valley*, 862-66; Munsell, *History of Luzerne, Lackawanna, and Wyoming Counties, 438T*.

30. Hitchcock, *History of Scranton*, 2: 623.

31. Kulp, *Families of the Wyoming Valley*, 2: 890-95; Chapman Publishing Company, *Portrait of Lackawanna County*, 268-69.

32. Hitchcock, *History of Scranton*, 2: 1-5.

33. Ibid., 1: 205; Stoddard, *Prominent Men [of] Scranton*, pp. 17, 36, ix, v.

34. For examples of the city loyalty of other urban elites, see E. Digby Baltzell, *Philadelphia Gentlemen* (Glencoe, Ill.: The Free Fress, 1958); Edward Pessen, *Riches, Class and Power before the Civil War* (Lexington, Mass., Toronto, and London: D.C. Heath and Co., 1973); and Edward J. Davies II, "The Urbanizing Region: Leadership and Urban Growth in the Anthracite Coal Regions, 1830-1885," Ph.D. diss., University of Pittsburgh, 1977.

35. Hitchcock, *History of Scranton*, 2: 30-31; Craft et al., *History of Scranton*, pp. 261, 262, 268-69; Luther Laflin Mills, Joseph H. Twitchell, Alfred Hand, Frederick L. Hitchcock, James H. Torrey, Eugene Smith, Edward B. Sturges, Charles H. Wells, James McLeod, and James A. Beaver, eds., *Henry Martyn Boies: Appreciations of His Life and Character* (New York, 1904), pp. 42-43, 54-55.

36. Craft et al. *History of Scranton*, pp. 272, 274-75; Hitchcock, *History of Scranton*, 2: 500; Chapman Publishing Company, *Portrait of Lackawanna County*, p. 136.

37. Throop, *A Half Century in Scranton*, p. 82n; Samuel P. Hays, "The Politics of Reform in Municipal Government in the Progressive Era," *Pacific Northwest Quarterly* 55 (October 1964): 157-69; Hays, "Political Parties and the Community—Society Continuum," 152-81; Hitchcock, *History of Scranton*, 1: 152-81.

38. For similar development in Wilkes-Barre, see Davies, "The Urbanizing Region." Scranton had wide city boundaries during the late 1800s; consequently its leaders had plenty of room to plan and create a healthy urban environment.

39. R.G. Dun Credit Ledgers, Pennsylvania, Luzerne County, 88: 239; 92: 142; 93: 275; 95: 47; Susquehanna County, 178: 65; Mills et al., *Henry Martyn Boies*, pp. 37-44, 53-55.

40. A minor problem arose by my including only organizations located in the Lackawanna Valley. Generally, of course, those people who held regional directorships outside

the region were also the most conspicuous businessmen inside the city. To have included all directorships held by Scrantonians would not have added new leaders but would merely have added directorships to those people already included in the economic elite.

41. For a study of the transition to formal training for mining employees, see Ray Ginger, "Managerial Employees in Anthracite, 1902: A Study in Occupational Mobility," *Journal of Economic History* 14 (Spring 1954): 146-57.

42. Alfred D. Chandler, Jr., "The Beginnings of 'Big Business' in American Industry," *Business History Review* 33 (Spring 1959): 1-30.

43. Ibid.

Chapter 5

1. Probably the best history of the Wyoming Valley before 1850 is Charles Miner, *History of Wyoming* (Philadelphia, 1845).

2. Miner, *Wyoming*, pp. 73-113; and Stewart Pearce, *Annals of Luzerne County* (Philadelphia, 1866), pp. 58-64.

3. Miner, *Wyoming*, pp. 114-34; Pearce, *Luzerne County*, pp. 64-66.

4. Pearce, *Luzerne County*, pp. 67-72; Horace Hayden, Alfred Hand, and John W. Jordan, *Genealogical and Family History of the Wyoming and Lackawanna Valleys, Pennsylvania* (New York and Chicago, 1906), 1: 48-51, 356; Oscar J. Harvey and Ernest G. Smith, *A History of Wilkes-Barre and the Wyoming Valley* (Wilkes-Barre, 1929), 4: 1866-67.

5. Pearce, *Luzerne County*, pp. 73, 100-119; Hayden, *Wyoming and Lackawanna Valleys*, 1: 48-51, 151-53.

6. Pearce, *Luzerne County*, pp. 73-99.

7. Miner, *Wyoming*, p. 139; Hayden, *Wyoming and Lackawanna Valleys*, 1: 50-51, 356-57; George B. Kulp, *Families of the Wyoming Valley: Biographical Genealogical, and Historical Sketches of the Bench and Bar of Luzerne County, Pennsylvania*, 3 vols. (Wilkes-Barre, 1885), 3: 1083.

8. Hayden, *Wyoming and Lackawanna Valleys*, 1: 151-53, 357-58; Harvey and Smith, *Wilkes-Barre*, 4: 1872, 1875.

9. Kulp, *Families of the Wyoming Valley*, 1: 2-13; 3: 1079-80, 1225-26; Hayden, *Genealogical and Family History*, 1: 10, 48-54.

10. Edward J. Davies, II, "Urbanizing Region: Leadership and Urban Growth in the Anthracite Coal Regions, 1830-1885," Ph.D. diss., University of Pittsburgh, 1977; interview by Edward Davies with Ralph Hazletine, retired director of the Wyoming Historical and Geological Society, October 1972; Pearce, *Luzerne County*, pp. 424, 426, 430-32.

11. Pearce, *Luzerne County*, pp. 370, 375-76.

12. Ibid., pp. 442, 470-75; Harvey and Smith, *Wilkes-Barre*, 4: 1887.

13. Henry C. Bradsby, *History of Luzerne County* (Wilkes-Barre, 1891), p. 482; J.A. Clark, *The Wyoming Valley and the Lackawanna Coal Region* (Scranton, 1875), p. 218.

14. For the evidence on Wilkes-Barre I am indebted to interview with Ralph Hazletine, October 1972, and Davies, "Urbanizing Region."

15. Edward J. Davies II, "Wilkes-Barre, 1870-1920: The Evolution of Urban Leadership in an Industrial Town," paper delivered at a seminar at the University of Pittsburgh, 1972; Davies, "Urbanizing Region"; and Davies, "Elite Migration and Urban Growth: The Rise of Wilkes-Barre in the Northern Anthracite Region, 1820-1880," *Pennsylvania History* 45 (October 1978): 291-314. I've discussed many of the comparisons that will follow with Professor Davies. We worked together compiling much of the data for the statistical comparisons: Davies worked on Wilkes-Barre and I did Scranton. I don't want to hold Davies

responsible for my interpretation of how Wilkes-Barre and Scranton compare; we've talked a lot about it and he disagrees with some of it.

16. Davies defined economic leaders as those having two directorships. I use two directorships in my definition if one included an officership. The caveat of the officership kept only four Scranton men from qualifying as economic leaders. I've checked into these four people and they are remarkably similar to the other forty in social characteristics. See Davies, "Wilkes-Barre, 1870-1920."

17. Davies, "Urbanizing Region."

18. Hayden, *Wyoming and Lackawanna Valleys*, 1: 3-7; Kulp, *Families of the Wyoming Valley*, 1: 2-13.

19. The elite dominance of voluntary associations in Cincinnati is also demonstrated by Walter S. Glazer, "Participation and Power: Voluntary Associations and the Functional Organizations of Cincinnati in 1840," *Historical Methods Newsletter* 5 (September 1972): 151-68. The connection between economic leadership and participation in voluntary associations is also supported in Edward Pessen, *Riches, Class, and Power before the Civil War* (Lexington, Mass., Toronto, and London: D.C. Heath and Company, 1973), pp. 251-80.

20. Davies, "Wilkes-Barre, 1870-1920"; see also Pessen, *Riches, Class, and Power*, pp. 169-204.

21. Scranton *Republican*, May 18 and 25, 1866, and June 8, 1966; Frederick L. Hitchcock, *History of Scranton and Its People*, 2 vols. (New York, 1914), 1: 360-62.

22. Scranton *Republican*, May 25 and June 8, 1866. Judging from the editor's earlier statements he was especially refering to Wilkes-Barre's administrative dominance over Scranton in his "brood of evils."

23. Scranton *Republican* 1880, 1884, 1889, April 13, 1866; Bradsby, *Luzerne County*, pp. 473-74, 520.

24. For detailed statistics on Wilkes-Barre's and Scranton's leaders, see Davies, "Wilkes-Barre, 1870-1920"; Burton W. Folsom, Jr., "Urban Networks: The Economic and Social Order of the Lackawanna and Lehigh Valleys during Early Industrialization, 1850-1880," Ph.D. diss., University of Pittsburgh, 1976, Chapter 4. Davies and I agreed on making 1880 the year for pinpointing economic leadership in Wilkes-Barre and Scranton.

25. Clark, *Wyoming Valley*, p. 219; Davies, "The Evolution of Urban Leadership in an Industrial Town"; and Folsom, "Urban Networks," Chapter 4.

26. Folsom, "Urban Networks"; and Davies, "Wilkes-Barre, 1870-1920."

27. Folsom, "Urban Networks"; and Davies, "Wilkes-Barre, 1870-1920"; Davies, "Urbanizing Region." For the residential propinquity of elites in other cities, see Pessen, *Riches, Class, and Power*.

28. Scranton *Republican*, May 10, 1880; *Scranton City Directory, 1880*; *General Index to Register's Dockets*, Lackawanna County, Estate No. 2277, Will book vol. 6, pp. 68-70.

29. Folsom, "Urban Networks," Chapter 4; Davies, "Wilkes-Barre, 1870-1920." For the philosophy of the Republican party see Paul Kleppner, *The Cross of Culture: A Social Analysis of Midwestern Politics* (New York: The Free Press, 1970); and Frederick C. Luebke, *Immigrants and Politics: The Germans of Nebraska, 1880-1900* (Lincoln: University of Nebraska Press, 1969).

30. Folsom, "Urban Networks," chapter 4; Davies, "Wilkes-Barre, 1870-1920."

31. Davies, "Urbanizing Regions"; Interview by Edward Davies with Ralph Hazletine, October 1972.

32. W.W. Munsell, *History of Luzerne, Lackawanna, and Wyoming Counties, Pennsylvania, With Illustrations and Biographical Sketches of Some of Their Prominent Men and Pioneers* (New York, 1880), pp. 215-17.

33. The impact of coal as an export in the Wyoming region resembled that of cotton in the South in several ways. Both coal and cotton production in the 1800s were labor intensive, and both failed to generate skills within the labor force. Neither industry was heavily

mechanized and neither had many backward or forward linkages to help their economies diversify. Since the largely unskilled and semi-skilled coal miners and cotton pickers were in great supply, they were paid low wages and couldn't buy many local services. The resulting weak infrastructure reinforced the adverse consequences of the single export and further prevented diversification. When the bust cycles came—cotton in the 1880s and coal in the 1920s—neither region had the flexibility to diversify its economy. Not surprisingly, both regions shifted into textiles, a labor-intensive industry, to supplement or substitute for the labor-intensive export. See Davies, "Wilkes-Barre, 1870-1920"; Morton Rothstein, "The Antebellum South as a Dual Economy: A Tentative Hypothesis," *Agricultural History* 41 (October 1967): 373-82; and Julius Rubin, "The Limits of Agricultural Progress in the Nineteenth-Century South," *Agricultural History* 49 (April 1975): 362-73.

34. Interview with Robert C. Mattes, April 1973; Clark, *Wyoming Valley*, pp. 92-129, 218-22; Pearce, *Luzerne County*, pp. 386-87.

35. Munsell, *Luzerne, Lackawanna, and Wyoming Counties*, pp. 215-17; Clifford M. Zierer, "Scranton as an Urban Community," *Geographic Review* 17 (1927): 426; Clark, *Wyoming Valley*, p. 218; Manuscript Census Returns, 1870, Luzerne County, M-593, Rolls 1368 and 1364.

36. *Industries of Pennsylvania: Wilkes-Barre, Scranton, Pittston, Plymouth, Carbondale, Kingston* (Philadelphia, 1881), pp. 304, 308, 314, 316, 318; David Craft, W.A. Wilcox, Alfred Hand, J. Wooldridge, *History of Scranton, Pennsylvania* (Dayton, Ohio, 1841), pp. 260-70, 272, 274-76; Hitchcock, *History of Scranton*, 1: 197; 2: 53-54; Munsell, *Luzerne, Lackawanna, and Wyoming Counties*, pp. 216, 408-9.

37. Craft et al., *History of Scranton*, pp. 260-62, 267; *Scranton City Directory, 1876, 1877, 1880*.

38. Craft et al., *History of Scranton*, pp. 262, 283-84, 360; Hitchcock, *History of Scranton*, 1: 228; 2: 278.

39. Craft et al., *History of Scranton*, pp. 267-68, 278, 277, 271.

40. Scranton *Republican*, April 13, 1866; Craft et al, *History of Scranton*, p. 280; Munsell, *Luzerne, Lackawanna, and Wyoming Counties*, pp. 331, 392B; Thomas Murphy, *History of Lackawanna County*, 3 vols. (Topeka and Indianapolis, 1928), 2: 682; 3: 1174.

41. Herbert G. Gutman, "Class, Status, and Power in Nineteenth-Century American Industrial Cities—Paterson, New Jersey: A Case Study," in Frederic C. Jaher, ed., *The Age of Industrialism in America: Essays in Social Structure and Cultural Values* (New York and London: The Free Press, 1968), pp. 263-87; Herbert G. Gutman, "The Reality of the Rags to Riches 'Myth': The Case of the Paterson, New Jersey, Locomotive, Iron and Machinery Manufacturers, 1830-1880," in Stephan Thernstrom and Richard Sennett, eds., *Nineteenth-Century Cities: Essays in the New Urban History* (New Haven and London: Yale University Press, 1969), pp. 98-124; Michael P. Weber, *Social Change in an Industrial Town: Patterns of Progress in Warren, Pennsylvania, from the Civil War to World War I* (State College: Pennsylvania State University Press, 1976).

Chapter 6

1. Robert J. Casey and W.A.S. Douglas, *The Lackawanna Story: The First Hundred Years of the Delaware, Lackawanna, and Western Railroad* (New York: McGraw-Hill Book Company, 1951), pp. 210-13. For a description of the difference in perspective between regional investors, such as those in Scranton, and the national capitalists in New York, see Samuel P. Hays, "Political Parties and the Community—Society Continuum," in William N. Chambers and Walter D. Burnham, eds., *The American Party System: Stages of Political Development* (New York: Oxford University Press, 1967).

2. David Craft, W.A. Wilcox, Alfred Hand, J. Wooldridge, *History of Scranton, Pennsylvania* (Dayton, Ohio, 1891); N.S.B. Gras, *An Introduction to Economic History* (New York and London, 1922).

3. W.W. Munsell and Company, *History of Luzerne, Lackawanna, and Wyoming Counties, Pennsylvania, with Illustrations and Geographical Sketches of Some of Their Prominent Men and Pioneers* (New York, 1880), pp. 439, 441, 452B; Frederick L. Hitchcock, *History of Scranton and Its People*, 2 vols. (New York, 1914), 1: 89-92, 202; 2: 660-61, 616, 639-43, 22-23, 5-6; Horace Hayden, Alfred Hand, and John W. Jordan, *Genealogical and Family History of the Wyoming and Lackawanna Valleys, Pennsylvania* (New York and Chicago, 1906), 2: 191-92; Samuel C. Logan, *The Life of Thomas Dickson: A Memorial* (Scranton, 1888); George B. Kulp, *Families of the Wyoming Valley: Biographical, Genealogical, and Historical Sketches of the Bench and Bar of Luzerne County, Pennsylvania*, 3 vols. (Wilkes-Barre, 1885), 1: 10-11. Carbondale's dominance over Dundaff is noticed by Emily C. Blackman, who observes that "Dundaff had high aspirations . . . but in 1836 they began to yield to the claims of Carbondale. . . ." The two Dicksons migrated from Dundaff to Carbondale in 1836 and Alfred Darte came in 1829. See Emily C. Blackman, *History of Susquehanna County, Pennsylvania* (Philadelphia, 1873), p. 396.

4. Munsell, *History of Luzerne, Lackawanna, and Wyoming Counties*, pp. 441-43.

5. Ibid., pp. 330A, 330B, 330G, 446, 462, 464A, 470, 470A; Hayden et al., *Genealogical and Family History*, 2: 111-12, 191-92; Hitchcock, *History of Scranton*, 2: 182-83, 616; *Scranton City Directory, 1880*.

6. These Carbondale businessmen who moved to Scranton and became economic leaders were Thomas and George Dickson, James Archbald, William Mories, Edward Weston, Horatio Pierce, Lewis Pughe, and William Richmond. For information on these men and their lives in Carbondale and Scranton, see Hitchcock, *History of Scranton*, 1: 202; 2: 660-61, 23, 639-43, 5-6; Munsell, *History of Luzerne, Lackawanna, and Wyoming Counties*, p. 438D; Hayden et al., *Genealogical and Family History*, 2: 70-71; Logan, *Thomas Dickson*, pp. 48-49, 70-71.

7. Munsell, *History of Luzerne, Lackawanna, and Wyoming Counties*, p. 438C-D; *Scranton City Directory, 1880*.

8. Hayden et al., *Genealogical and Family History*, 3: 111; Munsell, *History of Luzerne, Lackawanna, and Wyoming Counties*, pp. 440, 442, 446, 452B; Kulp, *Families of the Wyoming Valley*, 1: 84-88, 130-32.

9. Since these groups appear to have contributed little to shaping regional economic growth, their behavior is not central to this analysis. It is the elite that spearheads economic development and shapes city growth. In the Lackawanna Valley at least, the constant flow of leadership and of industrial capital into Scranton enhanced that city's dominance and reinforced Carbondale's subordinance (see Table 6.1). And possibly as a result, Scranton had substantially more opportunities than Carbondale did for social mobility for those groups below the elite.

For a good description of the problem, see Michael Weber, "Social Mobility in Nineteenth-Century America: Myth or Reality?" in Harold D. Woodman, ed., *The Forum Series* (St. Charles, Missouri: Forum Press, 1975).

10. Hitchcock, *History of Scranton*, 1: 89, 202; 2: 642, 278; Munsell, *History of Luzerne, Lackawanna, and Wyoming Counties*, p. 442; Hayden et al., *Genealogical and Family History*, 2: 71; Chapman Publishing Company, *Portrait and Biographical Record of Lackawanna County, Pennsylvania* (New York and Chicago, 1897), pp. 377-78, 944, 947, 121-22.

11. William B. Grow, *Eighty-Five Years of Life and Labor* (Carbondale, Pa., 1902), pp. 98-100; Chapman Publishing Company, *Portrait of Lackawanna County*, pp. 944, 947.

12. Logan, *Thomas Dickson*, pp. 10-11, 70-71; Hitchcock, *History of Scranton*, 2: 22-24; Lackawanna County, General Index to Register's Dockets, Lackawanna County, Will books, vols. 2: 319-21; 4: 212-16; 31: 258; Atlantic Publishing and Engraving Com-

pany, *Encyclopedia of Contemporary Biography of Pennsylvania*, 3 vols. (New York, 1889-1893), 1: 221-22.

13. John R. Durfee, *Reminiscences of Carbondale, Dundaff, and Providence Forty Years Past* (Philadelphia, 1875), pp. 39-40.

14. Alfred Mathews, *History of Wayne, Pike, and Monroe Counties of Pennsylvania* (Philadelphia, 1886), pp. 356-62. For the absence of Scrantonians in local Montrose businesses, see Rhamanthus M. Stocker, *Centennial History of Susquehanna County, Pennsylvania* (Philadelphia, 1887), pp. 298-99. Even in Waverly, which lay closer to Scranton than did Carbondale but nonetheless was outside the coal fields, no Scrantonian appeared as an officer in the town's chief enterprise, the Waverly Manufacturing Company. Munsell, *History of Luzerne, Lackawanna, and Wyoming Counties*, p. 458.

15. Munsell, *History of Luzerne, Lackawanna, and Wyoming Counties*, pp. 467-69.

16. Ibid., 464, 464A; Benjamin H. Throop, *A Half Century in Scranton* (Scranton, 1895), p. 236; Craft et al., *History of Scranton*, p. 276; Scranton City Directory, 1890.

17. Munsell, *History of Luzerne, Lackawanna, and Wyoming Counties*, p. 329; Henry C. Bradsby, *History of Luzerne County* (Wilkes-Barre, 1891), pp. 287, 314, 618-19, 624; M.J. McAndrew, *History of Hawley, Pennsylvania* (n.p., 1927), pp. 28-37.

18. Bradsby, *History of Luzerne County*, pp. 287, 314, 624. The other coal companies mining in and around Pittston, such as the Newton Coal Mining Company, the D.L.&W., and the Lehigh Valley Railroad were also owned outside of Pittston. For the lack of large wealth-holders in Pittston from 1850 to 1870, see the Manuscript Census Returns, Seventh, Eighth, and Ninth Censuses of the United States, 1850, 1860, 1870, Luzerne County, Pennsylvania, National Archives Microfilm Series, M-432, Roll 794 (1850); M-653, Roll 1135 (1860); M-593, Roll 1365 (1870).

19. Munsell, *History of Luzerne, Lackawanna, and Wyoming Counties*, p. 331.

20. Bradsby, *History of Luzerne County*, pp. 620-21.

21. Ibid., p. 623; Munsell, *History of Luzerne, Lackawanna, and Wyoming Counties*, pp. 331-32.

22. John W. Jordan, ed., *Encyclopedia of Pennsylvania Biography*, 32 vols. (New York: Lewis Historical Publishing Company, 1914-1967), 3: 748; 10: 32-34, 39-40; 12: 184-88; Hayden et al., *Genealogical and Family History*, 1: 19-22, 129-33, 165-70, 362-65, 488-90, 505-6, 528-29, 531; 2: 605-7, 610-12; Munsell, *History of Luzerne, Lackawanna, and Wyoming Counties*, pp. 330A, 330B, 330G, 331-32, 336; Bradsby, *History of Luzerne County*, pp. 623-24, 752, 1091, 1242, 1348; Dwight J. Stoddard, *Prominent Men of Scranton and Vicinity* (Scranton, 1906), pp. xlix, xxv; Hitchcock, *History of Scranton*, 1: 141; James O. Jones Company, *Eastern Pennsylvanians* (n.p., 1928), p. 359; Edward J. Davies, "Wilkes-Barre, 1870-1920: Evolution of Urban Leadership in an Industrial Town" (unpublished seminar paper, University of Pittsburgh, 1972); Manuscript Census Returns, 1870, Luzerne County, National Archives Microfilm Series, M-593, Roll 1365.

23. In this description I am influenced by Samuel P. Hays, "The New Organizational Society," in Jerry Israel, ed., *Building the Organizational Society: Essays on Associational Activities in Modern America* (New York: The Free Press, 1972), pp. 1-15.

24. Rowland Berthoff, "The Social Order of the Anthracite Region, 1825-1902," *Pennsylvania Magazine of History and Biography* 89 (September 1965): 261-91.

25. Ibid., p. 263.

26. Ibid., p. 262.

27. Rowland Berthoff, "The American Social Order: A Conservative Hypothesis," *American Historical Review* 95 (April 1960): 507. See also Rowland Berthoff, *An Unsettled People: Social Order and Disorder in American History* (New York: Harper and Row, 1971).

28. Berthoff, "The Social Order of the Anthracite Region," pp. 290, 275, 276, 291.

29. Berthoff, "The American Social Order," p. 500. This popular viewpoint is expressed

cogently in Louis Wirth, "Urbanism as a Way of Life," *American Journal of Sociology* 44 (July 1938): 1-24.

30. Walter S. Glazer, "Participation and Power: Voluntary Associations and Functional Organizations of Cincinnati in 1840," *Historical Methods Newsletter* 5 (September 1972): 151-68; Richard S. Alcorn, "Leadership and Stability in Mid-Nineteenth Century America: A Case Study of an Illinois Town," *Journal of American History* 61 (December 1974): 685-702; Joseph F. Rishel, "The Founding Families of Allegheny County: An Examination of Nineteenth-Century Elite Continuity," Ph.D. diss., University of Pittsburgh, 1975; Lee Benson, "Philadelphia Elites and Economic Development: Quasi-Public Innovation during the First American Organizational Revolution, 1825-1861," in Glenn Porter and William Mulligan, eds., *Working Papers from the Regional Economic History Research Center*, 1978.

Chapter 7

1. Bureau of Census, *Statistical Abstract of the United States, 1940* (Washington, D.C., 1941), pp. 143, 433.

2. David Craft, W.A. Wilcox, Alfred Hand, J. Wooldridge, *History of Scranton, Pennsylvania* (Dayton, 1891), pp. 266-80; *Report of the Scranton Board of Trade*, 1886.

3. Thomas Murphy, *History of Lackawanna County*, 3 vols. (Topeka and Indianapolis, 1928), 1:218-20.

4. Ibid., pp. 614-16.

5. Ibid., pp. 617-18; Craft et al., *History of Scranton*, pp. 283-84.

6. *Scranton City Directory*, 1880, 1921; Frederick L. Hitchcock, *History of Scranton and Its People*, 2 vols. (New York, 1914), 2: 53-55, 498-501; D.M. Singer's Clippings, Collection No. 1, LHS.

7. Luther Laflin Mills, Joseph H. Twitchell, Alfred Hand, Frederick L. Hitchcock, James H. Torrey, Eugene Smith, Edward B. Sturges, Charles H. Wells, James McLeod, and James A. Beaver, eds., *Henry Martyn Boies: Appreciations of His Life and Character* (New York: 1904).

8. Rowland Berthoff, "The Social Order of the Anthracite Region, 1825-1902," *Pennsylvania Magazine of History and Biography* 89 (September 1965): 261-91; Clifford M. Zierer, "Scranton as an Urban Community," *Geographic Review* 17 (1927): 428.

9. Hitchcock, *History of Scranton*, 1: 426-34.

10. *Scranton City Directory, 1921; Report of the Scranton Board of Trade, 1886;* Benjamin H. Throop, *A Half Century in Scranton* (Scranton, 1895), p. 175.

11. *Scranton City Directory, 1921*; Zierer, "Scranton as an Urban Community," pp. 419-21.

12. Interviews with Robert Mattes, director of the Lackawanna Historical Society, April 1973, and William Lewis, director of the Lackawanna Historical Society, July 1978, Scranton, Pennsylvania.

13. For two useful descriptions of the emergence of natural corporations, see Alfred D. Chandler, Jr., "The Beginnings of 'Big Business' in American Industry" *Business History Review* 33 (Spring 1959): 1-30; Glenn Porter, *The Rise of Big Business, 1860-1910* (Arlington Heights, Ill.: AHM Press, 1973).

14. *Scranton City Directory, 1876-77, 1880, 1881, 1890, 1920*; N.S.B. Gras, *An Introduction to Economic History* (New York and London, 1922).

15. *Scranton City Directory, 1921*; Thomas Murphy, *History of Lackawanna County*, pp. 812, 614-16, 218-20, 1173-75; Mills et al., *Henry Martyn Boies*, pp. 33-56.

16. Murphy, *History of Lackawanna County*, pp. 220, 1041-43.

17. Ibid., pp. 618, 125-26.

18. Murphy, *History of Lackawanna County*, pp. 127-29; Throop, *A Half Century in Scranton*, pp. 305-8.

19. Murphy, *History of Lackawanna County*, pp. 128-29; Berthoff, "The Social Order of the Anthracite Region."

20. In analyzing the Scranton economic elite in 1920, I have greatly benefited from reading Edward J. Davies, "Wilkes-Barre, 1870 and 1920: The Evolution of Urban Leadership in an Industrial Town." (Unpublished seminar paper, University of Pittsburgh, 1972).

21. For data on the children of the Scranton elite of 1880, see the sources for table 4.2 and *Scranton City Directory, 1920, 1921*.

22. The sons and sons-in-law of Scranton's 1880 elite who held corporate officerships were Paul and d'Andelot Belin, David Boies, Alfred E. and Charles R. Connell, James McAnulty, Joseph J. and Edmund B. Jermyn, Frederick J. Platt, George Sanderson, Worthington Scranton, Louis A. Watres, and Charles S. Weston.

23. See the sources in table 5.2.

24. Hitchcock, *History of Scranton*, 2: 660-63, 669-72, 7-9, 277-82.

25. Ibid., pp. 660-63; Chapman Publishing Company, *Portrait and Biographical Record of Lackawanna County, Pennsylvania* (New York and Chicago, 1897), pp. 205-7.

26. Samuel C. Logan, *The Life of Thomas Dickson* (Scranton, 1888); Hitchcock, *History of Scranton*, 1: 89-90, 254-55; 2: 22-24; Chapman Publishing Company, *Portrait of Lackawanna County*, pp. 456-57, 502-4; Mills et al., *Henry Martyn Boies*, p. 51; *Scranton City Directory, 1921*; Murphy, *History of Lackawanna County*, pp. 682-83.

27. Hitchcock, *History of Scranton*, pp. 10-13; Obituaries Notebook No. 7, p. 74, LHS; New York *Sun*, May 10, 1935; Interview with Robert C. Mattes, director of the Lackawanna Historical Society, April 1973, Scranton, Pennsylvania.

28. Obituaries Notebook No. 7, p. 40, LHS; R.G. Dun Credit Ledgers, Pennsylvania, Luzerne County, Vol. 96: 249.

29. Hitchcock, *History of Scranton*, 1: 254-55; 2: 10-13.

30. Hitchcock, *History of Scranton*, 2: 53-55, 30-32, 5-7, 188-91; *Scranton City Directory, 1920, 1921*.

31. Murphy, *History of Lackawanna County*, pp. 824-26, 816-17, 682-83, 129-30. Chapman Publishing Company, *Portrait of Lackawanna County*, pp. 776-77, 780-81, 783-87, 794-96, 805-6; *Scranton City Directory, 1920*.

32. The works which argue elite continuity over time include E. Digby Baltzell, *Philadelphia Gentlemen* (Glencoe Ill.: Free Press, 1958); Edward Pessen, *Riches, Class, and Power* (Lexington, Ma., Toronto, and London: D.C. Heath & Co., 1973); Ferdinand Lundberg, *The Rich and Super-Rich* (New York: Lyle Stuart Inc., 1968); John N. Ingham, *The Iron Barons: A Social Analysis of an American Urban Elite, 1874-1965* (Westport, Conn.: Greenwood Press, 1978).

33. *Scranton City Directory, 1921*.

34. Murphy, *History of Lackawanna County*, pp. 772-73, 1220-21.

35. Hitchcock, *History of Scranton*, 1: 426-34; Scranton *Republican*, May 18, May 25, and June 8, 1866.

36. For a description of the impact of these social issues on American politics, see Lee Benson, *The Concept of Jacksonian Democracy: New York as a Test Case* (Princeton: Princeton University Press, 1961); Paul Kleppner, *The Cross of Culture* (New York: Free Press, 1970); Frederick C. Luebke, *Immigrants and Politics: Germans and Politics in Nebraska 1880-1900* (Lincoln: University of Nebraska Press, 1969). My own contribution to this literature is "Tinkerers, Tipplers, and Traitors: Ethnicity and Social Reform in Nebraska during The Progressive Era" (forthcoming, *Pacific Historical Review*, 1981).

37. Murphy, *History of Lackawanna County*, pp. 212-16; Hitchcock, *History of Scranton*, 1: 478-81, 525-26. Interviews with Robert C. Mattes, director of the Lackawanna His-

torical Society, October 1972, and April 1973; Rowland Berthoff, "The Social Order of the Anthracite Region"; Robert H. Wiebe, *The Search for Order, 1877-1920* (New York: Hill and Wang, 1967).

38. Philipp V. Mattes, *Tales of Scranton* (n.p., 1973), pp. 43-44; Scranton *Republican*, March 30, May 25, and June 8, 1866.

39. Hitchcock, *History of Scranton*, 1: 431-34; Berthoff, "The Social Order of the Anthracite Region"; *Report of the Scranton Board of Trade, 1886*; Interview with William Lewis, director of the Lackawanna Historical Society, June 1978. *Scranton City Directory, 1920, 1921*.

40. Murphy, *History of Lackawanna County*, pp. 212-16; Interviews with Robert Mattes, director of the Lackawanna Historical Society, April 1973, and William Lewis, director of the Lackawanna Historical Society, July 1978, Scranton, Pennsylvania.

Chapter 8

1. For background information on the Lehigh Valley, see William J. Heller, ed., *History of Northampton County, Pennsylvania, and the Grand Valley of the Lehigh*, 3 vols. (Boston and New York, 1920).

2. Alfred Mathews and Austin N. Hungerford, *History of the Counties of Lehigh and Carbon, in the Commonwealth of Pennsylvania* (Philadelphia, 1884), pp. 23-42.

3. Ibid.; William G. Shade, "Pennsylvania Politics in the Jacksonian Period: A Case Study, Northampton County, 1824-1844," *Pennsylvania History* 39 (July 1972): 313-33.

4. Shade, "Pennsylvania Politics," pp. 313-33; Charles R. Roberts, John B. Stoudt, Thomas H. Krick, William J. Dietrich, *History of Lehigh County, Pennsylvania and a Genealogical and Biographical Record of Its Families*, 3 vols. (Allentown, Pa., 1914), 1: 43-46.

5. Joseph M. Levering, *A History of Bethlehem, Pennsylvania, 1741-1892, with Some Account of Its Founders and Their Early Activity in America* (Bethlehem, Pa., 1903); Gillian L. Gollin, *Moravians in Two Worlds: A Study of Changing Communities* (New York and London: Columbia University Press, 1967), pp. 50-109, 217-26.

6. Gollin, *Moravians in Two Worlds*, pp. 168-69, 186-96, 217-26.

7. Shade, "Pennsylvania Politics."

8. Anthony J. Brzyski, "The Lehigh Canal and Its Effect on the Economic Development of the Region Through Which It Passed, 1818-1873," Ph.D. diss., New York University, 1957, pp. 63-64; James T. Lemon, *The Best Poor Man's Country: A Geographical Study of Early Southeastern Pennsylvania* (Baltimore: Johns Hopkins University Press, 1972), pp. 81-82, *et passim*.

9. Mathews and Hungerford, *History of the Counties of Lehigh and Carbon*, p. 41; Uzal W. Condit, *The History of Easton, Pennsylvania from the Earliest Times to the Present, 1739-1885* (Washington, 1885).

10. Shade, "Pennsylvania Politics"; Mathews and Hungerford, *History of the Counties of Lehigh and Carbon*, p. 41; Condit, *History of Easton*, pp. 302-41; Levering, *History of Bethlehem*, pp. 683-717.

11. Fred Brenckman, *History of Carbon County, Pennsylvania* (Harrisburg, Pa., 1913), pp. 73-86; Jules I. Bogen, *The Anthracite Railroads: A Study in American Railroad Enterprise* (New York, 1927), pp. 108-10; Chester Lloyd Jones, *The Anthracite Tidewater Canals* (Philadelphia, 1908), pp. 7-13; Eliot Jones, *The Anthracite Combination in the United States, with Some Account of the Early Development of the Anthracite Industry* (Cambridge, Mass., 1914), pp. 10-22.

12. Mathews and Hungerford, *History of the Counties of Lehigh and Carbon*, pp. 596-97, 644-45; Jones, *The Anthracite Tidewater Canals*, pp. 13-17; Richard Richardson, *Memoir of Josiah White* (Philadelphia, 1873), pp. 31-85; Howard N. Eavenson, *The First Century and a Quarter of the American Coal Industry* (Baltimore, 1942), pp. 138-54.

13. Mathews and Hungerford, *History of the Counties of Lehigh and Carbon*, pp. 597-98; Jones, *The Anthracite Tidewater Canals*, pp. 13-17, 129-31.

14. Mathews and Hungerford, *History of the Counties of Lehigh and Carbon*, pp. 674-78.

15. Ibid., p. 657. Another source observed that "despite the natural advantages in the way, [Mauch Chunk] has continued to grow . . . and can now [1873] only enlarge itself by excavating sites from the precipitous rocks with which the narrow gorge abounds." *Guide Book of the Lehigh Valley Railroad* (Philadelphia, 1873), pp. 75-76.

16. Mathews and Hungerford, *History of the Counties of Lehigh and Carbon*, pp. 595-96, 671-74, 688, 700-704, 709-10. For a reconstruction of the Leisenring kinship group, see Burton W. Folsom, Jr., "Urban Networks: The Economic and Social Order of the Lackawanna and Lehigh Valleys during Early industrialization, 1850-1880," Ph.D. diss., University of Pittsburgh, 1976, p. 196.

17. Mathews and Hungerford, *History of the Counties of Lehigh and Carbon*, pp. 690, 704-5; John W. Jordan, ed., *Encyclopedia of Pennsylvania Biography*, 32 vols. (New York: Lewis Historical Publishing Co., 1914-67), 6: 2139-42; Davis Brodhead, "Asa Packer and the Lehigh University," *Magazine of American History* 13 (June 1885): 539; Manuscript Census Returns, Seventh Census of the United States, 1850, Carbon County, Pennsylvania, National Archives Microfilm Series, M-432, Roll 762. For a more elaborate view of the Packer kinship group, see Folsom, "Urban Networks," p. 199.

18. Mathews and Hungerford, *History of the Counties of Lehigh and Carbon*, pp. 612, 616-18, 620; Brenckman, *History of Carbon County*, pp. 413-16; Chapman Publishing Company, *Portrait and Biographical Record of Lehigh, Northampton, and Carbon Counties, Pennsylvania* (Chicago, 1894), pp. 262-63, 810, 813, 227-28; John W. Jordan, Edgar M. Green, George T. Ettinger, *Historic Homes and Institutions and Genealogical and Personal Memoris of the Lehigh Valleys, Pennsylvania*, 2 vols. (New York and Chicago, 1905), 2: 346-48; 1: 209-12; Manuscript Census Returns, Ninth Census of the United States, 1870, Carbon County, Pennsylvania, National Archives Microfilm Series, M-593, Roll 1320.

19. Bogen, *Anthracite Railroads*, pp. 109-10; Jones, *The Anthracite Combination*, p. 223. For another view of the comparative efficiency of canals and railroads, see Albert Fishlow, *American Railroads and the Transformation of the Ante-bellum Economy* (Cambridge, Mass., Harvard University Press, 1965).

20. Bogen, *Anthracite Railroads*, pp. 110-11; Mathews and Hungerford, *History of the Counties of Lehigh and Carbon*, pp. 601, 605. The L.C.&N., as might be expected, obstructed the legal progress of any railroad venture in the Lehigh Valley.

21. Bogen, *Anthracite Railroads*, pp. 110-12; Mathews and Hungerford, *History of the Counties of Lehigh and Carbon*, p. 601; Broadhead, "Asa Packer," pp. 540-42.

22. Bogen, *Anthracite Railroads*, pp. 110-21, 125; Mathews and Hungerford, *History of the Counties of Lehigh and Carbon*, pp. 601-5; Manuscript Census Returns, Ninth Census of the United States, 1870, Carbon County, Pennsylvania, National Archives Microfilm Series, M-593, Roll 1320.

23. R.G. Dun Credit Ledgers, Pennsylvania, Carbon County, vol. 36: 31, 42.

24. E. Digby Baltzell, *Philadelphia Gentlemen* (Glencoe, Ill.: Free Press, 1958), pp. 118-19; Mathews and Hungerford, *History of the Counties of Lehigh and Carbon*, pp. 608-11, 613, 736-37, 757-58, 777; Brenckman, *History of Carbon County*, pp. 232-22, 355; Lane S. Hart, *Annual Report of the Secretary of Internal Affairs of the Commonwealth of Pennsylvania, 1879-1880: Industrial Statistics* (Harrisburg, Pa., 1881), pp. 22-26.

25. One clear exception to this pattern is the independent William Lilly, the initial president of the First National Bank. Lilly came to Mauch Chunk in 1838 and became a coal operator in the Hazleton coal field northwest of Mauch Chunk. He married late in life to a woman outside the Lehigh Valley and had no children. Apparently he associated amicably with members of both groups, which may have contributed to his being Mauch Chunk's congressman in Washington for many years. Mathews and Hungerford, *History of the Counties of Lehigh and Carbon*, pp. 604, 676-78, 680-81, 689-90, 696, 699-700; Brenckman, *History of Carbon County*, pp. 499-502, 276-78; Atlantic Publishing and Engraving Company, *Encyclopedia of Contemporary Biography of Pennsylvania*, 3 vols. (New York, 1889-93), pp. 133-36; Manuscript Census Returns, Ninth (1870) and Tenth (1880) Censuses of the United States, Carbon County, Pennsylvania, National Archives Microfilm Series, M-283, Rolls 1107 and 1108.

26. Charles R. Roberts, John B. Stoudt, Thomas H. Krick, William J. Dietrich, *History of Lehigh County*, 2 vols. (Allentown, Pa., 1914), 1: 575.

27. Mathews and Hungerford, *History of the Counties of Lehigh and Carbon*, pp. 155-56, 237-41, 797-802; Roberts et al., *History of Lehigh County*, pp. 575-77.

28. Mathews and Hungerford, *History of the Counties of Lehigh and Carbon*, pp. 155-56.

29. Ibid., pp. 156-57, 240-41; *Annual Report of the Secretary of Internal Affairs, 1879-1880*, pp. 44, 46, 54-55.

30. Mathews and Hungerford, *History of the Counties of Lehigh and Carbon*, pp. 163-68.

31. Ibid., pp. 148-50.

32. Levering, *History of Bethlehem*, pp. 601-4; Condit, *History of Easton*, p. 13; Lemon, *The Best Poor Man's Country*, pp. 118-49.

33. Condit, *History of Easton*, pp. 445-47, 481, 492-93; *Guide Book of the Lehigh Valley Railroad*, p. 56.

34. Condit, *History of Easton*, pp. 468-69, 416, 417-18, 194-95, 312-13, 316-19, 325-26.

35. Ibid., pp. 468-69, 416, 417-18, 194-95, 312-13, 316-19, 325-26; R.G. Dun Credit Ledgers, Pennsylvania, Northampton County, 119: 477; Levering, *History of Bethlehem*, p. 724.

36. Gollin, *Moravians in Two Worlds*, pp. 156-96. For a description of the local cosmopolitan framework, see Samuel P. Hays, "Political Parties and the Community-Society Continuum," in William N. Chambers and Walter D. Burnham, eds., *The American Party System: Stages of Political Development* (New York: Oxford University Press, 1961). For an application of this model to economic development, see Julius Rubin, "Mobs, Markets, and Morality," Mimeograph, University of Pittsburgh.

37. Gollin, *Moravians in Two Worlds*, pp. 50-109, 217-26; W. Ross Yates, *Bethlehem of Pennsylvania: The Golden Years, 1845-1920* (Bethlehem, Pa., Bethlehem Book Company, 1976).

38. Raymond Walters, *Bethlehem Long Ago and Today* (Bethlehem, Pa., 1923), p. 64; Levering, *History of Bethlehem*, pp. 719-20, 722-24.

39. Levering, *History of Bethlehem*, pp. 722-24.

40. Walters, *Bethlehem*, p. 64; Heller, *History of Northampton County*, 1: 444; Levering, *History of Bethlehem*, pp. 722-24.

41. Lehigh Valley Railroad Company, *Annual Reports of the President and Directors to Stockholders, 1855 to 1863, from Manuscript Reports of Robert H. Sayre* (Bethlehem, Pa., n. d.), p. 9.

42. Ibid., pp. 9, 18; *Guide Book of the Lehigh Valley Railroad*, pp. 12-13.

43. Walters, *Bethlehem*, pp. 61-62; Atlantic Publishing and Engraving Company, *Encyclopedia of Contemporary Biography*, 1: 240-23; Jordan et al., *Lehigh Valley*, 1: 229-32,

234-37; Jordan, *Encyclopedia of Pennsylvania Biography*, 1: 215-16; John Ingham, "Elite and Upper Class in the Iron and Steel Industry, 1874 to 1965," Ph.D. diss., University of Pittsburgh, 1972, pp. 179-80; Manuscript Census Returns, Tenth Census of the United States, 1880, Northampton County, Pennsylvania, National Archives Microfilm Series, M-T 9, Rolls 1162 and 1163.

44. Clarence E. Beckel, ed., "Marriages and Deaths: Extracts from Bethlehem *Daily Times*, 1867-1890" (5 vols., clippings, Bethlehem, 1936), 5: 1545-46; 3: 845-46; 4: 1059; 1: 110; Times Publishing Company, *Directory of Bethlehem, South Bethlehem, and West Bethlehem* (Bethlehem, 1890); Bethlehem *Daily Times*, February 1, 1884, February 21, 1883, January 9, 1874; Peter Fritts, *History of Northampton County, Pennsylvania* (n.p., 1877), 213; Yates, *Bethlehem of Pennsylvania*; Ruth Hutchison, "The Fleeting Era of Opulence and Grandeur," in Bethlehem *Globe-Times*, December 23, 1967; Interview with Ruth Linderman Frick, Bethlehem, November 1975.

45. Hart, *Annual Report of the Secretary of Internal Affairs, 1879-1880*, pp. 54-55.

46. Levering, *History of Bethlehem*, pp. 728-30; Walters, *Bethlehem*, p. 62; Jordan et al., *Lehigh Valley*, 2: 1-4; Yates, *Bethlehem of Pennsylvania*, p. 93.

47. Yates, *Bethlehem of Pennsylvania*, p. 93.

48. Roberts, et al., *History of Lehigh County*, p. 263; Yates, *Bethlehem of Pennsylvania*, p. 93.

49. Jordan et al., *Lehigh Valley*, 1: 1-23; 2: 1-7; Condit, *History of Easton*, pp. 325-26; Mathews and Hungerford, *History of the Counties of Lehigh and Carbon*, pp. 180-86.

50. Levering, *History of Bethlehem*, pp. 727, 735, 738-39.

51. Mathews and Hungerford, *History of the Counties of Lehigh and Carbon*, p. 604; Bogen, *Anthracite Railroads*, pp. 126-27; Comencius Press, *The Bethlehem Iron Company of South Bethlehem* (Bethlehem, Pa., n. d.); *Philadelphia City Directory, 1880*.

52. Chapman Publishing Company, *Portrait of Lehigh, Northampton, and Carbon Counties*, p. 161; Levering, *History of Bethlehem*, p. 726; Atlantic Publishing and Engraving Company, *Encyclopedia of Contemporary Biography*, 1: 240-44; 3: 90-91; Jordan et al., *Lehigh Valley*, 1: 234-37.

53. For a description of the social life in Fountain Hill, see Hutchison, "The Fleeting Era," *Bethlehem Globe-Times*, December 23, 1967.

54. Allentown Board of Trade, *Past, Present and Future of the City of Allentown, Pennsylvania* (Allentown, 1886).

55. The existence of several cities in the Lehigh Valley that shared the functions of a regional center in 1880 is also reflected in the even distribution of population (relative to the Lackawanna Valley) of the major centers Allentown, South Bethlehem, Bethlehem, Easton, and Catasaqua. Francis Walker and Charles W. Seaton, Supts., *Compendium of the Tenth Census: 1880* (Washington, D.C., 1883), pp. 273-74, 276.

56. For a study of urban development before industrialization, see Lemon, *The Best Poor Man's Country*.

57. Baltzell, *Philadelphia Gentlemen*, pp. 96, 100, 112-13, 101, 119, 122, 125, 116, 127-128; Adna F. Weber, *The Growth of Cities in the Nineteenth Century: A Study in Statistics* (Ithaca [1963], 1899), pp. 255-63.

58. Jordan, *Encyclopedia of Pennsylvania Biography*, 17: 45-46; 13: 164-65; Baltzell, *Philadelphia Gentlemen*, pp. 119, 194; Albert N. Marquis, *Who's Who in Pennsylvania, 1939*, 2 vols. (Chicago, 1939), pp. 511, 943.

59. Jordan, *Encyclopedia of Pennsylvania Biography*, 13: 176-77; 17: 344; Brenckman, *History of Carbon County*, pp. 494-96; Poor's Publishing Company, *Moody's Manual of Railroads and Corporation Securities, 1924: Public Utilities Section* (New York, 1924), p. 2713.

60. Mathews and Hungerford, *History of the Counties of Lehigh and Carbon*, p. 711; Brenckman, *History of Carbon County*, pp. 478-80; Manuscript Census Returns, Carbon

County, Pennsylvania, 1880, National Archives Microfilm Series, M-283, Rolls 1107 and 1108.

61. Mathews and Hungerford, *History of the Counties of Lehigh and Carbon*, pp. 237, 241, 501-3; Roberts et al., *History of Lehigh County*, 3: 1312-13, 1407-11; 2: 404-5; 1: 595, 627-28; Chapman Publishing Company, *Portrait of Lehigh, Northampton, and Carbon Counties*, pp. 242, 131; *The Thomas Iron Company, 1854-1904* (New York, 1904); James F. Lambert and Henry J. Reinhard, *A History of Catasaqua in Lehigh County, Pennsylvania* (Allentown, Pa., 1914), pp. 38-45; William H. Glace, *Early History and Reminiscences of Catasaqua in Pennsylvania* (Allentown, Pa., 1914), pp. 19-28.

62. Roberts et al., *History of Lehigh County*, 1: 595; 2: 404; Glace, *Early History and Reminiscences of Catasaqua*, pp. 98-99.

63. See the sources in Table 8:3. Interview with Ruth Linderman Frick, Bethlehem, November 1975.

64. Historians have not supported the notion that sons of economic leaders are highly unlikely to match their father's achievements. For an example of this, see Edward Pessen, *Riches, Class and Power Before the Civil War* (Lexington, Mass., Toronto and London: D.C. Heath & Co., 1973). See also Heller, *History of Northampton County*; Bogen, *Anthracite Railroads*; Yates, *Bethlehem of Pennsylvania*.

65. R.G. Dun Credit Ledgers, Pennsylvania, Northampton County, 119: 581; 36: 97.

66. Robert F. Archer, *A History of the Lehigh Valley Railroad* (Berkeley: Howell-North, 1977), pp. 115-45; Bogen, *Anthracite Railroads*, pp. 126-32.

67. That Elisha Wilbur was not equal to his Uncle Asa Packer was apparently obvious to contemporaries. In 1879, the R.G. Dun Credit reporter observed that "it was under his [Packer's] protection that the men who compose this firm [E.P. Wilbur and Company] have during the past twenty years risen to occupy the prominent positions they hold today." R.G. Dun Credit Reports, Pennsylvania, Northampton County, 119: 581.

68. Archer, *Lehigh Valley Railroad*, pp. 146, 151, 152; Bogen, *Anthracite Railroads*, p. 126; E.G. Campbell, *The Reorganization of the American Railroad System, 1893-1900* (New York, 1968 [1938]), pp. 273-76.

69. Robert Hessen, *Steel Titan: The Life of Charles M. Schwab* (New York: Oxford University Press, 1975), pp. 164-66 (quotation on 165). The strategy of shifting from manufacturing rails to producing military ordnance was initiated by John Fritz, steel expert and general superintendent of Bethlehem Steel. Fritz's autobiography is a useful source for analyzing the business attitudes of the Packer group. See, *The Autobiography of John Fritz* (New York, 1912), pp. 173-74.

70. Hessen, *Steel Titan*, pp. 165-66; Information on the Packer group management of Bethlehem Iron was difficult to secure because the leaders were so secretive. The Dun Credit reporter observed that Bethlehem Iron was "a closed corporation. [They] publish no statement of their affairs [and] allow no one outside of their stockholders to know anything about them." This "closed system" approach is, of course, a characteristic of cautious and conservative leadership. See R.G. Dun Credit Ledgers, Northampton County, 122: 174.

71. Berthoff, "The Social Order of the Anthracite Regions." Some novelists have excellently conveyed the problems of patrician families with downwardly mobile sons. See, for example, Thomas Mann, *Buddenbrooks*, Samuel Butler, *The Way of All Flesh*, and John O'Hara, *Appointment in Samarra*.

72. Robert Hessen, "Charles M. Schwab, President of United States Steel, 1901-1904," *Pennsylvania Magazine of History and Biography* 96 (April 1972): 203-28; Hessen, *Steel Titan*, p. 167.

73. Walters, *Bethlehem*, p. 88. Hessen, *Steel Titan*, pp. 167-68. Contrasting the old and new leadership at Bethlehem Steel, John Fritz commented that "The Bethlehem Iron Company made many mistakes, but their refusal to go into the manufacture of structural material at the time alluded to [early 1880's] was to my mind the greatest. Later Mr. C.M.

Schwab acquired the entire property, and erected a structural steel plant, which is now in successful operation." Fritz, *Autobiography*, p. 175.

74. Hessen, *Steel Titan*, p. 169.

75. Ibid., p. 171.

76. Ibid., pp. 172-75, 182-84.

77. Ibid., pp. 186-87, 267.

78. Hessen, "Charles Schwab," p. 203; Heller, *History of Northampton County*, p. 276; New York *Times*, April 14, 1915; I am indebted to Robert Hessen's work for directing me to the New York *Times* article.

79. Hessen, *Steel Titan*, pp. 170-72, 177-78, 252; Walters, *Bethlehem*, p. 88.

80. Yates, *Bethlehem of Pennsylvania*, pp. 178, 282-83, 289-91, 207.

81. Ibid.

82. Walters, *Bethlehem*, pp. 88, 143-48; Yates, *Bethlehem of Pennsylvania*, pp. 282-317 (quotation p. 303).

Bibliographic Essay

Historians have long been writing city histories, but regional histories are something new. To do regional history requires broader vision: looking at more cities and towns, comparing growth rates and migration patterns. The sources needed to do this research are varied, too. So what I've done is to rank and then describe the primary sources I found most useful.

Federal Manuscript Census Schedules. The four manuscript censuses from 1850 to 1880 were indispensable to my work. Every ten years, census takers recorded information on each American household. They asked Americans their ages, birthplaces, occupations, education, real estate wealth, and personal wealth. Using this census, I could discover wealth holders and rank them *over time*. I could check the migration patterns of capitalists in my two regions and trace their eventual move to the regional center. More interestingly, I could see how the growth of industry created wealth for people at all levels of society—not just for the entrepreneurs.

City and County Histories. City and county histories used in tandem with the federal manuscript censuses create a potent source for regional history. City histories were written for most cities and some towns in the Lackawanna and Lehigh regions. Generally the plan for these histories was this: some entrepreneurs would sell "subscriptions" for a history of their city. Most prominent locals would pay to publish flattering descriptions and pictures of their families. Their fees would subsidize the printing of the book and they would each get a copy to show off to their neighbors. The virtues and defects of such works for historical research are obvious. On the plus side, city histories provide detailed biographical sketches of economic leaders, information on their families, their migration and career patterns, birth, death, religion, and sometimes political party. Such information transforms mere names into actual people with lives and careers. On the negative side, reading about these people is often

181

like reading about Greek gods. The grandiose comments sometimes border on narcissism and fabrication. In short, they are unreliable. Nonetheless, in cross-checking city histories with other sources, I almost always found the factual biographical data in the histories to be correct, and that was the information I needed most.

The R. G. Dun Credit Reports. Starting in the early 1800s the R. G. Dun Company (later Dun and Bradstreet) hired agents in almost every city and town in America to analyze the solvency of local capitalists and industries. The Dun reporters wrote candid financial evaluations and updates on all of Scranton's economic leaders and on all companies in the Lackawanna and Lehigh regions. In their evaluations of individual businessmen the Dun agents asked, Is he reliable? Who are his friends? What is he investing in? Reporting on companies, the Dun agents listed the partners or directors, the capital stock of the company, and its prospects for growth. Unlike the glamorous sketches of businessmen in city histories, the Dun Reports conveyed the unstable dynamics of capitalists risking big money in a welter of investments. Sometimes they made fortunes, sometimes they were bankrupt, and sometimes they did a little of both.

Personal Correspondence. I waded through the correspondence of the Scranton family and also the duPont's letters to their Scranton managers (Henry Belin and Charles duPont Breck). Most of this information is available and efficiently catalogued in the Eleutherian Mills Historical Library. Without reading these thousands of letters I never would have grasped the desperate reality of the Scranton's iron making and railroad building. The Scrantons' letters show the complexity, the riskiness, and the near bankruptcy of their pioneer experiment in industry. The disadvantages of their city's location, the novelty of their making iron with anthracite, the hostility of local settlers, and the skepticism of New Yorkers all come through in the letters. Of course, people will sometimes exaggerate in letters but the Scrantons' big debts, angry creditors, and broken-down blast furnaces tell a story of ambitious men with big problems. In any case, in studying the tie between entrepreneurs and city growth, there is nothing quite like reading what the entrepreneurs said about what they were doing.

Interviews. Unlike the other sources, these would answer my questions and serve me coffee. Robert Mattes and William Lewis, of Scranton, and Ruth Linderman Frick, of Bethlehem, were my sources and, in two cases, their knowledge spanned the entire twentieth century and part of the nineteenth. Since they personally knew some of Scranton's and Bethlehem's economic leaders I had the chance to gain first-hand insight into the lives of the men I was writing about. My interviewees also gave me opinions of the cities, their industries and institutions, and their past and future. Such conversation was obviously valuable, though understandably biased. The main problem was that I was asking twentieth-century people to tell me about nineteenth-century cities.

City Directories. After the 1850s Scranton and Bethlehem each had city directories published annually. A list of all urban dwellers and their jobs and addresses were provided therein. Major industries and businesses in town were also noted as well as occasionally boards of directors for local industries. Using city directories for Scranton and Bethlehem, I could find out exactly where local nabobs lived, who their neighbors were, and when they had moved to town. The Scranton city directory for 1920 helped me trace the sons and grandsons of Scranton's 1880 economic elite.

Newspapers. Newspaper were not much help in my research but they did give specific information on important events and people. For example, editors captured the intensity of Scranton's battle for a city charter—an important step in the competition with Wilkes-Barre. Also, by knowing when economic leaders in Scranton had died I could go to newspapers to check obituaries, pallbearers, and other information unavailable elsewhere.

Wills. An examination of the wills of several prominent capitalists in Scranton helped me understand how Scranton's wealthy men viewed their sons, the city of Scranton, and their old home towns. Scranton's economic leaders seemed to be equally generous to all their sons (partible inheritance). They were more loyal to their adopted Scranton than to their town of birth; sometimes they even urged their sons to stay in business in Scranton.

Histories of Institutions. Like newspapers and wills, institutional histories are mainly useful for filling in bits and pieces of ideas that could be developed more fully from other sources. Lodge 61 in Wilkes-Barre, the Honesdale Prebyterian Church, and the First National Bank and the Board of Trade in Scranton were all key institutions in those cities and all had books on their origin, membership, and development.

Annual Reports. Annual reports for the D&H, L.C.&N., and Lehigh Valley Railroad filled in a few gaps. They listed all officers and directors, discussed earnings, and briefly reported strategies for investments and for the location of branch plants. Annual reports often hid as much as they revealed. They glossed over tensions, failures, and incompetence while stressing the "achievements of management," both real and imagined.

Other Sources. Other sources were helpful, too. For example, I used the records of the Pennsylvania legislature to find the voting on the laws to enlarge Scranton's boundary and to separate Scranton from Luzerne County. Also, the state of Pennsylvania published an industrial directory that described the production and work force of most industries in the state. I used this directory for my sketch of Scranton in 1880. I also used the manufacturing section of the U.S. Census in 1880 to give me comparative statistics on the amount of coal mining and manufacturing done in the Lackawanna and Wyoming regions.

Most of these sources I've described are available for regions throughout America. Each region also has its own special set of surviving records that the historian can find if he will go to the region and look around. For example, in the Lackawanna Historical Society in Scranton and in the city library in Bethlehem I found books of newspaper obituaries; after reading them I had a much better notion of kinship and friendship ties among the leaders in both cities. Also in the Lackawanna Historical Society I found an 1850s map of Scranton that located and labeled all the industries, dwellings, and landowners in the city. I found similar maps for Towanda, Montrose, and Dundaff in the Eleutherian Mills Historical Library.

I learned a lot by just visiting cities and towns in my two regions. Touring these cities and talking with the natives may be vintage 1980 but it does give some insight into 1880. To see Joseph Scranton's house is almost to believe, as one reporter said, that it "will serve for centuries to illustrate to future generations the make and style of the men whose successes under difficulties have been the greatest and most striking of the age." To visit Asa Packer's restored and preserved mansion in Mauch Chunk (now Jim Thorpe) is to get a real glimpse of the man. To view Mauch Chunk from his mansion, as he must have done, is to see and feel the empire he dreamed about and created.

One final thought: the sources I found and the way I used them were limited only by my imagination. My approach to regional history is not definitive, it's only a starting point.

Index